W9-AUV-822

Praise for *The Value of a Whale*

'A sorely needed corrective in an era of climate politics dominated by dollars and models. Adrienne Buller's *The Value of a Whale* is critical reading for the important task of prying the future out of the hands of corporations and technocrats.'

Olúfẹ́mi O. Táíwò, author of *Reconsidering Reparations* and *Elite Capture*

'Why do so many of the alleged solutions to climate crisis fail to deliver? In this tightly argued, precise and deeply researched book Adrienne Buller looks inside the heads of "green" capitalists, exposing how non-solutions proliferate. Read this brilliant exposé if you want to understand not only how some of the world's most powerful people think and act but also how their solutions differ from what is really needed to secure a safe and abundant future for everyone.'

Amelia Horgan, author of *Lost in Work*

'This is a witty, lucid and beautifully written critique of that contradiction-in-terms, "green capitalism". It explains why, despite the farcical diminuendo of climate denialism, so little has changed. Its searching inquiry into the puritanical reduction of all living matter to economic value, which underpins most government responses to ecological catastrophe, incisively debunks one of the most dangerous illusions going. This is the book we have long needed.'

Richard Seymour, author of *The Twittering Machine*

'A wonderfully readable attack on the worldview that argues for adding a dollar value to nature in order to save it. An accessible account of a new phase of capitalism that we all need to understand.'

Professor Simon Lewis, author of *The Human Planet*

'At last! A wonderfully refreshing antidote to the notion that market forces can solve the climate and nature crises, and the deadly assumption that every idea must be evaluated in terms of markets, finance, property or profit. Elegant, incisive and fierce, Buller systematically takes apart the false solutions that dominate mainstream analysis, from carbon offsets to the commodification of nature, and gives us the tools to challenge their dominance and to broaden our understanding of what's both possible and necessary.'

Caroline Lucas MP

'Buller offers essential context for understanding how economic dogmas and market-driven statecraft have warped our understanding of and responses to the climate crisis – or lack thereof. Crucially, she also presents a practical roadmap for course-correction. *The Value of a Whale* is an accessible and expertly curated guide to the increasingly slick, green face of capitalism in the twenty-first century. This book should be required reading for everyone from climate activists to policymakers and concerned citizens looking to salvage our collective prospects for a liveable future.'

Kate Aronoff, author of *Overheated*

'This is a book for anyone troubled by our lack of progress on the climate crisis, from young activists to hard-headed CEOs and investors that face losing control of companies as the climate breaks down. In her persuasive analysis of net zero policies that narrowly prioritise efficiency, market pricing and offsetting – and with unusual clarity and scrupulous integrity – Buller comes to unsettling conclusions. Read this before it is too late.'

Ann Pettifor, author of *The Case for the Green New Deal*

'*The Value of a Whale* is an urgent and honest intervention, casting a magnifying glass over the institutions, insider groupthink and non-solutions distracting and deflecting from the radical ideas and compassion we need to secure a safe planetary future. For too long, our response to ecological crisis has been steered by mainstream economic thinking that is not fit for purpose, to the exclusion of other vital perspectives. As Buller compellingly argues, we are long overdue a reset.'

Farhana Yamin, Visiting Professor at UAL and Associate Fellow, Chatham House

The Value of a Whale

Manchester University Press

The Value of a Whale

On the Illusions of Green Capitalism

Adrienne Buller

Manchester University Press

The right of Adrienne Buller to be identified as the author of this work has been
asserted by them in accordance with the Copyright, Designs and Patents Act
1988.

Published by Manchester University Press
Oxford Road, Manchester M13 9PL
www.manchesteruniversitypress.co.uk

British Library Cataloguing-in-Publication Data
A catalogue record for this book is available from the British Library

ISBN 978 1 5261 6263 2 paperback

First published 2022

Typeset
by Cheshire Typesetting Ltd, Cuddington, Cheshire

Contents

Preface

I wrote much of this book from my sister's home in the foothills of Oakland, California. It was August in a summer of record drought across the Pacific Northwest, fanning wildfires so immense their smoke cast the sun behind a dense red haze above my father's home 4,000 kilometres east in Northern Ontario. Despite constant insistence of the exceptionalism of the fires, North America was not unique in playing host to 'unprecedented' blazes. Across Turkey and Greece, and within the Siberian Arctic Circle, fires raged for weeks, sending tourists and residents flocking to the sea, and unleashing bursts of methane from scorched permafrost. In the same summer, floods tore through Central Europe, causing hundreds to lose their lives and prompting one resident to say the quiet part out loud: 'You don't expect people to die in a flood in Germany. You expect it maybe in poor countries, but you don't expect it here.'[1]

Nor was she wrong; the climate and environmental crises are delivering wholeheartedly on their promise to claim the lives and livelihoods of those least implicated in their creation. Heavy rains in the summer of 2021 brought deadly flooding and landslides to an already embattled Rohingya people at refugee camps in Bangladesh; in Jacobabad, Pakistan, temperatures coupled with suffocating humidity inched past the upper limit at which the human body is capable of cooling itself, a decade ahead of scientific predictions. Echoing the premature arrival of these predictions, I was gripped by the distinct feeling that – while I had anticipated this kind of summer in my middle age and had spent years mentally preparing for it – I hadn't been ready for it so soon. As it turns out, it's deceptively easy to become adjusted to catastrophe.

In a particular shot of irony, it later emerged that the Bootleg Fire raging in Oregon and California had torn through thousands of square kilometres of forest designated for the 'carbon offsets' of companies including Microsoft and BP. The basic premise of an offset is that individuals or corporations can purchase the entitlement to continue polluting or burning fossil fuels by paying someone else to 'offset' it in some way. In many cases, this takes the form of tree planting or forest management, such as the Klamath East forest offset in Oregon, owned and operated by the Green Diamond Resource Company. Not content to try to unpick the dubious assumptions and, often, practices underlying these schemes, the Bootleg Fire instead sent these claims toward carbon neutrality quite literally up in smoke. I envy it that.

The destruction of thousands of acres of the Klamath East forest is the essence and the irony of the green capitalist model, as well as a window into its future. Carbon offsets embody the logic of what I define in this book as 'green capitalism'. Green capitalism is an effort to address environmental catastrophe through new paths to accumulation while minimising disruption to our current economic systems and modes of living, irrespective of whether the actions taken actually lessen the damage they claim to or cause other harms in the process. Green capitalist solutions are predicated on the continuation of the destructive processes, systems and economic relations that have both delivered us into this state of crisis and severely delayed action to stymie it.

Amid the chaos and loss of that summer, I felt a seductive sliver of hope that compounding disasters might finally spur action on the environmental crisis. This hope is, however, an eternally fickle one. Many hoped that Hurricane Sandy, effective as it was at rocking a centre of global capital and power, might do the same. And though they are increasing in both frequency and devastation, we have had summers like these before, with little result. For many around the world, this level of disaster is now a routine that simply isn't reported nor reaches the ears of those of us in the enclave of the affluent Global North. Ultimately, we shouldn't need catastrophe to spur us to action on the climate and nature crises. We have had robust, evidenced consensus on their causes and trajectories for decades. And yet here we are.

I was born at 359ppm (meaning 359 parts per million of CO_2 in the atmosphere); twenty-three years later, this concentration had crept, unabated, above 400ppm. On the day I wrote this note, it had reached 413. The last time the concentration of carbon dioxide in the atmosphere was above 400ppm was some 16 million years ago, when the world looked radically different.[2] I say this not because we have surpassed some mythical threshold of climatic change beyond which there is no hope (though many groups place the threshold for 'safety' at 350ppm). I say this to underscore just how drastically we have changed the composition of the atmosphere in a few decades alone – decades in which we understood the origins of this crisis, and what we could do about it. And still, here we are.

How can it be that – with all our knowledge, capabilities, and ever-expanding public concern and dismay over the deteriorating health of our climate and natural world – we remain so mired in this mess? How can we, despite countless government pledges and programmes and a groundswell of civil society, remain quietly on course to sacrifice swathes of this planet's people and lifeforms to the demands of an affluent and powerful minority? These are the questions that motivate this book.

What follows is not an account of sinister denialists or overt obstructionism (which others have robustly and eloquently documented elsewhere),[3] but rather of false prophets and false solutions to these crises – however well intended (or not) they may be. This is a story of ineffectual efforts, distractions, and piety to the status quo. I hope that in telling it, I can contribute to some understanding of why – despite more policies, international conferences, and Elon Musks than ever – we are still where we are. And maybe how we can move on from here.

Acknowledgements

Writing is always a collaborative process – writing a book especially so. There are many people who helped me along the way, and too many more to name whose own work and thinking have greatly influenced what's written here. First, thanks are due to those who generously gave their time to reading and offering input to bits and pieces: Kate Aronoff, Ulrich Brand, Ben Braun, Rosie Collington, Frédéric Hache, Ann Pettifor and Markus Wissen. Your expertise much improved the text, and many of you have offered me time and support far beyond this specific project. To my team at Common Wealth, thank you for accommodating your absentee colleague for so long, and for picking up my slack without complaint. To Mat Lawrence, in particular, thank you for your generosity, guidance and friendship. You've made this process immeasurably easier. Thank you to Tom Dark at Manchester University Press for seemingly inexhaustible patience, thoughtful editing, and most of all for believing so strongly in this project. To my anonymous reviewer, thank you for your thoughtful challenges to the arguments and ideas made throughout this book. It is much better for them.

Acknowledgements

To a community of friends who encouraged and nourished me throughout the writing process – Tilly Cook, Vicky Foing, Danny Magill, Adam Rutledge, Eleanor Salter, Hallam Tuck, Alexa Waud – thank you. Thanks are also owed to my parents for their encouragement and often (accidentally) devastating feedback along the way. Thank you to Robin and Mark for offering their home to me for weeks to write in the tough early stages, and to Robin, in particular, for being a constant inspiration, distraction and source of joy. Finally, to Matthew, without whose love, patience and probably unjustified belief in me this book might never have been finished, thank you.

This book is dedicated to Betty.

 # Introduction: what's the value of a whale?

A team of researchers at the International Monetary Fund (IMF) recently posed a simple question: what is the value of a whale? The researchers settled on an even $2 million per specimen (great whales only), summing to an impressive $1 trillion for the existing global 'stock'.[1] They based their calculation on whales' contributions to eco-tourism revenue (ironically detrimental to whale populations themselves) and their robust capacity for carbon sequestration: over their lifetimes, on average great whales capture the equivalent of 33 tonnes of carbon dioxide – more per pound than a tree. Recognising the potential for this stock, if allowed to return to its pre-whaling population, to sequester 1.7 billion tonnes of CO_2 per year, the IMF researchers earnestly suggested investment in whale conservation over other carbon capturing methods. They estimated the cost of such conservation at a modest $13 per person on Earth. $13 – that's the value of a whale, as it turns out, to you or me.

I was seven years old when I first remember seeing a whale in the wild. On a diesel-belching ferry from Tsawwassen, British Columbia, staring out across the damp horizon, suddenly there it was. A fleshy, smooth, gunmetal grey lump rising out of the jet dark Pacific, a plume of mist, and it was gone. The encounter couldn't have lasted more than a few seconds, but standing in my high-vis raincoat I remember having the distinct feeling that I had just had the curtain lifted on another world. Ever since, I've spent every moment in which I'm lucky enough to find myself by the sea furtively scanning the horizon, hoping for another silent communion. Perhaps more than most, I am fixated on the fate of the whale. Their fate, however, is increasingly a barometer for our own.

Whales were once considered a great success story of conservation. The twentieth-century commercial whaling industry oversaw the slaughter of some 3 million whales, reducing the populations of some species by 90% and driving the traditional ways of life dependent on them to near extinction.[2] Eventually, as whale oil was replaced by fossil fuels, and following the International Whaling Commission's moratorium on the practice in 1986, many populations began to recover. Today, whales face new threats. Intensified global shipping channels disrupt their ability to communicate by flooding migratory paths with noise. In oceans warming and acidifying from an unrelenting flow of carbon into the atmosphere, their food sources and habitats are rapidly dwindling. In part because they are so large and their lives so long, whales are uniquely exposed to the pollution with which we flood the ocean, storing the signatures of our impact on the planet in their flesh. Some whales' blubber has accumulated levels of heavy metals and other toxins so high that their beached bodies need to be formally disposed of in hazardous waste facilities. Despite having been banned some forty years ago, PCBs – the chemicals found in coolant fluids and electrical appliances – today threaten half of the world's orca populations with extinction, accumulating in their blubber as it ascends the food chain before being passed on to their calves, extending their reach long after we prohibited their use. They have also accumulated in toxic levels in the breastmilk of Inuit mothers living on a traditional diet. Microplastics are ubiquitous in the bodies of belugas in the remote reaches of the Arctic Ocean.[3] Organisations tracking the deaths of beached whales report increasingly horrific contents lodged in their stomachs. As Rebecca Giggs documents in her book *Fathoms: The World in the Whale*,[4] a few years ago a beached whale was found on the Spanish coast with an entire collapsed greenhouse in its gut.

Confronted with these threats, against the ever-present backdrop of deepening climatic crisis, I admit I have wondered: should we welcome the IMF's effort to encourage investment in whales' preservation – all while capturing carbon without the need for vast and costly facilities? It's a reasonable sounding question set within reasonable sounding parameters, but even for those without a particularly strong penchant for whales, I would venture that the idea of trying to put a price tag on one seems intuitively strange. Plugging variables into a spreadsheet to evaluate the cost-benefit of saving a species like you would a hostile takeover is a tough equivalence to take seriously. Many might recoil at the idea of attaching a dollar value to a sentient life form; some likely think $2 million is too steep. Perhaps many more don't particularly care. I hope to convince you that all of us should, because however one might presently feel about the monetisation of great whales, this is not the only such calculation circulating the halls of political and economic power.

World leaders and financiers gather with growing frequency at elite conferences to earnestly debate how best to monetise

3

and trade 'ecosystem services' – that is, the clean water or breathable air a healthy environment provides us. Building markets for trading molecules of carbon dioxide is the top priority of innumerable climate conferences. Proposals have been drawn up for intergovernmental frameworks on 'biodiversity offsetting', whereby the destruction of a biodiverse ecosystem can be struck from the ecological balance sheet by developing an ecosystem of equivalent 'value' somewhere else. Whales, elephants, peat bogs, breathable air – little has escaped the covetous gaze of the world's actuaries. In short, these are not fringe efforts. Increasingly, they reflect the default position of those pulling the levers on our responses to possible climate and environmental catastrophe.

Neither are they new. As early as 1996, a team of researchers determined that the global environment's value was approximately $33 trillion, roughly double global GDP at the time.[5] A more recent survey by the World Economic Forum determined that some 50% of global GDP 'is moderately or highly dependent on nature',[6] effectively bringing the total 'value' of the entirety of Earth's ecosystems to about $44 trillion. A big number to be sure – but not much more than the total market capitalisation of the S&P 500 (a financial index containing the 500 largest public US companies). These sorts of headline-grabbing estimates and $2 million whales might make it easy to dismiss these efforts as the economic equivalent of clickbait, or the hobbyhorse of financial analysts (it's difficult to see, for instance, how half of all GDP would be undisturbed by the collapse of natural systems and, by extension, the collapse of the other half of GDP). But the idea that prices, markets, and clever financial products offer the solution to ecological crisis is the guiding framework of climate and environmental

4

governance. For as long as the climate and nature crises have featured on the political agenda, a fixation with markets and narrow economic priorities has shaped not only how those in positions of power – governments, policymakers, even prominent non-governmental organisations (NGOs) – respond to them, but the very way they (and many of us) engage with and conceive of them. In doing so, this tunnel vision has diminished our collective ability to imagine alternatives.

In 1990, the Intergovernmental Panel on Climate Change published its first landmark report, collating the scientific consensus on the climate crisis and highlighting the urgency of immediate and decisive reductions in carbon emissions. Cumulative emissions at the time of writing are 60% higher than they were at the time the report was published, and continue to rise apace.[7] This failure to 'bend the emissions curve' in the interim does not reflect a period during which consensus on the effects and implications of unabated emissions and their primary basis in the use of fossil fuels was not cemented. Certainly, a not-insignificant number of years within this period were marred by some groups' outright denial of the climate and nature crises; wilful obstructionism with respect to any proposed legislation equipped with any teeth for addressing them; robust lobbying and marketing campaigns from industry; the dissemination of misinformation, conspiracy theories and misrepresentations by well-funded 'think tanks'; and an apparent lack of sufficient public outcry (at least reaching the ears of those in power).[8] But for many years, the window has been closing on the effectiveness of this kind of behaviour. Outright denial is increasingly a figment of the fringes, and even the most right-leaning of political parties have suddenly found themselves in need of a stance on the greatest crisis facing humanity. Many now pay lip service to the central importance of 'sustainability' and conservation. Indeed, in some cases, fascist and nationalist parties have embraced environmentalism as a centrepiece of their politics; a representative of France's National Rally, for instance, recently laundered xenophobia and anti-migrant politics with green detergent, claiming 'borders are the environment's greatest ally ... it is through them we will save the planet.'[9]

In the private sector, Exxon once openly led the denialist charge, having obscured their own conclusions on the scientific origins of the climate crisis, spread disinformation, and waged well-funded lobbying campaigns for decades (a practice, it should be noted, that has not ended).[10] Now, they champion their nominal investment in algal fuel at every opportunity. Meanwhile, BP's and Shell's PR campaigns are adorned with the language of 'nature-based solutions' and slow-motion footage of redwood forests and lush mangrove swamps captured on drones. Over the course of the COVID-19 pandemic, 'sustainable' or 'ESG' (environmental-social-governance themed) investing enjoyed an unprecedented boom, with the ballooning savings of the wealthy flooding at record pace into funds sold as ethical or environmentally conscious. Businesses now voluntarily disclosing their carbon emissions and sustainability data number in the thousands, while in the UK a formerly climate-sceptic Prime Minister known for ridiculing 'eco-doomsters'[11] now champions his party's plan to use 'free markets, innovation and prosperity' to tackle climate change.[12] In short, compared to the landscape of even just a few years ago, politics and public attitudes, at least on the surface, look radically different. In many ways, this is a good thing. Changing the terms of public acceptability and debate is a helpful precondition for change.

The strange irony of this moment is that we are at once more aware of and committed to action on our planetary crisis than ever before, and yet we continue to fall woefully short of what we are capable of – let alone what must be done. As the gavels fell on the 26th Conference of the Parties in Glasgow (COP26) in November 2021, few felt buoyed by the outcome, despite the self-laudatory tone of some envoys. The long-standing commitment of wealthy nations to deliver $100 billion per year in climate finance to low-income countries by 2020 was still unmet; language referring to fossil fuels in the agreement suffered rounds of assault and manipulation by powerful governments; funds for the climate-related loss and damage already being suffered around the world were struck from the text; and even the loftiest of voluntary pledges – still lacking in plans for meeting them – could not bring temperature projections within 1.5 degrees Celsius, widely accepted as the upper limit of safety for global heating. Despite all the outward progress in the positions of politicians and business even since the Paris Agreement was signed, the final pledges emerging from the COP26 climate summit in Glasgow were, for the first time in history, enough to give us just a 50% chance of keeping warming below its 2 degrees Celsius target – and even then, only in the optimistic case that all of them are met.[13] Among the few new points of agreement was finalising Article 6 of the Paris Agreement: the establishment of agreed rules for carbon markets.

This book is motivated by a straightforward question: why – despite unprecedented public knowledge and concern, as well as commitment (at least rhetorically) from governments; despite the raft of technological solutions and policies we've devised; and despite the immediate suffering of so many as the impacts of ecological emergency hit – do we remain so off course from a habitable future and safe present for so many? The answer is somewhat less straightforward. In seeking it, this book does not aim, first and foremost, to add to the existing accounts of bad faith actors and corruption directly stymying progress on ecological action (though these are of course features of our problem, and there are many excellent accounts of their role).[14] My contention is that the forces holding us in our current state of suspended animation are no longer, primarily, as insidious as that. Instead, this book makes the case that our present challenge is less a plague of overt denial than of self-defeating adherence to flawed assumptions and 'solutions'. Led increasingly, as this book explores, by the interests and influence of a swollen finance sector, ours is a world defined by the imperatives of 'the economy' – conceived of as a discrete unit distinct from the environment in which it functions – rather than one where a thriving economy is a vehicle for life to flourish. Indeed, myopic and narrowly defined impacts on 'the economy' are often the only lens through which climate and environmental policies are designed and their success appraised.

The central target enshrined in the Paris Agreement, for example, is the progeny of economics. Before its reification by the Paris Agreement, the idea of limiting warming to 2 degrees has been widely attributed to economist William Nordhaus: in a 1975 paper on the economics of climate change, Nordhaus 'thinks out loud' about what might constitute a reasonable limit of global temperature rise for humanity to achieve,[15] after which the 2 degrees Celsius target began to percolate through the halls of influential policymakers.[16] Now among the world's most prominent economists, Nordhaus has dedicated much of his subsequent career to exploring the impacts of climate scientists' projections, weighing them against his particular economic considerations in an effort to determine where an appropriate balance between the two might lie, arguing in his 'Nobel'[17] acceptance speech that a 4 degrees Celsius rise in temperature would in fact be 'optimal' based on the cost-benefit analyses of his now famed DICE (Dynamic Integrated Climate-Economy) Model.

Nordhaus's models and analyses will be explored in depth in subsequent chapters. For the moment, to understand the questions motivating this book, there are two essential takeaways from Nordhaus's story. The first is that, in lieu of robust scientific determination or principles of global justice, it was an economist's thought experiment that shaped what remains a central pillar of global climate policy nearly 40 years later. The second is that although many on the spectrum of climate denial cite his work as justification for delaying or scrapping climate action, Nordhaus himself does not deny the reality of climate change – far from it. Indeed, his career has been dedicated to grappling with its implications. But that Nordhaus does not deny the science of climate change is precisely the problem, one that is not unique to his work. Rather, Nordhaus resides among a large cohort whose role in compromising vital and urgent action on the climate and nature crises stems not from their denial of the need for it, but of their work's commitment to understanding this profoundly human crisis through an almost puritanically economic lens. The road to hell is paved not only with good intentions, but with the incentives, efficiencies, and tidy cost-benefit analyses of many more and less well-meaning economists, politicians, businesspeople, financial institutions, civil servants and NGOs.

Rather than appraise our economy from the perspective of supporting life – recognising the ways in which our economic institutions and systems currently drive social and ecological crisis – instead we appraise life, and any action taken to protect it, in economic terms.[18] Crucially, this is not just the case for the policies and proposals of the political right. Across the political spectrum, from left-leaning politicians to progressive civil society groups, few can escape the pressure to frame and evaluate every idea in the language and imperatives of markets, finance, property or profit. In part, this constraint derives from a degree of crude necessity – negotiation often demands that we communicate in the language of our opponents to make ourselves heard, and admittedly, I do so in many parts of this book. But it cuts much more deeply than that. The primacy of market mechanisms, private property rights, and financial imperatives have changed the boundaries within which ecological crisis is debated and understood. The received wisdom of market forces holds sway over our understanding of how to address crisis in systems, both natural and social, whose complexity can't be forcibly collapsed into the greyscale of spreadsheets. As a result, the horizons of what is possible, what we are capable of, and what we are allowed to hope for have been needlessly shrunk. Indeed, they have changed the way many of us understand, relate to, and make sense of this incredible planet we inhabit.

And yet, even when measured against the metrics of those same economists and the policymakers they advise, we've made little progress. Emissions trading schemes – a crowning achievement of climate policy from the EU to California – have yet to deliver more than a modest impact on overall emissions, while generating several new problems in the process.[19] The booming carbon offset market, meanwhile, is plagued by issues of both ethics and efficacy. The economy continues to stutter from one anaemic 'recovery' to another, while wealth accrues in outrageous quantities to those lucky enough to own and control assets. As a consequence, staggering degrees of inequality, both intra- and inter-nationally, generate ethically and ecologically untenable distributions of consumption and waste. And underneath all of it, the invisible hand of the market continues to raise the natural thermostat.[20] An economist at the US Federal Reserve recently wrote – easily missed, in the footnote of a 30-page briefing on inflation – that for the purposes of his briefing, he would regrettably 'leave aside the deeper concern that the primary role of mainstream economics in our society is to provide an apologetics for a criminally oppressive, unsustainable, and unjust social order.'[21] In what follows, I pick this concern back up. Freeing ourselves from the assumptions, imperatives and misleading pragmatism of mainstream economics is long overdue. This book aims to make a contribution to doing so.

What this book is and is not

This book is intended as a stock-take of our collective responses to the climate and ecological emergencies. The hope is to carve out, to the fullest extent I can, an answer to the question posed above: why is it that we are so perilously off course for a future (and for many, a present) of ecological and climatic safety? My focus is not on the forces seeking to undermine the scientific consensus, though there are several, nor those actively resisting any advance of a programme seeking to confront a rapidly changing climate and degraded environment, though these too must be reckoned with. Rather, it is on those actors wielding outsized influence over the global response to ecological crisis, from mainstream economists to NGOs and financial titans, and the solutions they advocate, alongside the institutions and frameworks that structure the global economy in their image and interest. In sketching an answer, I necessarily sketch, in part, some vision for how things might be different, but this is not the primary aim of this book. Rather, my aim is to shed light on the resolute failure of the institutions and entities that govern our economies to 'follow the science' on ecological emergency, no matter how liberally they may parrot this line. For anyone else grappling with this book's question, I hope to offer some answers or, at the very least, some food for thought.

This book is about 'green capitalism', which I argue is the project guiding much of the global response to ecological crisis and the unprecedented threat to capitalist systems it presents. It is an imperfect term, but I use it to describe the union of two defining pillars: first, the effort to preserve existing capitalist systems and relations in response to this unprecedented threat, and second, ensuring new domains for accumulation in the transition to a decarbonised and ecologically sustainable economy.

The first chapter begins by interrogating the basic assumptions, rules and frameworks that guide mainstream, market-centric economic thinking. These are the foundations of green capitalist thought, informing most climate and environmental governance and the institutions that generate it. This provides the foundation for the second chapter's examination of the defining environmental policies and programmes pursued by many of the world's powerful political-economic institutions and governments, namely carbon pricing and carbon offsetting regimes. It is within this chapter that the programme of 'green capitalism' begins to take shape. Together, the first chapters explore how the flattening tendency and appeals to scientific objectivity of neoclassical economics, in combination with the depoliticising tendencies of market-centric governance and thought, serve to erase the inescapably political nature of ecological crisis and obscure the essential role of power in determining the contours of our responses to it.

The third chapter maps a critical and relatively nascent site of power in the global economy and, importantly, in the design of the green capitalist programme: the asset management industry. Once a niche industry serving the wealthy, asset managers now sit at the helm of Wall Street's immense power, with a consistently growing influence over policy including, saliently, the way many governments and international institutions are designing their responses to ecological crisis. The chapter examines the historically distinct combination of incentives, governing logics, and mechanics that drive this vast and highly concentrated industry, exploring the outsized impact of a small cohort of enormous firms. There are countless firms and industries at play within the messy politics of ecological crisis, not least the fossil fuel giants; however, their role is not documented here for the same reasons that I don't focus on the efforts of denialist politicians: first, these efforts have been catalogued in considerable detail elsewhere; and second, though they remain influential, they are not the primary entities shaping the green capitalist project as it is defined here, oriented as it is toward a particular set of 'solutions'.

The fourth chapter delves into the increasingly central role of the asset management industry in policymaking and in practice, namely within an essential new site of green capitalist effort: the booming 'sustainable finance' industry. If the focus of the book, and particularly these chapters, is skewed toward actors in the Global North, it is because, unjust as this reality is, the sites of power shaping green capitalism remain primarily within Northern governments, firms, NGOs and Northern-dominated international institutions like the IMF and World Trade Organization. Moreover, most international finance and exchange is governed by the legal systems of just two jurisdictions, New York State and England, whose respective capitols play host to most of the world's powerful financial and legal firms.[22] It is, therefore, to a large extent within these two sites that the programme of green capitalism is being defined and legally encoded, and where efforts to contest it should, at least for the time being, be directed.

In the fifth chapter, the horizon is extended beyond Wall Street and the City of London to the global level of finance and exchange, exploring how the institutions and systems that govern the international economic sphere presently undermine not only effective action to confront ecological crisis but also, critically, the ability to secure justice in doing so. As the chapter argues, confronting profound inequalities in both wealth and power within the global economy is neither optional nor a distraction from the challenge at hand, as efforts to do so are often described. To the contrary, doing so is a question of both justice and material necessity. The final chapter brings this material question to light, highlighting how the emerging green capitalist policy programme – from nature as a financial asset to the untenability of 'decoupled' growth – comes up at every turn against the physical constraints of a global economy marred by inequality, and a natural world whose complexity cannot be efficiently priced and traded, nor converted to terms compliant with optimising financial risk profiles.

The book thus has two primary aims. The first is to cohere the ideas, policies and relevant actors that make up the prevailing response to the climate and nature crises under a single banner, arguing that they all ultimately suffer from a particular set of biases and serve a particular set of interests. The second is to explore how these ideas and policies are self-defeating when it comes to grappling with the existential threat posed by a changing climate and the collapse of biological diversity; at best, they are a distraction for which we have no time, but at worst they are actively sabotaging the desperate fight for a future that can offer both justice and ecological stability. Together, my hope is that these amount to a useful resource for those who are concerned, terrified or incensed by deepening ecological crisis and injustice, and who seek, like me, to understand the seemingly insurmountable stasis gripping our systems and institutions of governance. Naming an adversary is not tantamount to vanquishing it, but it certainly doesn't hurt. Doing so is the project of this book.

The book concludes by asking what could lie beyond the constraints within which we have been needlessly confined. The shape of what comes next is not fixed. Evidence confirming that we have the ability to sustainably support a thriving quality of life for everyone on this Earth, and then some, continues to mount – provided we can accept that present distributions of consumption, wealth and waste are not only unjust, but also untenable.[23] As Aaron Benanav elegantly puts it, 'abundance is a social relation'[24] much more than a technological or material absolute. It is eminently possible to build an economy that supports thriving life rather than supplanting it. It is also far from guaranteed.

*****

Off the west coast of British Columbia around the same time as my first whale encounter, a young orca, perhaps disoriented

15

by the clamour of an increasingly trafficked coastline, became separated from its pod. The whale – later named Luna (Tsux'iit to the Mowachaht/Muchalaht First Nations people) – became a local darling. Scores of admiring whale-watching expeditions tracked Luna's exploits, and jubilant sightings were a regular feature in local media. People across the province felt a genuine connection to the ebullient young whale. Hollywood A-listers even produced a film about his struggle. Years of contentious debate were fought over the risks the whale posed to industry and shipping channels, and local authorities eventually approved a mission to transport Luna back to his community – an effort resisted by the Mowachaht/Muchalaht First Nations government of the region, who recognised Luna as the reincarnation of their late chief who had died just three days prior to the whale's appearance, and who had expected to return after death as an orca.

Luna's ability to capture the public imagination was unsurprising. After all, the whale has long been a source of awe, fear, wonder – one of the remaining symbols of the wildly unknown world we occupy. Whales occupy central roles in many Indigenous societies, from the Chukchi people of Chukotka at the North-Eastern tip of Russia to the Bequia of St. Vincent and the Grenadines. Cave walls in the Chilean desert bear in brilliant iron-oxide 1,500-year-old drawings of whale hunts. Baleen giants swallow ships whole and evade the harpoons of sailors across the pages of English literature. Every summer, hundreds of whale-watching boats flood the coastal waters off Alaska carrying eager tourists from the dozens of cruise ships that traverse the route. Whales are at once alien and, to our delight, infinitely anthropomorphisable, forming close communities with complex language. They are also intimately woven throughout the history of capitalism. Though initially hunted for their meat, by the nineteenth century, whales had become the essential commodity of imperial and industrial expansion. Whale oil, a by-product of boiling their blubber, illuminated ships and rapidly growing cities. The rendered bodies of millions of whales lubricated the machines and fertilised the fields of an ascendent industrial capitalism. Today, they occupy the spreadsheets of researchers at the IMF.

Just a few years after he was first recognised, while playing with a friendly tugboat, Luna was killed in the ship's propeller. Scientists estimate that within 30–50 years, there may be no orcas left off the coasts of the world's industrialised nations.[25] In their vastness, their ancientness and their intense strangeness, whales have long filled us with delight, wonder, fear. Now they wash up on beaches with bellies full of plastic waste in banal confirmation of our mastery over the last wild places. That mastery is rapidly approaching the end of its tenure. To understand where we go from here, we first have to ask: how did we get here? Why are we still here?

1

Gatekeepers: economics and the collapse of possibility

> Good policies must lie somewhere between wrecking the economy and wrecking the world. –William Nordhaus[1]
>
> No, no, you're not thinking. You are just being logical. –Niels Bohr[2]

In *Seeing Like a State*, James C. Scott documents the early efforts of forestry scientists in eighteenth- and nineteenth-century Germany.[3] For the German state, the forest was an essential source of fiscal revenue, whose precise management and exploitation was therefore an essential task. To maximise the productive yield of the nation's forests while ensuring a stable supply of trees for the long term, researchers in the burgeoning field began to analyse Germany's forests, measuring the distributions of trees' ages and circumferences in an average plot of land. Over time, scientists developed the concept of 'Sustained Yield Management', a mathematical framework that modelled the optimal schedule for planting and harvesting trees, as though managing crop rotation.[4] At the core of the model was the *Normalbaum*, a mathematically abstracted ideal tree with average traits deemed to be representative of its particular species. By evaluating the yields to be had from particular distributions of trees, scientists determined they could

best meet their goal by planting precisely spaced trees of a certain age in regimented blocks to create a uniformly aged forest
comprised of a single species, either Norwegian spruce or the
Scotch pine – cash crops with quick growth trajectories.[5] To
eliminate the threat of pests and ensure the soil's nutrients were
directed solely toward the trees, the chaotic undergrowth characteristic of a natural forest was ruthlessly cleared, while dead
or hollowed trees which had played host to forest animals were
removed. Over time, the *Normalbaum* moved 'from abstraction
to reality'.[6]

For a period, the Germans' experiment in forest management was, by its own measures, a runaway success. Rows upon
rows of even and virtually symmetrical plantings were much
easier for minimally trained, low-paid workers to both manage
and harvest. The uniformity of the trees made lumber yields
unprecedentedly reliable to calculate and obtain, while creating
new opportunities for experimentation to optimise their methodology. Both pragmatically and aesthetically, the Germans'
'forests' came to be celebrated as a major achievement in
science, replicated not only domestically but around the world,
from Australia to India and British Columbia.[7] It was not to last.
While the first 'crop rotation' of trees was staunchly productive,
by the time the second planting reached maturity – roughly 100
years after the method was first put into practice, owing to the
lifetimes of trees – cracks had begun to show. The uniformity
of the trees and their spacing turned out to be more amenable to the pests plaguing the chosen species, while rendering
the trees more vulnerable to disease and damage from storms.
Clearing out both fauna and the forest floor, meanwhile, also
cleared the soil of its nutrients. By the time the second generation of trees was coming of age, the impact on both survival and

growth was devastating – so devastating in fact that it merited a new word: *Waldsterben*, meaning 'forest death'.[8] Ultimately, the razor-sharp focus and organised elegance of German forestry science that had made it so celebrated became its downfall – the consequence of reducing the phenomenal complexity of old-growth forests to a single, optimised variable. Having forcibly excluded as much of this complexity as possible from their model, it was only a matter of time before everything cast aside came roaring back.

The experience of German forestry – made even more impactful through its replication across the world – offers a cautionary insight into the risk, to borrow from Scott, of 'dismembering an exceptionally complex and poorly understood set of relations and processes in order to isolate a single element of instrumental value.'[9] Admittedly, all models and analyses involve a certain degree of abstraction, selecting relevant variables and attempting to measure their interactions. Indeed, as a practice, science relies on it; without abstracting away some of the noise of complex phenomena, we would scarcely be able to study them in any meaningful way. The trouble for German forestry science was that the reduction of this complexity was so extensive as to swiftly shift from the experiment's source of rigour to its demise.

With respect to ecological crisis, one might reasonably expect that the analyses most adhered to by politicians and the numerous other institutions that govern our response to it – such as the World Bank or offices of the United Nations – would be those that reflect the science of the ecological phenomena confronting us. However, while these models regularly prompt sober press conferences from political leaders, and undoubtedly inform our 'targets' and 'ambitions' (albeit alongside other considerations), in practice it is far more often an economic model that ultimately shapes the policies and decisions taken. The co-optation of scientists by the fossil fuel industry and their sowing doubt on the science of the climate crisis is by now a well-documented story. It is also a practice that, thankfully, is becoming slowly confined to the annals of history. Only a dwindling number of politicians, even among conventionally denial-rich and vocal circles, now deny the hard science of the climate crisis. Instead, the earnest refrain to 'listen to the science' is by now a cliché.

The role played by professional economists in direct policy obstruction and climate denial is less traversed. When, in the 1980s, governments first began to consider whether and how they should address a changing climate, the economics pro-fession was on hand to provide the analysis demonstrating, for example, that the cost of curbing emissions or shifting to renewable energy was too great to justify (analysis, it should be emphasised, often funded by major fossil fuel producers).[10] In the fraught decades since, from proposals for carbon pricing in the United States to basic environmental protections and the adoption of the Kyoto Accord, a handful of economists and consulting firms have published report after report in response to emissions-curbing proposals that project job losses number-ing in the hundreds of thousands and caution of the inevitable loss in GDP they will incur.[11]

Like the coterie of fossil fuel-backed scientists routinely wheeled out to dispute the scientific consensus, so too has a vocal team of economists lent the perceived authority of their discipline to the interests of oil companies and reticent politicians. In the process, they created years of delay and wasted time while cementing an enduring perception among policymakers and the wider public of an essential trade-off between a stable climate and environment, and a healthy economy. There is nothing wrong, in principle, with using economic insights in evaluating our response to ecological crisis – understanding how a radically changing world will impact our lives and wellbeing, mediated through economic interaction and exchange, is important for deciding in what ways we respond to crisis, as well as what form the alternative economic future we must build should take. There are, however, two essential problems with the way economics is currently employed in the swirling mass of debate over how we should address ecological crisis.

First is the extent to which narrowly defined economic measures (for instance, rates of aggregate GDP growth or tallies of public-sector debt) are routinely prioritised to the neglect, or at the direct expense, of concrete needs and lived impacts. Often, this prioritisation is weaponised against the actions we must take to both mitigate and adapt to deepening ecological crisis, as in the common (as well as frequently inaccurate or disingenuous) refrain that policies designed to curb emissions will necessarily place unliveable burdens on working people or load debt on future generations. But, as this chapter explores, economic analyses built on substantial degrees of abstraction are also at the centre of the 'solutions' that presently dominate the policy discourse, such as carbon pricing. Herein lies the second essential problem: the extent to which these solutions centre a single and narrow school of economic thought, to the near-total exclusion of the rich diversity of perspectives available to us, and which we desperately need to hear and heed to secure a future that is not just liveable, but wonderful to live in.

Free markets, double government

Overt obstructionism and conflicts of interest within the economics profession have undoubtedly cost us years of inaction and obfuscation on the urgency of the ecological crisis, which we did not have to spare. This is not, however, the focus of this chapter. Instead, I argue that today, the most significant impact of economists and economic thought on our approach to the climate and nature emergencies is their invocation, with varying levels of good faith, in service and in support of action on these crises. The more potent and widespread threat to action comes not from obstruction so much as the pursuit of false 'solutions' – the solutions of what throughout this book I identify as an emergent 'green capitalism'. From the commodification of nature to carving out new pathways for 'green' accumulation and financial speculation, the reason for our continued failure to mitigate the risk of catastrophe – despite historically high levels of belief in 'the science' and professed public support for action – is the adherence, at every turn, to economic imperatives over other needs. In short, the trouble is not economists' advocacy against action so much as the nature of the 'action' that mainstream economics prescribes.

This chapter explores how, through a series of critical junctures in recent history, a mainstream 'market-centric' economic consensus on the climate and nature crises both emerged and was cemented. These are the assumptions, frameworks and ideologies which structure the emergent 'green capitalism' we increasingly inhabit. 'Mainstream' and 'market-centric' are both imperfect terms, with exact boundaries that are difficult to draw, and which capture multiple traditions of thought.

23

For clarity and expediency, however, throughout this book I use the term 'market-centric' (interchangeably with 'mainstream') to denote the combination of two perspectives: neoclassical economics and neoliberal statecraft. I use 'neoclassical' here to describe a school of economic thought that adheres to several core assumptions about how the economy and wider world operates, and methods for studying it. For the purposes of this discussion, the most important of these include: economic entities as 'rational maximisers' making decisions based on (theoretically perfect) information; the price mechanism as the superlative conveyor of information, with the corollary that markets are the optimal vehicle for delivering efficient outcomes; the prioritisation of efficiency over other outcomes; and a methodology centred around mathematical modelling of an often highly abstracted economy and world. From carbon pricing, to 'sustainable finance', to the very modelling that informs the pathways of Intergovernmental Panel on Climate Change (IPCC) reports, neoclassical ideas are the essential foundation of most policy programmes and 'solutions' to climate and environmental breakdown advanced by Global North governments and prominent international institutions.

The use of economics in the design of and politics surrounding climate and environmental governance is and has always been political. There is no escaping the inherent subjectivity of the assumptions and choices that permeate economic analyses. Nor is there any denying the effect of politicians and ideological projects in elevating certain economic perspectives and practices over others. Despite this, the received common sense, including within the institutions most influential in shaping our response to the climate and nature crises, is that the economic sphere is and should be kept distinct from the political.

This is not by accident. It is the product of the second pillar of the 'market-centric' or 'mainstream' consensus: the neoliberal framework for governance. Though the term is so regularly and variably used as to have lost some of its meaning, as historian Quinn Slobodian articulates, the neoliberal project was a purposive effort to insulate the economic sphere from interference by democratic demands, which neoliberals viewed as damaging to economic prosperity and growth.[12]

Beginning in the 1970s and enduring over the past several decades, the framework of neoliberal statecraft and governance has produced an artificial separation between the political and the economic through a strategic ideological, intellectual and political effort. Its architects described a system of 'double government', with one set of laws, norms and institutions for the market, and another for the political. As Slobodian writes, the aim and effect of this division – leaving some sovereignty over domestic social affairs to nation-states while limiting sovereignty over the economic sphere – was to 'satisfy mass demands for self-representation while preserving the international division of labour and the free search for profitable markets.'[13] Many elements of the 'neoliberal consensus' will be recognisable: the privatisation of public assets and services in the UK under Margaret Thatcher; President Reagan's 'regulatory relief' agenda; the crushing of organised labour on both sides of the Atlantic; the deregulation of finance in the world's financial hubs (namely London and New York); and the pursuit of an increasingly liberalised, global marketplace wherein capital and finance move freely in their pursuit of returns. But where common sense on neoliberal governance has often misconstrued it as an approach based on a small state and limited government 'interference', to the contrary, neoliberalism has both built new and reworked existing institutions and intellectual and legal architectures 'to encase the global market from interference' from the sovereign nation-state and the democratic populace.[14] As David Harvey summarises, neoliberalism can be understood as:

A theory of political economic practices that proposes human well-being can best be advanced by liberating individual entrepreneurial freedoms skills within an institutional framework characterised by strong private property rights, free markets, and free trade. The role of the state is to create and preserve an institutional framework appropriate to such practices.[15]

Leading neoliberal thinkers like Friedrich Hayek argued that states and individuals had insufficient knowledge of the unknowably large and complex economy to be able to engage in effective economic planning, instead advancing the idea that the economy can be best governed only by the price mechanism and market forces.[16] The project of neoliberalism has a lengthy history extending back to intellectual circles in the inter-war period who, responding to perceived state protectionism at the time, primarily in the form of trade barriers, sought to liberate and globalise the economy from the perceived hindrance of national sovereignty.[17] In this sense, though it has become cast in a depoliticised light – a programme of technocracy and 'value-free' efficient governance – neoliberalism has always been a political project whose goal (in many ways, if still incompletely, achieved) has been to prevent 'too much' democracy or, in the words of neoliberal scion Milton Friedman, the 'internal threat' stemming from the inherent ignorance of 'men of good intentions and good will who wish to reform us.'[18]

Over time, a consensus has formed that the state should, where possible, limit its role to supporting the action of markets. Meanwhile, deference to (or strategic leverage of) economic imperatives and authority has become a political fixture, from the technocratic authority of the European Commission and the European Union's commitment to 'green growth', to the constant justification in economic terms of climate and environmental action within international institutions such as UN climate negotiations or the World Bank. Even in ostensibly radical proposals such as the Green New Deal resolution advanced by Congressperson Alexandria Ocasio-Cortez and Senator Ed Markey, various progressive policies are interspersed with the language of markets and profit, from providing 'adequate capital' to private businesses, to prioritising sufficient 'returns on investment' to the public purse from capital grants and 'ensuring a commercial environment'.[19]

The economics profession has been instrumental to the maintenance and continued success of this project of governance, particularly by cementing the impression that a planned and state-or-otherwise coordinated approach to transitioning the global economy away from fossil fuels is a futile endeavour. The default position is one of constant assurance that no action taken to avert the possibility of catastrophic ecological damage will damage 'the economy', understood through the impossibly narrow frame of GDP growth – itself inappropriately conflated with human welfare as well as a historically recent and contestable objective. Over the past few decades, the combined tenets of neoclassical economic thought and neoliberal statecraft have narrowed and cemented the parameters within which climate and environmental policy is permitted to operate. In this sense, mainstream or 'market-centric' economics has been an essential tool in the advance of green capitalism as the answer to our mounting ecological crises. The project of green capitalism is intellectually enabled by the work and the enduring intellectual authority of market-centric economics and statecraft, which serve to present the prevailing economic arrangements and systems as somehow natural, inevitable and unassailable. The impact of this tunnel vision has been profound: by viewing the world through the lens of a narrow set of economic imperatives, the influence of market-centric economics has been to fundamentally alter the way the state functions and society understands itself – from our relations to each other to our position in the natural world. In doing so, it has severely and needlessly restricted the capacity to imagine necessarily radical alternatives. To invert the wisdom of the late Raymond Williams, by continuing to cleave to the myopic worldview of market-centric economics in addressing ecological crisis, we risk making despair convincing, rather than hope possible.

The greatest market failure ever seen

Within mainstream economics, the climate and nature crises are defined overwhelmingly in the terms of 'market failure'. The seminal 2006 Stern Review on the Economics of Climate change – a document of near-biblical importance for policymakers – described climate change as 'the greatest market failure ever seen.' A market failure describes the failure to price in the 'externalities' of an economic activity: the consequences of said activity that impact upon others not involved within the activity or transaction. Because the cost of these impacts is not priced, they remain 'external' to the market, which is therefore unable to produce an optimal outcome. Externalities may be positive, such as the air pollution avoided by an individual's decision to walk to work, or more often negative, as in the case of carbon emissions, which impact every living being on Earth in the form of climate change, whether or not they contributed to or benefited from the production of those emissions.

For Stern and much of the economics profession, the climate crisis is understood as both an archetypal and extreme example of a market failure, insofar as the enormous true costs of carbon emissions are not reflected in the monetary costs of the actions that produce them, from massive agro-businesses engaged in widespread deforestation to frequent flyers taking regular trans-Atlantic flights. In this framework, because the adverse effects of carbon emissions are external to the market, it over-produces them. The solution, therefore, is simple: the costs of these externalities must be 'internalised' – that is, brought into the market via the price mechanism. Once appropriately priced, the logic goes, market actors incentivised by profit will both effectively and efficiently (two terms which, as we will see, are critically distinct) shift economic activity away from high-emitting areas to reduce their costs. The idea that the externalities of emissions and environmental damage can be fully internalised to the market, which will then eliminate them, is a fundamental logic underlying the governance approach of green capitalism, embodied in its flagship policy: the carbon price.

The economics of climate change literature is dominated by discussion of carbon pricing, while prominent figures, from Bill Gates to William Nordhaus, champion its merits in their widely selling books. Among politicians of varying stripes and a suite of the world's powerful institutions from the United Nations to the World Bank, carbon pricing has long been the default policy position despite years of resistance, patchy implementation and questionable results. Its popularity is not impossible to understand. There is an intuitive appeal to the idea of putting a price on carbon; after all, our continued failure to do so leaves major polluters unimpeded from wreaking outsize damage on our shared planet, which seems an immense moral failure. For many, the simplicity and elegance of the idea, often contrasted with the purported messiness and inconsistency of a regulatory or 'command-and-control' approach, also holds practical appeal. Similarly, the idea that the cost of emitting will be distributed in proportion to how much one emits – that is, those who consume more carbon and do more damage will pay proportionately more – speaks to a sense of fairness. Though less widespread in mainstream policy and discourse, the same logic is also frequently and increasingly applied to pricing ecological damage through concepts such as 'natural capital' and 'ecosystem services' – proposals for monetising the benefits such as breathable air or clean water that nature currently offers us freely. Ecosystem services and the economic approach to nature are discussed in depth in Chapter 6.

For mainstream economics, there is little question of the capacity, in the words of political economist Servaas Storm, for the market's 'invisible hand' to 'adjust the natural thermostat.'[20] Once implemented, the argument goes, the consistent and likely painful signal stemming from a steep carbon price that sufficiently embodies its social impact in the form of high costs will necessarily push profit-seeking firms and capitalists to innovate and adapt, and individuals to shift to decarbonised sources of energy. In his recent book *The Spirit of Green*, William Nordhaus claims 'Economics points to one central and all-important truth about climate-change policy … For any policy to be effective, it must raise the market price of CO_2.'[21] Similarly, as influential economist Martin Weitzman wrote with stirring conviction in his response to the 2006 Stern Review:

One can only wish that U.S. political leaders might have the wisdom to understand and the courage to act upon the breath-takingly simple vision that steady pressure from the predictable presence of a high carbon price reflecting social costs (whether imposed directly through taxes or indirectly via tradable permits) would do more to unleash the decentralized power of capital-istic American inventive genius on the problem of researching, developing, and finally investing in economically efficient carbon-avoiding alternative technologies than all of the piece-meal command-and-control standards and patchwork subsidies making the rounds in Washington these days.[22]

The time of the Stern Review was a heyday for the popular-ity of carbon pricing as a policy tool. Major institutions from the International Energy Agency to the World Bank strongly advocated its use in policy papers around this time, while the European Union's flagship Emissions Trading Scheme began its pilot phase in 2005, entering into full force in 2008. Perhaps most profusely in favour of a carbon price and the market-based approach was the UN Development Programme, which in a 2007 report stated: 'this is not the time to come back to a system of massive quotas and bureaucratic controls because of climate change. Emission targets and energy efficiency controls have an important role to play, but it is the price system that has to make it easier to achieve our goals.'[23]

The enormity of the support for the concept's elegance, its efficiency, and its supposed pragmatism raises the question: why is there not already a global price on carbon (or indeed ecosystem services)? Or, more modestly, why has no jurisdic-tion managed to enact a carbon price effective enough to bring their economy in line with the trajectory of a safe future? This is an urgent question, with a complex answer. The next chapter discusses in depth the various mechanisms for putting a price on carbon, as well as the practical and theoretical issues that have undermined them. For the time being, however, I begin with the carbon price because it embodies the core tenets of market-centric economic thought on the climate and nature crises. It is also a policy emblematic of green capitalist logic: carbon pricing offers, in theory, a pathway for addressing environmental breakdown that preserves capitalist social and economic relations. Better still, it does so by creating a new, state-facilitated route to profit-making. It is telling that the origins of carbon markets can be found in 1960s proposals for 'pollution markets', developed by a heady blend of economists, large environmental NGOs, business groups and financial titans such as Richard Sandor, the so-called 'father of financial futures'.[24] Within the carbon price thus sit the twin logics of the green capitalist framework: first, the hypothetical and, as I argue throughout this book, impossible project of preserving the architecture and arrangements of wealth and power that define contemporary capitalism; and second, the identification and construction of new sites for accumulation within an economy and world that must change rapidly to secure climatic and ecological stability.

Efficiency evangelism

Carbon pricing is emblematic of both the way in which market-centric economics understands the climate and nature crises, and of its inability to materially grapple with them. At the heart of both is the singular value that mainstream economics places on the pursuit of efficiency in designing solutions. In a recent report commissioned by French President Emmanuel Macron, two economists specialising in the field wrote: 'Carbon pricing has the advantage of focusing on efficiency in terms of cost per tonne of CO_2, without the need to identify in advance which measures will work.'[25] Similarly, as quoted above, Weitzman argued that the price mechanism was the superior approach to climate policy, to be contrasted with supposedly 'command-and-control' style regulation, on the grounds that it would provide the most economically efficient solutions. There is perhaps no better summary of the centrality of efficiency to neoclassical economic thinking than that provided by William Nordhaus, arguably the most prominent economist working on the issue of climate change, when he wrote: 'Efficiency is the staple diet of economists, who eat it for breakfast, lunch, and dinner.'[26] But to set aside for a moment the question of whether any of the preceding claims to the efficiency of carbon pricing are empirically valid, what is distinctly absent from this array of praise is a justification for the implicit assertion that efficiency should be our primary consideration in designing and evaluating policies to confront climate and ecological crisis.

Within neoclassical economics, efficiency implies the most effective use of resources in satisfying various outcomes and needs. This sounds reasonable enough as a principle for policymaking. The trouble with efficiency, however, is that it does not in any sense require an ethical or fair outcome, nor, as in the case of climate policy discussed below, does it necessarily imply an effective outcome – that is, an outcome in which emissions are reduced as swiftly as possible. Indeed, as Partha Dasgupta and G.M. Heal argue with respect to intergenerational distributions of resources: resource allocation can be efficient and yet be 'perfectly ghastly' from an ethical perspective.[27] Moreover, though cast as a neutral concept, deciding where to establish the boundaries of efficiency involves several subjective decisions – a theme returned to below. The surface-level definition of efficiency as simply the least-cost path to a given target obscures essential decisions about how the target was determined (for instance, why should we focus exclusively on rapid emissions reduction, rather than deciding speed cannot compromise justice, distributional concerns, durability of reductions and so on), and which variables are or are not counted as 'costs' in the calculus.[28] This omission raises vital questions: who is at the table when these decisions are made? Whose perspectives and needs are considered, and whose, such as the world's poor majority, are ignored or discounted?

Though critical, injustice is not the only problem with centring cost-efficiency in evaluating climate and environmental policy. Confronting the threats of climate and ecological breakdown will require us to remake the infrastructures and arrangements of the entire global economy, from the obvious, like energy and transport systems, to the fertilisers and methods we use to raise food or the extent of our exploitation of land and resources. This is a Herculean task, and our time is short. In this context, prioritising the most cost-effective and efficient use of resources seems intuitively misguided. As Cedric Durand writes:

> Given the existential threat posed by climate change ... our concern should be with the effectiveness of reducing greenhouse gases rather the efficiency of the effort. Instead of using the price mechanism to let the market decide where the effort should lie, it is infinitely more straightforward to ... provide a consistent reduction plan to ensure that the overall goal will be achieved in time.[29]

In effect, as Durand argues, considering the scale, complexity and existential quality of the challenge we currently face, the idea that 'efficiency' should be a priority is difficult to defend. Our primary concern must be ensuring that climatic and ecological stability occurs, and that in doing so we do not generate profound injustice – not what the cost will be. Ecological crisis is not a problem for which we have the luxury of time for price signals to gradually shift economic activity. There is, therefore, a certain irony in the fact that mainstream economists have helped undermine the prospects for their totemic solution, carbon pricing, to be effective as a standalone or even primary policy approach. In short, by providing the intellectual foundations for procrastination and diverting policymakers' attention from more direct and effective strategies such as stringent regulation of emissions, they have enormously shrunk the window of time within which we must achieve increasingly extraordinary reductions in emissions and a transformation of global production and consumption. And, as the next chapter explores, by reducing the complexity of the challenge to a question of efficiency concerning a single issue – reducing carbon emissions – a misplaced emphasis on the efficiency achievable through the price mechanism ignores that some forms of carbon reduction are far more durable, effective (inasmuch as they swiftly and directly reduce emissions) and just than others.

Why, then, is efficiency the priority, implicit or otherwise, of policy approaches in the context of an existential crisis with profound implications for justice and equality? Certainly, an economically efficient allocation of resources in addressing ecological crisis might be an unobjectionable feature of a well-designed plan. But why, in the face of a genuinely existential crisis with profound time pressures and already-existing impacts and harms throughout the world, should efficiency be placed above the far more pressing issue of effectiveness, or, as this book will argue, its corollaries: justice and equality? As Richard Lane has documented, a convincing justification for 'the iron law of efficiency' as the essential test of 'the viability of environmental regulation' is sorely lacking; by contrast, the central role for economic efficiency in environmental policymaking has been cemented not by evidence so much as assertions by its advocates.[30] In other words, by simply asserting that efficiency is necessary, and that market-based mechanisms are efficient while direct regulatory approaches are inefficient, the assertion has become accepted 'fact' in the common sense – the assumption is the conclusion.

In the past, even substantially smaller transformations than the one we now face – for instance the electrification of national economies such as the United Kingdom's – have been of sufficient complexity and pressing need as to demand a public-led approach in both planning and delivery. There is simply no example of a market-based transformation that comes close to resembling the scale and complexity demanded by the global replacement of fossil-fuel based infrastructure. Doing so means abandoning as our guiding priority the central drive of the market-centric economic frameworks that inform the decisions made by policymakers the world over, and economists' 'staple diet': economic efficiency. Despite this, as the next chapter explores, cost efficiency remains the guiding principle of the green capitalist policy programme.

Abstracting catastrophe

The introduction to this book recounted the role of a thought experiment published by William Nordhaus in the 1970s in the origin story of the 2 degrees Celsius target that would become cemented as the safe limit for global warming, enshrined in the Paris Agreement on climate change. What was the basis of Nordhaus's conclusion? *Prima facie*, one might reasonably assume the target was the product of a review of the best available science, and selected as a means for minimising damage, suffering, and loss of life and livelihood. One would be disappointed. As Professor Steve Keen has documented, the idea that 2 or, more shockingly, 3 or more degrees of warming could be 'optimal' is instead the product of cost-benefit analysis of the projected impact of the climate crisis on the global economy. These cost-benefit analyses are intended to provide a supposedly 'pragmatic' guide for policymakers to ensure that our response to the climate crisis is economically cost-efficient, balancing the costs of action for today's population with the benefits received by those in the future of averting climate impacts. These analyses are omnipresent in the landscape of climate policy and governance, featuring within the calculations that inform the scenarios of the IPCC, the global scientific authority on the climate crisis whose synthesis of climate science and pathways for curbing emissions inform the targets and strategies of governments around the world. They are also, however, analyses based on economic models and assumptions so abstracted as to bear little, if any, resemblance to the real world, the living beings within it, or the systems they inhabit.[31]

As Nordhaus wrote in one of his earliest papers on the subject, attacking the work of another economist: 'most scientists would require empirical validation of either the assumptions or the predictions of the model before declaring its truth content', rather than simple 'subjective plausibility.'[32] This is, however, precisely what much mainstream economic work on the climate crisis has relied on, and features in the assumptions that underlie Nordhaus's and others' (widely used) models. For instance, after first acknowledging that 'human societies thrive in a wide variety of climatic zones' early in his influential 1991 paper on the economic impacts of climate change – the frameworks of which have since come to inform the IPCC's economic synthesis – Nordhaus proceeds to exclude nearly 90% of all economic activity from his analysis. His justification for doing so is that these activities take place in 'carefully controlled environments that will not be affected by climate change.'[33] The industries assumed to be negligibly affected – and therefore excluded from subsequent estimates of how GDP will be impacted by a changing climate – featured not only mining (a decision later reversed), but also manufacturing, financial services and insurance, among several others.[34] In short, because these activities were determined to take place indoors, it was assumed that a potentially catastrophic change in global temperatures – displacing millions, causing widespread failure in agricultural systems, subjecting enormous regions of the global coastline to inundation by saltwater, and beyond – wouldn't affect them.

Were Nordhaus not so immensely influential a figure, perhaps the findings of this paper could have been disregarded. However, the original 1991 paper is, to borrow from a paper co-authored by none other than Nicholas Stern (author of the Stern Review), 'a landmark in economic research' – a genuine first of its kind, which 'opened the [economics] profession to a new field of application – climate change', and has informed an enormous volume of influential research since.[35] The 2014 IPCC report, for instance, repeats the notion almost verbatim: 'For most economic sectors, the impact of climate change will be small relative to the impacts of other drivers', such as labour pressures, population changes, and other more conventionally economic factors.[36] Certainly, those sorts of factors presently have a greater effect on GDP than do climatic impacts, though this is arguably already beginning to change.[37] However, with respect to advancing climate crisis, present factors influencing the economy cannot be assumed to be representative of a future of potentially radical ecological destabilisation.

In spite of this, the IPCC's 2014 report concludes that 'economic activities such as agriculture, forestry, fisheries, and mining are exposed to the weather and thus vulnerable to climate change'.[38] As Keen notes, the implication that direct exposure to weather is the sole vehicle through which the climate crisis might affect economic activity is an astonishing finding in a major report from the world's authority on climate science and pathways forward. It should be said: unpicking technical problems with economists' calculations of how ecological crisis will impact GDP growth as the lens through which we criticise mainstream climate economics is itself problematic, insofar as it reinforces the idea that GDP and similar measures should be upheld as the means through which we understand and make judgments on policies and actions. There is a rich body of work arguing for entirely different and more representative measures for doing so; however, for the sake of engaging with these ideas on their own terms, and because we presently exist within a system in which these measures prevail, throughout this book I will at various points uncritically employ such concepts without being directly critical of the concepts themselves.

The extent of the abstraction present in Nordhaus's (and, years later, the IPCC's economic conclusions) also leaves out of consideration the complexity of our globalised economy, in which no single industry could be considered immune to impacts elsewhere, nor in other industries. Trade, finance, insurance, various forms of transport, government services – none of these activities, unjustifiably excluded from consideration, are wholly independent of one another. To assume that substantial hits to the agricultural or mining industries would not also significantly impact finance, for example, is, in a word, bizarre. Nonetheless, the assumption that the majority of global GDP will be only lightly impacted by climate change continues to be asserted.[39] Meanwhile, the impacts of ecological decline and biodiversity collapse have, until recently, often failed to feature. Put differently, to abstract away the interconnectedness of the global economy and the inherent complexity of the climate crisis and its relationship with ecological breakdown is to create an elegant calculation of nothing.

That Nordhaus's lauded DICE model (Dynamic Integrated Climate-Economy model), prescribes 3.5 degrees Celsius of warming by 2100 as 'economically optimal' should immediately set alarms ringing. A world in which global average surface temperatures have increased by 3.5 degrees Celsius does not imply that the average temperature in any given town or region around the world is simply 3.5 degrees higher. To the contrary, the Earth is warming highly unevenly, with the Arctic and oceans having borne the brunt of warming to date, keeping other parts of our planet's surface much cooler than they would otherwise have been. In the near term, this has temporarily softened the blow of a warming world; in the long term, however, the disproportionate heating currently shouldered by these critical ecosystems could trigger devastating climatic and environmental 'tipping points' with unknowable and potentially irreversible implications, such as permafrost thaw, mass coral die-off, or the cessation of ocean currents. Three degrees of warming could inflict droughts 'persistent enough to cripple the world's food supply', while according to climate scientist Kevin Anderson, four degrees is likely 'incompatible with an organised global community.'[40] It's difficult to see how either could be economically 'optimal'.

I should emphasise that Nordhaus – though uniquely influential and acclaimed – is not alone in producing this kind of analysis. There is a wide and enduring gulf between economists and scientific reality when it comes to the climate and nature crises, which extends far beyond one person. For example, a paper published in the Proceedings of the National Academy of Sciences examined the implications of a world 6 degrees Celsius warmer and concluded that global per capita consumption in such a context would be reduced by just 1.4%[41] – a remarkably modest figure that is irreconcilable with the scientific consensus on climatic tipping points and the catastrophic conditions of a world 6 degrees Celsius warmer. The combined impact of widespread permafrost thaw, the cessation of vital ocean currents, a net-emitting Amazon rainforest and the loss of the Greenland ice sheet – to name a few – together constitute an utterly unimaginable future in which planetary conditions would resemble those not seen for tens of millions of years. The idea that 6 degrees of warming – double the 3 degrees Celsius scenario most scientists consider 'catastrophic' – would have only a marginal impact on global consumption requires, to say the least, a robust justification.

Unfortunately, as Keen and several academic peers enumerate in a response to the paper, the analysis is built on foundations from prior studies that either ignore the scientific consensus on tipping points, or neglect to consider them altogether.[42] For instance, one reference study underlying the analysis finds that the collapse of ocean currents would produce 'modest but by and large positive effects on human welfare' through a subtle cooling effect.[43] Science, meanwhile, suggests the stalling of ocean currents would bring devastation, including severe disruption to the rainfall patterns in India and West Africa, which are critical to agriculture in those regions.[44] These complex and unpredictable interactions are widely ignored by prevailing economic models of the climate crisis such as DICE, which tend instead to focus on aspects of a changing climate that can be smoothly modelled, such as the interaction between rising temperatures and agricultural yields.[45] Nor do prevailing models have the capacity to account for the possibility that the effects of a changing climate are self-reinforcing, a possibility that creates a 'nontrivial risk of catastrophic threats to human life on Earth', and which therefore makes attempts to quantify an 'economically optimal' degree of global heating 'a dangerous delusion', in the words of Lord Adair Turner (himself hardly an economic radical).[46]

The subjective science

There has long been a chasm between economists and scientists in anticipating and describing our potential futures. Incidentally, a 1994 survey conducted by Nordhaus of both economists' and scientists' expectations regarding the impact on global GDP of damages from the climate crisis was among the earliest studies to document this disconnect in perspective. The study found estimates from natural scientists were a stark 20–30 times above those made by mainstream economists.[47] While several scientists warned of the risks of collapsing the complexity of climatic and ecological disruption into a single aggregate figure, one economist responding to the survey simply asserted their confidence that 'the degree of adaptability of human economies is so high' that the economic impact of the climate crisis would be 'essentially zero' in most scenarios.[48]

At a more fundamental level, the survey also highlights how subjective decisions regarding the types of economic measures we use can substantially impact what we find. In his survey, Nordhaus asked respondents to anticipate a change in global GDP from climate impacts, effectively asking respondents to aggregate a vast array of granular and geographically uneven impacts into a single figure, despite several respondents having no expertise in the science or modelling of climate change. As one respondent, a climate scientist, put it:

> I marvel that economists are willing to make quantitative estimates of economic consequences of climate change where the only measures available are estimates of global surface average increases in temperature. As [one] who has spent his career worrying about the vagaries of the dynamics of the atmosphere, I marvel that they can translate a single global number, an extremely poor surrogate for a description of the climatic conditions, into quantitative estimates of impacts of global economic conditions.[49]

Though some may seem extreme, the sorts of assumptions and abstractions I have outlined are neither an academic curiosity nor a practice of the economic fringes. The mainstream economics approach to climate and environmental policy and modelling is populated not only with abstractions that collapse the complexity of our globalised economy, climate and biosphere into improbably simple predictions, but also with countless subjective decisions disguised in the language of objectivity. Subjective decisions about assumptions or principles are, in and of themselves, both inevitable and reasonable; where problems arise is in their erasure, or their treatment as incontestable truths. For no issue is this more pronounced, nor more divisive, than the discount rate. Among the many complexities policymakers cite in shaping their approach to climate and environmental governance (or to excuse inaction) is that the investments and changes we make today will impact those living many generations into the future, positively and negatively.

From the perspective of science, maximising upfront investment is the surest route to a habitable and secure planetary future. For many political figures, however, the question of intergenerational value distribution is thorny, and a potent rhetorical tool for arguing against climate and environmental regulation and investment. Listen to any right-leaning figure discuss the issue, and it doesn't take long for a familiar (if somewhat contradictory) set of questions to be raised. For instance, why and to what extent should those today pay for benefits that will supposedly only be enjoyed by those in the future? Alternatively, how can it be fair for us to undertake investment today that will leave future generations 'burdened' by debt? For economists, these questions can be resolved through the derivation of some equivalence between money spent today and the value it creates in the future to make cost-efficient decisions regarding how to respond to climate breakdown or biodiversity collapse. In other words, does investing $100 today to receive the equivalent of $150 of value many years in the future (whether this is an actual investment return, or the calculated value of avoiding the costs of severe drought, for example) make economic sense?

For mainstream economists, this is perhaps the essential question of the climate crisis – one whose answer depends on the concept of 'present value'. Within mainstream economics, it is received wisdom that $1 is worth more today than it is in the future. Through the combination of my assumed preference for having money now, my ability to invest the dollar for returns, and the assumption that societies will invariably grow wealthier over time, my $1 will devalue with each passing year, such that within ten years it might be worth the equivalent of 80 cents today. But how can we know exactly what that value will be at some future point in time? Through the application of a 'discount rate', it becomes possible to calculate the theoretical present value, in monetary terms, of a cost or a benefit that we predict will occur sometime in the future, by 'discounting' its value by a certain amount each year. The higher the discount rate, the greater the relative weight given to costs and benefits in the present, and vice versa. With respect to addressing ecological crises from biodiversity collapse to rising surface temperatures, discount rates are at the crux of contentious debates over how much we should spend, in the present, to avert impacts that will be felt by others in the future. In other words, they purport to help us determine how to balance the costs to society, today, against the benefits that will be felt in the future as a result of, for instance, preventing the shutdown of ocean currents or mass desertification.

Discount rates are, ultimately, a matter of choice; there is no official 'appropriate' discount rate within the economics discipline that tells us at what rate present value declines over time.[50] For this reason, they have long been at the centre of heated debate even among mainstream economists otherwise aligned in their view of how the economy functions. Upon publication of the landmark Stern Review, for instance, a spate of reviews by prominent economists, including Nordhaus, Weitzman and

45

several others, leveraged significant criticism against Stern for his supposedly extreme choice of discount rate which, at the unconventionally low 1.4%, they believed gave too much weight to the future at the expense of those living in the present.[51] By contrast, advocates of more radical action on the climate crisis have argued that inappropriately high discount rates have been weaponised to argue against environmental and emissions regulations.[52] By focusing debate on these technical disagreements, discounting serves to depoliticise the inherently political and profoundly impactful economic choices underlying climate and environmental policies, transforming 'an ethical and political choice about sharing resources with future generations into a technical debate over the choice of an interest rate.'[53] Prominent mainstream economists such as Partha Dasgupta have acknowledged that, in an ethical sense, the assumption of 'societal impatience' that underlies discounting is likely 'indefensible'. As Dasgupta writes, to assume an annual discount rate of 2% (a standard in economics literature), 'is to say that the felicities of the next generation (35 years down the road) ought to be awarded half the weight we award our own felicities. Justifying that is difficult',[54] – unless, as such calculations do, one assumes continued economic growth, effectively in perpetuity.

Despite these significant ethical concerns, the choice of discount rate is a key element in countless policy and investment decisions, determining how and to what ends resources are allocated. With respect to the climate crisis, its most influential role is in the calculation of the Social Cost of Carbon (SCC) – a measure the Chief Economist on President Obama's Council of Economic Advisers described as 'the most important figure you've never heard of.'[55] Expressed as the monetary cost of the damages inflicted by every additional unit of carbon emitted, the SCC is the prevailing economic measure for policymakers of the impact of emissions on the economy, and it features heavily both in the design of climate-related policies, and the politicking required to secure their approval. Generally, the SCC is calculated based on the output of 'Integrated Assessment Models' (IAMs, discussed in more detailed below), which model the nature of the atmospheric changes of each additional tonne of emitted carbon and, ultimately, project the damages to the economy and to human wellbeing that will result from these changes.[56] With respect to the mechanics of its modelling, the SCC represents the value, expressed in monetary terms, of the damages avoided by mitigating CO_2 emissions. In other words, it measures the difference between unabated carbon emissions and the lesser damages that would result if we undertook efforts to cut emissions.

While the SCC is upheld as a standard of objectivity in policy, ultimately its calculation is imperfect, inherently subjective and, consequently, politically contestable. To begin, the SCC can, by definition, be based only on those sectors of the economy for which we have sufficient data to be able to reliably predict climatic impacts, such as changes to agricultural yields, sea level rise and corresponding coastal property loss, changes to labour productivity, and other sectors of the economy with the easy-to-model relationships to a warming world.[57] Consequently, its calculation neglects many critical industries for no reason other than that data is lacking, as well as those aspects of human wellbeing that cannot be measured in a conventional economic sense. By necessarily reducing impacts to a dollar value, many of the things we most cherish – our mental wellbeing, access to nature, thriving ecosystems, and so forth – and whose value is intrinsic and unmeasurable, rather than monetary, are excluded from the decision-making frameworks and justifications of governments throughout the world.

Moreover, as discussed below, there are important limitations to these models owing to a range of questionable assumptions underlying their design. While the SCC is a widely used decision-making tool for policymakers, it is ultimately an applied output derived from complex IAMs, which integrate a range of models – both economic and scientific – to generate a monetary value based on a cost-benefit analysis of climate scenarios. The core of the IAM is the 'damage function', which establishes a relatively simple relationship between gradual events such as temperature and sea-level rise and economic impacts. At this stage, it should be unsurprising that these functions embody a set of simplifying assumptions that, while useful from the perspective of economic model and data limitations, are nonetheless difficult to reconcile with scientific consensus or with good sense. For instance, the major damage functions are calculated in an additive sense, meaning the cost implications for different sectors and regions are treated as independent, and summed to a total figure; as such, they entirely neglect the immense complexity of the interactions between climate impacts, between sectors of our globalised economy, and between unquantifiable social impacts and the welfare of the economy.[58] Similarly, the functions are calibrated toward estimating the impacts of a mean equilibrium shift such as surface temperature or sea level, but are substantially less well attuned to events characterised by extremity, such as heatwaves, or 'stochastic variability' (in other words, unpredictability), such as freak storms. Despite the potential for these events to cause untold devastation, as Frank Ackerman, Elizabeth Stanton and Ramon Bueno write:

'Conventional economic analysis does not appear to be stymied by the problems of irreducible uncertainty and catastrophic risks', which Nordhaus himself admits are poorly captured by economic models like DICE.[59]

More troubling than these simplifications are the assertions of various equivalences between wholly inequivalent impacts, regions and goods. For example, while IAMs largely offer estimates of global economic damages, the studies of impact that underlie the model are primarily analyses of wealthy, industrialised Northern economies, namely the United States and European Union. The data and analysis of impacts on these regions is then extrapolated to the rest of the world, despite enormous divergences between these and lower-income economies; the scale and immediacy of the threat posed to them by climate and ecological crisis; and their capacity to adapt to a changing climate or to rebuild after catastrophic events. Similarly, most IAMs assume a significant degree of 'substitutability' between various environmental goods, meaning that something of value, if lost, can be readily replaced by something of equivalent monetary value. In other words, by reducing all the variables within the model to a monetary value, IAMs assume that the losses that occur from climate impacts, such as loss of coastline, coral bleaching or a decrease in arable land, can be fully substituted by equivalent monetary gains elsewhere in the form of, for instance, increased consumption and incomes.[60] Methodologically, these equivalences are difficult to calculate and justify, even for more conventionally monetisable goods, like crop yields; when it comes to non-transactional but invaluable goods such as health, biodiversity or access to nature, however, the idea that losses in these areas can be offset by higher consumption or incomes becomes absurd.

Perhaps most alarming is that cost-benefit analyses frequently assign a value to human life (termed the 'value of a statistical life', or VSL). The VSL originated in Cold War analyses comparing the costs of different military operations (in other words, weighing up loss of life). Today, the value generally ranges from $8–11 million per life, based on various studies that assess how much people are willing to pay to avoid life-threatening risks, or how much financial incentive they require to be convinced of taking those risks, such as a higher salary for higher-risk jobs.[61] To be clear, the VSL does not, in a strict sense, 'put a price on a life'; rather, it represents the marginal benefit of preserving a life based on how much a society is willing to pay to do so. This does not mean, however, that when it comes to its use in studying the climate and ecological crises, the variable does not have profound ethical implications. Most saliently, because its underlying calculus depends on measures such as income or GDP, the lives of those in lower-income nations (or indeed, lower-income regions within a country), have a lower VSL.[62] The assumptions and simplifications underlying these analyses thus lead to a harrowing policy conclusion: that actions taken to protect the lives of those in lower-income countries are less cost-effective and, by extension, less worthwhile. Indeed, in the logic of the VSL, any action that might reduce economic productivity, such as environmental regulation or limits on working hours, are more costly (and by extension, less justifiable) the lower the VSL of a country. In short: some lives are, explicitly, worth less.

The SCC and the main IAMs underlying it offer a window of insight into the extent to which the economics of our ecological crisis – despite efforts to paint these models with the brush of objectivity – are inherently subjective, and profoundly political. The SCC is routinely invoked as an objective measure of value to mollify politicians resistant to climate policy and couch the benefits of these policies in economic terms. In the US alone, the SCC has been used to evaluate dozens of regulations based on a cost-benefit analysis of policies that would mitigate carbon emissions, including as justification for the Obama administration's decision to enact fuel economy regulations for cars – a move staunchly resisted by many Republicans on economic terms. However, its history in legislative and policy-making decisions provides considerable insight into just how malleable economic models are to the whims of politics: in 2017, the Trump administration issued an executive order to change the official method of calculating the SCC, resulting in a cost per unit of carbon 90% lower than under the preceding administration,[63] which was subsequently used to justify rolling back those same fuel economy regulations.[64] In a sense, the Trump administration's nakedly political decision to change the underlying variables for the US government's official SCC offered an unexpected dose of intellectual honesty with respect to how economics is wielded to serve ideologically driven policy agendas. The use of the mainstream economic discipline – its prestige, the ostensible objectivity of its analysis and sober authoritativeness of its prominent figures and institutions – has been among the most potent forces in the delay, dilution and overt obstruction of the political and policy programmes required to both mitigate catastrophe in the future, and strive for justice in the present. Painted with the brush of objective science and rationality and enveloped in the mythology that there is no alternative, mainstream economics continues, with great effect, to cleanse our ecological crisis of its profoundly political origins and resolutions.

51

A bloodless abstraction

Indeed, despite its naturalisation as an essential priority in the economic mainstream, the reification of economic growth as both an imperative and the central measure of a government's success, with the implication that hindering it is detrimental to human wellbeing, are recent inventions. Because growth is often understood as part and parcel of the fundamental need for expansion that defines capitalist enterprise and systems, the active and political decisions underling its centrality have often been obscured. Though growth has always defined capitalist economies, its diffusion as the overriding goal for government did not spring spontaneously from the ascendance of capitalism as the world's dominant economic system. Indeed, in a review of economic writings between 1870 and 1940, historian H.W. Arndt found 'hardly a line … in support of economic growth as a policy objective.'[65] Accelerated economic growth is a historical anomaly, having taken off only in the nineteenth century.[66] The expansive measurement and prioritisation of economic growth meanwhile, as evaluated by GDP, began only in the aftermath of the Second World War. Confronted by the astonishing spike in the consumption of resources, particularly metals and oil, precipitated by the war effort, the public became concerned with the depletion of natural resources, and the United States government established a forum tasked with finding a solution: the Paley Commission.[67]

Prior to the Second World War, public discourse and political concern in the United States over the concept of resource scarcity was virtually absent. The impact of the war effort, however, and intermittent shortages in various key fuel sources that followed it, radically upset this equilibrium. Beginning in the late 1940s, an influential report from a prominent think tank on the question of American self-sufficiency was followed by 'a glut of popular books' devoted to the suddenly urgent question of resource scarcity alongside renewed fears about an exploding global population and the pressures this might place on the planet.[68] Grappling with the supposedly imminent drying up of key resources now became an essential policy priority for the US government, which was charged with evaluating the risk of resource shortages as well as generating proposals for resolving them.

While the Paley Commission was not the sole arbiter of the United States' (and subsequently the world's) pivot to prioritising aggregate economic growth, as documented by Richard Lane, its influence served three key functions: first, it cemented the idea of 'the economy' as a discrete entity whose operation was defined by theoretically limitless growth. Second, it was a vital step in formally establishing economic growth, hitherto a subjective value, as the defining priority of government; indeed, despite its remit to examine resource shortages, the commissioners opened their report – entitled 'Resources for Freedom' – with the following assertion: 'we share the belief of the American people in the principle of growth. Granting that we cannot find any absolute reason for this belief we admit that to our Western minds it seems preferable to any opposition'.[69] Finally, through a technical revision in how resource scarcity was calculated, the report both intellectually validated and politically prioritised not only growth but also the acceleration of globalisation and American imperialism in the extraction and provision of resources, particularly overseas fossil fuel development.

Through a mathematical sleight of hand, the report changed the calculation of scarcity from an absolute to a relative definition, such that price rather than absolute physical values became the limit of resource availability. In other words, it began to create a consensus according to which resource abundance was a function not of absolute supply, but of the cost and profitability of extraction. The result was to make the increasingly salient question of resource governance not the management of a finite pool, but rather ensuring constant growth of demand and 'exploration' for new and less expensive sources, largely overseas. As Lane articulates, the effect of this inversion was to sever 'the direct connection between material resources and the growth of the economy … no longer bound by physical and material constraints, the economy was understood as free to continue a trajectory of continuous growth.'[70] Six years after the publication of the Paley Commission's findings, policymakers followed, and Henry Kissinger published a report in which he affirmed that 'our nation is dedicated to economic growth', while then-presidential candidate John F. Kennedy campaigned on a 5% growth rate.[71]

Lane argues that these outcomes in and of themselves have been pivotal in defining the trajectory of the climate and nature crises, precipitating the 'great acceleration' of resource consumption, fossil fuel use, and exploitation of nature that defined the latter half of the twentieth century and the so-called 'golden age' of capitalism. Used to describe the post-war explosion of capitalist growth, the period of the great acceleration was defined by an astonishing remaking of the planet and global society: plastic production rose from 1 million to 300 million tonnes, much of it discarded into waterways to endure for hundreds of years; the number of cars expanded from 40 million in the 1940s to over 1.2 billion today; primary energy use more than quintupled; marine fishing rose from approximately 15 million tonnes to a high of over 70 million tonnes per year; half of global forests were razed; and mankind became the single most important regulator of the chemical cycles governing and sustaining life, namely carbon, sulphur and nitrogen.[72] I am not making a causal claim, here, that the Paley Commission established growth as a priority *ex nihilo*, nor that it was necessarily the impetus for the 'great acceleration'. As noted above, growth is inherent to capitalist economic functioning, and its continuation serves the accumulative drive of capitalist firms.

Rather, above all, the Paley Commission offers a stunning insight into the potent and often unseen pathways by which technocratic redefinition and inescapably political economic analysis, treated as incontrovertible and 'objective', have served to justify and politically legitimise actions and priorities that cannot be reconciled with ecological stability. As Richard Seymour expresses: 'the 'obviousness' of the universal human striving for growth is on a par with the 'obviousness' of America's preference for functioning democracy in Iraq: a non-scientific, ideological conception.'[73] Through a simple redefinition in response to an ostensibly technocratic question some decades ago, the Paley Commission helped re-cast ideology as an innate imperative. In doing so, it contributed to the construction of our immensely precipitous present. Rather than reflecting some 'natural' set of governance priorities birthed autonomously from 'human striving since time immemorial'[74] and the accumulative drive of a capitalist economy, the establishment of limitless 'growth' as a central policy goal both reflected and facilitated the political atmosphere and priorities of its time (including, saliently, the assertion of liberal capitalist societies as a hegemonic global order). It was through active and political decisions that by the middle of the twentieth century, mainstream economics became 'crystallised as a bloodless abstraction in which nature figured, if at all, as a storehouse of resources waiting to be used.'[75]

Economics is, in its essence, a social science and a political practice. Its ultimate subject, human interaction, is inherently unpredictable. Subjective decisions underlie the many assumptions, abstractions and conveniences found within mainstream economic models of the impacts of climate and environmental crisis. Subjectivity and analytical simplifications are not, in and of themselves, problematic. By definition, models and analysis demand some reduction of our unknowably complex world into a more measurable and predictable form, with the understanding that an amount of certainty and representativeness is lost along the way. Each of these steps involves discretionary choices, particularly for a science as social as economics. Sometimes, these abstractions are so extreme as to be indefensible. But mostly, the trouble begins when we forget this subjectivity, or purposefully obfuscate it to serve political ends. As a discipline, the neoclassical perspective that informs much of climate economics has often proven far happier to imagine the tidy elegance of what could be, rather than engage with the messy complexity of what actually is. The continued triumph of market-centric, neoliberal governance over alternatives, meanwhile, has served to wash government's hands of responsibility for action, willingly and needlessly yielding this power to the price mechanism while affording outsized legitimacy and intellectual authority to a narrow set of economic imperatives within the institutions that govern our economies and lives.

2

Sirens: distraction and dispossession in carbon markets

Between equal rights, force decides. –Marx, Capital Vol. I[1]

Perhaps more than any other policy proposal for grappling with climate breakdown, the carbon price has enjoyed the constant attention and endorsement of policymakers, academics and the media. There is also, arguably, no other policy proposal which better encapsulates the twin imperatives of an emergent green capitalism: the search for means of addressing ecological crisis which prescribe minimal, if any, disruption to existing economic relations and systems; and the pursuit of new domains of accumulation amidst an otherwise unprecedented threat to economic returns, profit and growth.

In the years up to and surrounding the 2008 Financial Crisis, the inevitability of carbon pricing seemed undeniable. The European Union's flagship Emissions Trading Scheme came into full force to much fanfare. The world's powerful international institutions, from the World Bank to the United Nations, were unabashedly effusive in their support for the idea. In the United States, the American Clean Energy and Security Act of 2009 (informally referred to as the Waxman-Markey Bill) sought to establish a pricing system comparable to the EU's cap-and-trade scheme. Admittedly, the Waxman-Markey Bill met with fierce resistance from across the political spectrum and made uncomfortable allies out of high-emitting industries and green groups, whose shared resistance (albeit for different reasons), helped crush it in the Senate. This setback notwithstanding, however, given the furore of activity around this time – even among climate-sceptical polities like the United States – in support of carbon pricing mechanisms, one might reasonably be asking: what happened? Why aren't we, some 10–15 years down the line, living in a world governed by effective and elegant carbon pricing systems?

This chapter explores the concept of carbon pricing and its frequent bedfellow, carbon offsetting, as totemic policy 'solutions' of green capitalism. In doing so, it examines why the two have thus far failed (and are doomed to continue failing) to achieve material progress against a deepening climate crisis. Ultimately, as this chapter will argue, despite its intuitive logic and appeal, the theoretical elegance and 'breath-taking simplicity' of the carbon price has been thwarted by the messiness of reality, and a necessary grounding in the physical constraints of nature. Importantly, while the development and advocacy of pricing and market-based policies is most advanced within the sphere of limiting carbon emissions, the same logics and policy designs increasingly feature in proposals for addressing other elements of the ecological crisis, from biodiversity loss to deforestation. While the specific details of these evolving policies will be examined in detail in Chapter 6, the essential contradictions and limitations of carbon pricing discussed here also apply.

For want of an effective carbon price

There are two main methods for pricing carbon. Conceptually the simpler of the two, the carbon tax establishes a predetermined cost per unit of carbon, which can be applied in various ways, for instance on absolute emissions or via a sliding scale such as carbon intensity. Under a carbon tax, the only fixed variable is the rate at which carbon is priced; the extent to which overall emissions are lowered by that price is ultimately left up to 'the market'. By contrast, within the carbon market approach, typified by the European Union's 'cap-and-trade' model, an absolute emissions cap is often set by the body governing the market in question, and emissions allowances are handed out to entities falling under the market's purview, such as heavy industrial firms. Each firm can then emit as much as it has permits for, or trade with others for additional allowances they will not use – creating, in theory, the most 'efficient' distribution of emissions reductions from a cost perspective. Typically, the overall level of emissions permitted – the 'cap' – is lowered over time by the governing body, while the actual price of carbon is determined by the market as it trades scarce allowances for emissions at a variable price. In theory, this price is meant to be driven by supply and demand of permits (alongside the gradually declining cap) to generate 'efficient' distributions of the right to emit; in practice, however, these dynamics are often overwhelmed by price fluctuations driven by trading in derivatives of the actual carbon allowances – that is, financial products whose valuations are based on movements in the price of the underlying asset, in this case carbon allowances (discussed further below).[2]

Under carbon pricing systems, then, while the absolute cap for emissions or the price of carbon in the case of a tax is a fixed political determination, the more fluid question of how permits are allocated or how economic activity shifts becomes depoliticised – handed over to the private authority and will of 'the market'. In the case of the EU Emissions Trading Scheme (ETS), this transfer of authority to the market, coupled with generous allocation of free permits, has meant that many large firms in high-emitting sectors have extracted enormous windfall profits from the mechanism, estimated at EUR50 billion since the scheme began in 2008.[3] Thus, rather than adhering to the 'polluter pays' principle that is meant to underlie and justify carbon pricing, in practice the world's foremost carbon pricing scheme has inverted this logic, such that polluters frequently profit, rather than pay.[4]

On its own terms, the evidence in support of the efficacy of carbon pricing schemes – let alone their fairness – is hardly inspiring. In a comprehensive review of implemented carbon pricing schemes across a range of jurisdictions, academic Jessica Green made the simple observation that although the academic literature on the economics of climate change is heavily populated by papers on carbon pricing, shockingly few actually consider *ex post* evidence of their effectiveness. As Green documents, since 1990 just 37 studies (among a wider literature comprised of thousands of articles) have analysed the real impacts of carbon pricing schemes, with a majority focusing on the EU's ETS, the oldest and most well-known such scheme. The aggregate finding on the extent to which the schemes have decreased emissions is hardly uplifting at 'between 0% and 2% per year'.[5]

Data from the EU ETS (about which there is by far the most) shows a modest annual reduction in the EU's overall emissions of between 0% and 1.5%, despite the scheme's position as the jewel in the crown of the EU's climate policy.[6] The EU's official figures celebrate that for those industries covered by the scheme, emissions have fallen by closer to 40% since it came into force. However, the extent to which emitting sectors have been excluded from the scheme, including as the result of effective lobbying, has meant that as a proportion of the EU's total emissions, the contribution made by the ETS is just 3.8% over its 15 years of operation, and despite enormous regulatory effort and capacity being dedicated to its construction and operation.[7] In contrast to both the perilously steep cuts in emissions by 2030 advocated by the Intergovernmental Panel on Climate Change (IPCC) and the effusive praise doled out to carbon pricing schemes by commentators and economists,[8] these are hardly figures in support of the utility of carbon pricing, even when evaluated on its own terms. Indeed, when asked by a reporter at the press conference unveiling the IPCC's 2018 report on pathways for 1.5 degrees Celsius whether a carbon price would be sufficient to reach this, one of the report's lead authors simply laughed.[9]

Despite this, many policymakers and powerful institutions continue to champion the virtues of carbon pricing as if the mere belief in its efficacy is tantamount to evidence for it. For instance, the 2017 High Level Commission on Carbon Pricing concluded in its report that 'Carbon pricing is an effective, flexible, and low-cost approach to reducing greenhouse gases (GHGs)', despite, as Green's research makes clear, a lack of robust evidence to support this claim.[10] An article in the International Monetary Fund's research publication about carbon prices, meanwhile, reads: 'Their principal rationale is that they are generally an effective tool for meeting domestic emission mitigation commitments.' The same article continues by listing the theoretical mechanism of the carbon price as though it is robustly evidenced, claiming: 'Because these taxes increase the prices of fossil fuels, electricity, and general consumer products and lower prices for fuel producers, they promote switching to lower-carbon fuels in power generation, conserving on energy use, and shifting to cleaner vehicles, among other things ... Carbon taxes also provide a clear incentive for redirecting energy investment toward low-carbon technologies like renewable power plants.'[11] Evidence in support of such claims is lacking; for instance, within the EU ET, the bulk of emissions reductions achieved to date were found to have been the result of switching from coal to natural gas fuel sources, rather than investing in and shifting activity to decarbonised technologies or to the 'innovation' that carbon pricing advocates are so fond of championing.[12] Nonetheless, within the literature and popular discourse on carbon pricing, such assertions are commonplace.

Advocates of carbon pricing chalk up the limited progress delivered by existing schemes to persistent 'teething problems' in instituting them. In this view, failures are governments' rather than the market's, nor can they be attributed to problems inherent to carbon pricing's design. In the case of the EU ETS, for instance, the scheme's underwhelming performance is regularly ascribed to what many consider the overly generous allocation of free emissions permits to the firms regulated by the market.[13] In more extreme instances, policies like rent controls have been maligned as preventing carbon prices from working as intended because they prevent landlords from hiking rents to reflect their investment in insulation, double-glazed windows, or solar panels (never mind that in many places, homeowners are eligible for direct subsidies to do so, while renters are not).[14]

Public resistance can also be pointed to as a cause of limited progress, particularly as it has bred a reticence among politicians to make the unpopular choice of putting a price on carbon that is sufficiently steep within a sufficiently brief (read: immediate) timeframe. And certainly, resistance to those carbon pricing regimes already in existence has often been incredibly high. In Canada, a federally instituted carbon price has been challenged by individual provinces with carbon-intensive industries such as oil-producing Alberta and economic hub Ontario, ultimately prompting a fraught, if unsuccessful, legal challenge in the country's Supreme Court. In the US, proposals to enact carbon markets have met with enormous resistance in both houses of Congress, and often on a state-by-state level. Moreover, the political hostility surrounding the fate of the Waxman-Markey proposal has left a lingering unwillingness among politicians to pursue further carbon pricing legislation.[15] In Australia, meanwhile, a hotly contested carbon pricing scheme introduced in 2011 was swiftly repealed just three years later by incoming Prime Minister Tony Abbott, who toured the country claiming the policy was 'economic vandalism.'[16]

Unfortunately for the prospects of effective carbon pricing schemes, resistance has regularly come from across the political spectrum. Free-market acolytes and fossil-fuel guzzling corporations have (until recently, in certain key instances) consistently challenged carbon prices on the grounds of competitiveness or of stifling jobs and economic growth. Liberal environmental groups, meanwhile, have mounted resistance to efforts such as the Waxman-Markey Bill on the grounds that they were unduly generous to major polluting corporations, particularly the coal industry.[17] And as the *gilets jaunes* protests throughout France demonstrated with blazing clarity, an unfairly designed tax which adds unmanageable costs to those already struggling under an economic system geared in favour of elites is an intolerable injury.[18] None of these explanations, however, really hits at the core of the carbon pricing problem. Certainly, political resistance has slowed the implementation of these programmes, but even where their implementation has been successful on the surface, meaningful results remain scarce: in California, often hailed as the 'most successful' carbon pricing scheme in the world, promising emissions reductions attributed to the scheme turned out to be the result of other more direct regulatory efforts, such as investments in energy efficiency and 'clean standards' for electricity and vehicles.[19]

Decarbonisation in isolation

As is the case with many elegantly conceptualised and modelled economic policies, for the carbon price, theoretical elegance has consistently been complicated by the constraints of reality. Public debate among economists and *Financial Times* columnists on the carbon price would suggest the sole question holding back the success of carbon pricing is the question of the ideal price for effective emissions reduction, and indeed, to date, no one seems able to agree. According to William Nordhaus, present carbon prices should sit at approximately $40 per tonne and increase over time to bring the planet in line with future warming of 3 degrees Celsius[20] (a future which, it should be emphasised, science and even mainstream publications like *The Economist* accept would be catastrophic).[21] Also per Nordhaus's models, to bring the price of carbon in line with a world 2 degrees Celsius warmer (still a future which, relative to 1.5 degrees, subjects millions more to devastating impacts, and still a model which fails to incorporate the non-trivial risk of catastrophic events) would require a carbon price of $200 per tonne. Separately, a survey of policy experts from 2019 found ideal prices ranging from $80 to $300 per tonne,[22] though many estimates are more conservative than even this lower bound. Some estimates for a carbon price in line with the 1.5 degree pathway range as high as $14,300.[23] According to the IMF, as of 2020 the actual global average carbon price stood at roughly $2 per tonne.[24] Beyond these speculative prices, existing schemes worldwide have thus far failed to arrive at a price on carbon that comes close to reflecting its true social and ecological cost, with most falling below even the most conservative estimates of the Social Cost of Carbon (SCC).

There are many who argue, reasonably, that even if a carbon price doesn't represent the true (and arguably incalculable) SCC, it is nonetheless a worthwhile endeavour: in other words, while not sufficient, putting a price on carbon is an essential weapon in our arsenal. In support of this argument is the assumption that even if the price of carbon is far lower than its true social cost, because carbon prices – whether in the form of a tax or trading system – efficiently drive firms from high- to low-emitting activities, beginning with those firms for which it is least costly to make the shift, even a too-low carbon price can 'push the market in the right direction in a least-cost manner.'[25] There is also an intuitive ethical appeal to the notion that major emitters and polluters should be charged commensurately for their profiting from ecological destruction. Indeed, to continue failing to price emissions associated with highly profitable and destructive enterprise such as fossil fuel extraction, or with excessive consumption by the global wealthy, seems like a moral and practical failure. However, there are many reasons to be cautious: even if a carbon price could be designed to be fair in terms of distributional cost impact (and there are reasons to doubt this), there remain inescapable limitations that undermine the theoretical effectiveness and implementation of even partial carbon pricing systems, and which, to my mind, risk making their use a dangerous crutch or distraction, rather than a helpful-if-alone-insufficient tool.

As economists Eric Lonergan and Corinne Sawers succinctly put it, when it comes to the urgency, complexity and economic mechanics of decarbonisation, advocates of carbon pricing seem to be reading from 'the wrong chapter of the textbook.'[26] Namely, the assumption of swift and cost-efficient transfer from high to low-emitting economic activity disregards the immense inertia that defines our fossil-fuel based economy, particularly within industrial sectors like cement and steel – both of which are carbon-intensive and necessary materials for decarbonised infrastructure, from renewable transport to energy efficient homes. The logic of the carbon price in terms of driving the transition to low-carbon technologies is that it levels the playing field for new sectors and technologies by adding a fee to legacy fossil fuel activities that better reflects their true cost. It should be noted that there is evidence to suggest that positive supports, such as incentives and feed-in tariffs for renewable energy, are more effective in this regard;[27] however, setting that aside for the moment, an inescapable problem arises from the reality that cost is only one obstacle to decarbonisation.

Firms – let alone entire sectors – cannot decarbonise in isolation; nor is it always possible for individuals to readily move toward alternative products or services as carbon pricing advocates envision. The vast majority of economic activity relies on a highly embedded energy system and fossil-based economy whose complexity and structural role in mediating basic needs demand foresight and careful planning to disentangle while minimising disruption – planning the invisible hand of the market is unable, by definition, to do. Empirical evidence suggests a critical factor determining a technology's value to consumers is not simply demand, but the 'regime' or infrastructure in place to support it.[28] To put it another way, smartphones are valuable only insofar as there are infrastructures such as physical cellular networks and networks of other users to enable and merit their use, respectively. Indeed, the motorcar didn't take off quickly after it was invented (despite many qualities that made it far more desirable than, for instance, a horse drawn carriage); rather, cars only became popularised after the widespread dissemination of traffic laws and paved roads.[29]

Thus, for the magic of the market to support, via a carbon price, a consumer-driven transition from high- to low-carbon energy sources, there would first need to be the infrastructures and systems in place to accommodate that transition. As it stands, there remain grave mismatches between the needs of decarbonised technologies and our existing systems. In light of this, Lonergan and Sawers argue the appropriate time for a carbon price is toward the tail-end of the decarbonisation process, rather than as an early and primary tool.[30] Both infrastructures – from electricity networks to cities designed around the personal car – and institutional frameworks like wholesale electricity pricing are built around fossil fuels and require coordinated government planning and effort to change. In other words, for the 'invisible hand' to function requires substantial support from the much more visible hand of public investment and coordination.

Herein lies a second problem for the market-based logic of the carbon price, one which confronts its core claims of market-based action and low-interference efficiency. There is substantial agreement across mainstream economists that for a carbon price to be effective, it must be uniform and universal with respect to both industries and geography.[31] Debates about 'carbon border adjustments' in the EU, which would effectively apply a carbon price to imported goods that policy-makers view as under-cutting EU-manufactured goods, speak to the technical challenges of unilaterally enacting a carbon price.[32] This reality does not, however, bode well for the political expediency assumed to stem from a 'lighter touch' market-based approach. As political economist Servaas Storm writes: 'paradoxically, the artificial creation of a global carbon market demands a far more sensitive, centralised and powerful state apparatus for measurement and enforcement than is needed for conventional regulation.'[33] This reality is doubly problematic for our ability to realise a theoretically effective carbon pricing regime, as it implies both substantial institutional costs with respect to global negotiation and implementation, as well as making political resistance likely from those who should in theory be most ideologically aligned with the market logic of carbon pricing.

The externalising machine

Beyond questions of efficacy, the essential fault in the market-based approach to ecological crisis is its virtual guarantee of delivering injustice, both domestically and globally. As the *gilets jaunes* demonstrations highlighted, politicians are perfectly willing to enact a carbon pricing mechanism that generates economically unjust outcomes. In some cases, schemes have attempted to mitigate unjust redistributive outcomes domestically through a rebate or 'dividend' system, in which cash dividends are paid out to the public to make up for the increased cost imposed by a carbon tax. Praise for the combined efficiency, fairness and assumed popularity of such programmes among economists is lavish: a statement signed by over 3600 economists in support of carbon dividend programs describes itself modestly as 'The Largest Public Statement of Economists in History.'[34]

Available evidence, however, suggests redistributive add-ons to carbon taxation regimes do little to improve their public acceptability, with support instead cleaving along traditionally political lines.[35] In short, technocratic appeal simply cannot evade the storm of political complexity surrounding climate and environmental policy, including the need to create the impression of justice and fairness among those on the receiving end of a policy. Moreover, the piecemeal nature of carbon pricing schemes implies that only those within the jurisdiction in question are entitled to the carbon dividends, even though the impacts of the carbon price – whether via 'carbon border adjustments' that penalise imports or the offsets that prop up carbon markets – are frequently felt beyond the borders of that jurisdiction. Importantly, ensuring just outcomes with respect to how both the costs and benefits of the transition to a decarbonised and ecologically sustainable economy are distributed is not an exclusively ethical consideration, though the moral implications are important. Justice is also pragmatic and materially necessary.

As has been demonstrated by widespread resistance to carbon pricing regimes in many areas, in a pragmatic sense, distributive justice – meaning an economically fair distribution of burdens and benefits – is necessary, at least in public perception, to generate popular democratic support for climate policy and initiatives. It is a commonly held idea that climate politics is defined by a quintessential 'collective action problem': in other words, countries have struggled to implement effective climate policies because of concerns over 'free riding' at the international level. Instead, evidence shows that the critical factor determining the viability and implementation of climate policy is distributive conflict – that is, conflict over the 'dramatic renegotiation of the institutions that structure economic and social activity' demanded by economy-wide decarbonisation, alongside negotiation over the new cohorts of economic winners and losers this will inevitably create.[36] It's here that the green capitalist framework begins to dig its own grave. Through its adherence to the ideas and demands of 'elites' – corporations, prominent billionaires and other celebrities, technocratic politicians, financiers, economists, and so on – whose support for carbon pricing and similar 'solutions' reflects their will to preserve the institutions and distributions that currently define society and ensure they remain the economic winners, green capitalist approaches neither generate widespread support nor dispel the perception so powerfully fomented by politicians like Donald Trump that climate policy is by and for elites.

Materially, the simple elegance of a single uniform carbon price is undermined by the fact that not all carbon emissions (nor all solutions) are created equal. It matters, deeply, whether emissions are the product of the demand for SUVs and the convenience of private car journeys among the affluent of the Global North or the gas boiler heating the home of a low-income family that can't afford to replace it, but a uniform

70

carbon price does not, by design, discriminate between these sources. Nor does a uniform carbon price reflect the fact that the wealthy are far more likely to be able to absorb higher costs and therefore maintain the demand for and use of many carbon intensive products and services. In California, the uniform carbon price enforced by its cap-and-trade scheme has led to uneven and unjust distribution of emissions reductions, with reductions in some areas contributing to a relative increase in emissions and associated pollutants in areas populated predominantly by communities of colour.[37]

It also matters whether the incentivised changes are permanent or simply fleetingly cost-efficient. As Larry Lohmann writes: 'Equating CO_2 reductions that result from different technologies ... makes it possible, indeed necessary to make climatically wrong choices in the name of molecule prices', for instance by failing to discriminate between permanent elimination of fossil fuels in the energy mix, and temporary but lower-cost adjustments like routine improvements in energy efficiency.[38] Here again, the 'elegance' of the carbon price is that, in applying a uniform price per unit of carbon, it does not try to distinguish between these sources; instead, it is interested in least-cost emissions cuts, prioritising near-term cost efficiency over long-term ecological imperatives. As noted above, most emissions reductions achieved to date in the EU ETS are the result of switching from coal to gas, rather than longer-term decarbonising shifts.[39] Similarly, because the emissions associated with activities like supply-chain deforestation have substantial overlaps with other ecologically critical phenomena such as biodiversity collapse, eliminating these practices first should be a priority – a question of sequencing that is utterly ignored by a uniform carbon price. Carbon pricing is likewise disinterested in addressing economic inequalities, either domestically or internationally, within which the origins of our ecological crisis, as well as its resolution, are located.[40]

Thus, the 'solutions' and lower-carbon alternatives that putting a price on carbon might engender have no guarantee of delivering outcomes that are effective – that is, which drive rapid and permanent decarbonisation. Even more certain is their disinterest in justice. For example, the drive to reduce carbon intensity by moving from concentrated crude oil production to highly distributed fracking risks creating widespread health problems for nearby inhabitants.[41] Similarly, as the next section explores, the scramble for biofuel based energy sources and carbon offsets has already generated food crises and land grabs among subsistence agricultural and Indigenous communities in the Global South.[42] Ultimately, these failures reflect the fact that capitalism is, by design, an 'externalising machine' – constantly in pursuit of mechanisms through which profits can be maximised by minimising or altogether evading the true costs of economic activity.[43] Rectifying these issues – from devising and implementing carbon tax or pricing mechanisms that don't penalise the poor or create other social and environmental externalities to negotiating, agreeing and monitoring a hypothetical global carbon pricing scheme – would demand enormous coordinated action from governments, both domestically and internationally. On its own terms, given that cumbersome bureaucracy and the necessarily incomplete knowledge of the state is precisely what the 'breathtaking simplicity' of carbon pricing is meant to avoid and overcome, it's worth asking: why bother?

The capitalist state

It is a question too often ignored. Confronted with ever-escalating public support for and scrutiny of government action on the climate crisis, the candle for carbon pricing continues to burn brightly. At the COP26 climate conference in Glasgow, establishing unifying rules for carbon markets was a top priority, ultimately celebrated, including by prominent environmental NGOs, as a success story.[44] Meanwhile, in 2020 the American Business Roundtable, a lobbying organisation comprised of the CEOs of the largest American corporations, came out in favour of a price on carbon despite generally pushing back against climate policies such as the Clean Power Act in previous years.[45] Tellingly, several fossil fuel giants have recently reversed on their extensive histories of lobbying against and systematically undermining carbon pricing, with BP, Shell, ExxonMobil and the American Petroleum Institute publishing statements on the need for a carbon price. Recent boldly worded position statements stand in stark contrast to their lobbying efforts even within the past five years: for instance, the American Petroleum Institute, the fossil fuel industry's lobbyist organisation, described the Paris Agreement as 'aggressive', and stated as recently as 2020 that it would oppose 'any regulations or taxes that would increase the price of US oil and gas exports.'[46] Similarly, in 2018 fossil fuel firms spent $30 million campaigning against a ballot to establish a carbon tax in Washington state – double the amount raised in support of the tax by a ragtag billionaire cohort including Michael Bloomberg, Bill Gates, Tom Steyer and Laurene Powell Jobs, widow of Steve Jobs.[47]

Though it's impossible to know for certain, this union of billionaires, corporate and financial giants, and fossil capital seems unlikely to be the product of chance. To the contrary, it seems capital may have come to conclusions about carbon pricing similar to those I have articulated here (albeit with what I assume to be rather different motivations): for constituents of the green capitalist alliance from prominent billionaires to major corporations, the carbon price is a gradual and comparatively painless policy solution which preserves existing economic relations and structures while also offering a new route to accumulation within a competitive market. As an attractive bonus, it also offers a compelling branding opportunity in response to consumer pressures. For others, more insidiously, it is a convenient distraction from genuinely impactful legislation. Perhaps no one has expressed this position more clearly than a PR representative for ExxonMobil when they joked, in a leaked interview, that the firm's support for a carbon price was 'an easy talking point', before affirming that 'nobody is going to propose a tax on all Americans … it gives us a talking point that we can say, well, what is ExxonMobil for? Well, we're for a carbon tax.' His conclusion? 'A carbon tax is not going to happen [in the US].'[48] However, while this brand of hollow endorsement may serve the interests of fossil capital, it does less to explain the enthusiasm of governments the world over, as well as a gamut of major international institutions, for carbon pricing.

When it comes to the motivations of the state, it is Marx who provides the clearest insight. Advanced capitalist states face a pair of intimately linked, if occasionally conflicting, imperatives: supporting accumulation (that is, the central process of capitalism) while securing legitimacy for the state and existing system in order to reproduce it. In the case of carbon pricing, as Gareth Bryant argues in his masterful book on the political economy of carbon markets, 'economic notions of "market failure" tend to displace attention away from the origins of, and disperse responsibility for addressing, climate change.'[49] Just as states faced severe crises of legitimacy following the 2008 Financial Crisis and the sweeping economic damage it engendered, so does the spectre of the climate crisis pose a challenge to states' legitimacy and democratic consent. In this sense, carbon pricing is an ideal pursuit, allowing states to 'take action' on the climate crisis in a way that enjoys substantial legitimacy among elite and influential cohorts such as the economics profession and corporate sector, even if it accomplishes little in terms of environmental impact.

Indeed, one of the fundamental qualities of the market-based approach rather than a direct regulatory approach is the simple diffusion of responsibility: if a market-based policy fails to deliver on its intended outcomes, the sheer volume of actors involved distributes accountability by design. A lack of, or constraints on, political ambition affects all policymaking; however, market-based policies make it much easier for policymakers to evade the spotlight when those policies fail to deliver. Thus, through carbon pricing, states and political operatives can visibly respond to democratic demands for action while minimising individual accountability and, crucially, avoiding direct confrontation with fossil capital or with the underlying economic dynamics in which ecological crisis originates, namely the accumulative, expansionary and externalising drives of capitalism, and the vast global inequalities those drives continue to widen.[50]

To borrow from Friedrich Hayek, a founding father of neoliberal thought: 'the fundamental principle' of economic liberalism is that 'the prince and the pauper are free in law to sleep beneath the bridges of Paris.'[51] In other words, within the liberal ideal, a government should limit itself to ensuring legal, formal equality, rather than undertaking futile efforts to deliver substantive material equality. Indeed, liberalism is, by its definition, largely unconcerned with material inequality provided the conditions of formal equality are met – an indifference that has enabled the continued proliferation of the numerous and profound injustices that presently scar the global economy, and which will only widen as ecological crisis continues to unfold along uneven social, racial and geographic lines. It is also an essential principle underlying the advance of the carbon price as a totemic 'solution' of green capitalism: provided that, under a system of carbon pricing for instance, everyone is equally free to participate, there is little reason to care, as theorist Stuart Hall elegantly puts it, that the prince 'is "free" to go home to his palace, [while] the beggar has nowhere else to go.'[52]

Within carbon pricing, the liberal capitalist states of the Global North have found an ideal solution to the contradicting demands they face, while capitalist firms have found a new route by which to satisfy their underlying drive toward accumulation. By establishing rights to pollute the atmosphere that can be bought, sold and converted into novel financial assets, new pathways for profit and speculation are created, while the need for states to impose meaningful regulation can be met in a cosmetic sense without the risk of alienating the corporate and capitalist base to which they are in various ways beholden. In the process, all the political and value-laden questions associated with decarbonisation – improving public health, escaping our dependence on fossil fuels, limiting further environmental impacts – are reduced to the singular goal of curbing emissions in order to make the question of governing emissions into a market-compliant unit.[53]

76

The offset obsession

The unimpeded pollution of the atmosphere by (overwhelmingly) Northern economies in recent decades represents a profoundly unequal enclosure of what is a global commons: the resilience of the atmosphere to our interference, and its capacity to maintain stable conditions for life to thrive. In this sense, the world's poorer economies have been dispossessed of their shared rights in this extraordinary privilege. This is not, however, the only sense through which a carbon pricing-based approach represents dispossession on a vast scale. Whether in the form of a carbon tax or cap-and-trade schemes, carbon markets, as well as the policy programmes advanced by many governments and intergovernmental institutions, often require the incorporation of 'carbon offsets'. Anyone who has taken a flight within the past few years is likely to have been offered the option to purchase an 'offset' for their personal emissions, probably in the form of (ostensibly) newly planted trees. From 'sustainable' clothing brands to meal kit subscriptions and Amazon deliveries, claims of carbon neutrality are now as ubiquitous as they are hollow.

Offsets can take a variety of forms, but fundamentally they offer a mechanism for firms (or individuals, voluntarily) to continue emitting, while paying for the privilege of doing so by 'offsetting' this carbon in some way. Offsets broadly fall into two categories. The first are negative emissions or emissions removal offsets, for instance through tree plantations intended to draw carbon down from the atmosphere over their assumed lifespans. The second (and more intuitively dubious) are 'avoided' emissions, which represent the projected emissions prevented by stopping an activity from taking place, such as

77

cutting down a woodland for grazing or, in the positive sense, paying for a firm's use of renewable instead of fossil fuel energy sources. Importantly, save for a specific UN deal for the aviation sector, there is presently no regulation at the international (or, indeed, the national level) of offsets; rather, the system has, to date, been left to the private sector, with a suite of firms vying to corner the market of offset verification and provide the best (voluntary) standards and stamp of approval.

Despite this lack of regulatory scrutiny or consistency, carbon offsets are now an essential lubricant in the functioning of carbon markets and pricing schemes, both voluntary and involuntary. In theory, they enable firms to avoid penalties or to undertake actions that supposedly bring their overall economic impact closer to 'net zero', which describes the state at which emissions are balanced by carbon drawdown. Net zero is the target of countless individual corporate emissions pledges, as well as the endpoint prescribed by the IPCC for global emissions at mid-century to remain within safe temperature limits. Because net zero does not specify how large the scale of emissions and drawdown should be provided they are equal to each other, carbon offsetting regimes have become an integral component of governments' plans for bringing their economies in line with net zero as painlessly as possible. Mark Carney, former governor of the central banks of both England and Canada and a scion of green capitalism, asserts that the offset market must grow by fifteen-fold to support reaching net zero by 2050.[54]

Private sector titans from financial giants to oil majors are overwhelmingly keen on both offsets and the 'net zero' targets they help facilitate. Shell, for instance, has made 'Nature-Based Solutions' its flagship policy, adorning its public-facing platforms and advertising materials with glossy images of woodland; BP, meanwhile, announced its own 'net-zero' policy with a commitment to fully offset the emissions associated with its facilities and production by 2050 (though emissions associated with the end use of its product, which comprises the vast majority of the firm's emissions, it only aims to cut by half).[55] Both Shell and French oil major Total have begun trading 'carbon neutral' fossil gas, with Total incorporating a payment of some $600,000 toward forest management and an operational wind farm as part of a $17 million dollar gas trade.[56] As a result of these and countless other pledges, the voluntary carbon market in which offsets are purchased and traded has exploded, topping $1 billion in 2021.[57] This all might seem relatively unobjectionable; we are now so late in the pathway toward mitigation that most IPCC projects assume substantial carbon drawdown if we are to stabilise atmospheric carbon at a safe level and mitigate the risk of catastrophe. For some, the explosion of voluntary offsets is therefore cause to celebrate, and a perfect example of the neoliberal vision of governance: creating the conditions for private actors to thrive and, motivated by the drive to profit, innovate to reduce the cost burden of the task at hand. Under competitive conditions, firms will continue to enter into the offset market of their own volition, obviating the need for binding legislation or bureaucracy. Meanwhile, market forces, unleashed, will allocate resources with optimal efficiency.

Smoke and mirrors

If only it were that simple. As with the enthusiasm of billionaires and ExxonMobil for carbon pricing, the enthusiasm of the private sector for voluntary offsetting regimes should be viewed with a healthy scepticism, to say the very least. Despite becoming a billion-dollar industry spanning the global economy and with participation by the world's largest corporations, offsets within the voluntary carbon market are entirely unregulated, from the calculations underlying the carbon they supposedly draw down or avoid, to their implementation on the ground. The result is a Wild West of trading, speculating and profit-making. For example, the $600,000 paid by Total to make the ludicrous claim of 'carbon neutrality' on a $17 million shipment of liquified natural gas was in part directed to a forest management project in Zimbabwe. Rather than paying for the restoration of a forest or carbon-trapping wetland, the funds supported local volunteers and workers to manually clear the thick underbrush as a wildfire preventative measure. The scale and value of the offset were then determined based on the emissions theoretically avoided between a scenario in which the forest goes up in flames, and one in which it doesn't.

The lack of equivalence is astonishing, and indefensible. On one side of the equation, around the world, Total's fossil gas fuels countless fires, spewing hundreds of thousands of tonnes of carbon into the atmosphere and generating vast revenues. On the other, a comparative pittance of cash supports some clearing activity that may have happened anyway, and has no guarantees of preventing a wildfire, which similarly might never have happened. The maths are difficult to justify, nor is there any requirement at present for Total to do so. Even for the offset company, South Pole, which helped to develop the project and sold the carbon credits to Total, the sorts of claims Total and other corporations make toward carbon neutrality are frequently outrageous. Indeed, in the choice words of the organisation's co-founder: 'it's such obvious nonsense.'[58]

In fairness, much of Total's offset purchase was derived not from the forest project but from a wind farm in China, under the premise that the money would ensure the use of wind power to support local energy needs, theoretically avoiding the need to use coal-fired power. Here again, actual emissions are meant to be 'offset' by the theoretical maximum difference between existing plans (the use of wind power in the region) and an imagined alternative scenario (the use of coal power), raising the necessary question: did the trade actually prevent the use of coal power? Given that the wind farm in question had been operational for more than a decade prior to the trade, it seems unlikely it would have stopped all operations had it not been for a small payment from Total.[59]

Both projects linked to Total's 'carbon neutral' gas perfectly capture the dubious practices surrounding carbon offsetting regimes, as well as pointing toward the criteria for what might constitute an effective project of carbon drawdown or avoidance. Taking the concept of offsetting on its own terms, the first requirement for an offset's existence to be justifiable is material impact: in short, does the project actually have the capacity to curb carbon emissions? The second, and much more regularly violated, requirement, is additionality – in other words, is the offset credit contributing to a material reduction in carbon that would not have happened otherwise? In the case of Total's not-at-all-carbon-neutral fossil gas shipment, one would be hard pressed to claim these requirements were satisfied. Unfortunately, this is the case for much of the offsetting industry, in large part because the additionality of avoided emissions is difficult to prove, reliant as these claims are on a hypothetical counterfactual scenario. The result is a system incredibly open to abuse, including by long-standing environmental institutions

81

and authorities. In the United States, for instance, the Nature Conservancy, the world's largest corporate environmental NGO with nearly $1 billion in revenue in 2020, has been routinely criticised for its role in the offset market and the questionable additionality of its projects. Investigations into several of the Nature Conservancy's US-based offsets found the credits being sold were based off purported conservation of land already under the organisation's protection (the organisation has accumulated some 125 million acres over its 70 years in operation), or owned by wealthy landowners already committed to maintaining the woods.[60] Both the Conservancy and the landowners pocket cash from the exchange without having to undertake any new protection efforts; the carbon ledgers of polluting corporations are 'balanced'; and emissions continue, unabated.

In principle, materiality should be easier to prove for some projects. After all, it's relatively straightforward to prove that your funds have enabled a forest to be planted or prevented a wetland from being purchased by property developers. But even in these ostensibly more straightforward cases, offsetting continues to raise far more issues than it resolves. A necessary assumption underlying the calculations of embodied carbon surrounding countless tree planting projects and pledges at the heart of the offsetting industry is that the trees in question will both survive to maturity and endure long enough to capture some theoretical maximum of carbon, generally set at 100 years. With a horizon this long, there are no guarantees this will be the case – particularly amidst accelerating ecological breakdown and a rapidly warming climate. The summer of 2021, for example, saw record blazes tear across the Pacific Northwest, sending thousands of square kilometres of forest up in smoke.

Among these were several offset credits purchased by the likes of BP and Microsoft within a forest project managed by the Green Diamond Resource Company.[61] This was hardly a lone instance; just a few years prior, the Trinity Timberlands offset project in California was so ravaged by wildfires that the entire programme was abandoned.[62]

When an offset goes up in flames, it's doubly bad for the climate: not only have the emissions that merited the offset in the first place accumulated in the atmosphere, but all the carbon stored within the trees, wetland or other ecosystem in question is sent spiralling upward. Even absent the increasingly frequent and severe blazes, droughts and invasive species outbreaks that will characterise deepening ecological crisis, the private articulation and management of these projects means there is no guarantee that the land will remain designated for forest or other carbon-sequestering ecosystems for anywhere close to the 100-year horizon. Investigations into offset projects have found that in some instances, more forest has been destroyed after the establishment of the offset's 'protection' programme than was originally sold in the credit.[63] One highly fraught project in Cambodia, for example, sold credits based on a pledge to protect a region that, when credits entered the market in 2008, was 88% forested; a decade later, satellite imagery showed this forest cover had been halved.[64]

Though its status as a household term is relatively recent, the concept of the carbon offset is far from new, nor simply struggling with teething problems. The first carbon offset dates to 1989,[65] while offset markets were first given an official rubber stamp in the 'Clean Development Mechanism' (CDM) of the Kyoto Protocol (the predecessor to the Paris Climate Agreement). Within the CDM, high-income Northern countries could purchase offset credits from low-income states. If you were to ask any Northern government at the time, the deal worked for everyone: Northern industry could pay to avoid having to undertake the far more challenging, costly and materially complex task of decarbonising, while poorer Southern economies received cash for their own development and decarbonisation efforts. Unfortunately, for many of the same reasons discussed above, a report prepared for the European Commission found that a full 85% of all offset programmes under the CDM had failed to generate a meaningful reduction in emissions.[66] Despite this, industry and governments alike, including the European Commission, continue to tout the merits and necessity of offset programmes, even while an ongoing abject lack of oversight means the burden of proof that a project offers any enduring or legitimate environmental protection is phenomenally low. Why?

In part, because it is politically easy. Just as carbon pricing enables capitalist states to evade the difficult questions surrounding decarbonisation and ecological degradation, so too does the concept of offsetting sidestep confrontation with the industries and inequalities at the root of the climate crisis. It is for this reason that offsetting finds such positive reception in the private sector, whose operations need not change significantly so long as they continue to reap enormous profits with which they can purchase a handful of offsets. Meanwhile, as the next sections outline, the harms of offsetting are often invisible – transferred to people and regions deemed less valuable by globalised capitalism.

At the same time, offsetting has brought to bear a world in which money really can grow on trees. To facilitate the uninterrupted consumption of the global affluent and the

unimpeded ecological damage doled out by fossil-based production, an enormous new sector replete with NGOs and
new for-profit entities has sprung up, offering a novel route
for profit-making within a supposedly 'green' economic future.
For private companies, it offers a commercial opportunity out
of a crisis that was previously almost exclusively perceived as
a threat. British pharmaceutical firm Novartis, for example, is
almost laudable in their transparency about the motivations of
their offsetting projects, extolling the success of the firm's Santo
Domingo Estate project in Argentina based on their ability to
'turn the plantation into a commercial asset.'[67] Thus, from the
depths of the ocean of corporate reputation to be cleansed has
sprung a new fount of value. In the process, a new accumulative regime supports green capitalist states in adhering to the
mantra of 'green growth' and in affirming that our ecological
crisis can be confronted without a fundamental reckoning with
the economic consensus.

Accumulation by dispossession

Carbon offsets are a distillation of a fundamental blind spot
within the green capitalist architecture: the indivisible link
between carbon emissions – abstracted as some disembodied
quantity in an imperceptible atmosphere – and the intensely
embodied reality of their production and mitigation (a concept
we will return to in more depth in Chapter 6). In the calculus
of offset providers and the firms purchasing them, just as their
ability to emit is seemingly interminable, so too is the availability of offsets with which to erase their impact. This is, however,
true only within the confines of a spreadsheet. Take Shell's
much-publicised 'net zero' pledge and their recent, fervent turn

advocating 'nature-based solutions' – industry jargon for off-setting programmes based on tree planting and other 'natural' carbon sinks. Shell's commitment to net zero supposedly incorporates not just the emissions associated with their production facilities and operations, but also the full Scope 3 emissions associated with their products, meaning the full life cycle of emissions associated with the oil and gas they sell. Despite this ambitious pledge, the company plans to make remarkably little adjustment to its total production and to continue exploring for new oil and gas reserves. To do so, they've committed to undertake an expansive investment in 'nature-based solutions' – so expansive, in fact, that it would require an area of land for reforestation three times the size of the Netherlands by 2030 alone to offset the planned emissions associated with just one corporation.[68] Elsewhere, Shell has begun to create its own scenarios for how the world might reach the targets of the Paris Climate Agreement, akin to those created by the IPCC or the International Energy Agency. The oil major's aspirational-sounding 'Sky 1.5' scenario predicts fossil fuel use will remain widespread to the end of this century (and presumably beyond, as this is merely the terminus of the scenario). Within the scenario, global temperatures temporarily surpass the 1.5 degrees Celsius target, to be brought back down through carbon removal in the latter half of the century, which would require an area of land dedicated to reforestation the size of Brazil, alongside 22 other types of 'nature-based solution'.[69]

Accompanying the scenario's publication are softly lit drone photographs of woodland, lush mangrove forest and rolling hills – halcyon images that conceal the violence and neo-colonial programme implied by the scale of Shell's imagined future. Carbon offsets work in theory because carbon in the atmosphere is global, meaning there is no need for an offset to be located anywhere near the source of the emissions it is ostensibly meant to net out. In practice, this means offsets are overwhelmingly purchased by individuals, governments and corporations of the high-income Global North in order to facilitate their continued enclosure of the atmospheric commons, while the offsets themselves involve the sequestration of land in the Global South in service of this atmospheric enclosure. While in some instances, some funds may be transferred to communities surrounding offset projects, as Total's 'carbon neutral' gas deal underscores, these values are often trivial compared to the profits that offsets enable firms to reap, as well as the savings they make in avoiding the need to decarbonise their operations. This is, at its core, a neo-colonial effort: enclosing the resources and land of lower-income countries to service accumulation and consumption in wealthier areas. In and of itself, this is an injustice. When coupled with the disruption of and direct violence routinely inflicted upon communities living near these projects, it is even more so.

Between 2000 and 2010, under the United Nations' 'REDD' scheme (Reducing Emissions from Deforestation and Degradation), a beleaguered offsetting programme implemented by the UN, some 500 million acres of land across Africa, Asia, Latin America and the Caribbean were 'acquired or negotiated under deals brokered on behalf of foreign governments or transnational corporations.'[70] Though the REDD programme itself has fallen out of favour, it has been more than supplemented by the explosion of the voluntary carbon market and the trend toward 'net zero' commitments from heavily polluting industries. For example, in 2019, oil giant Eni published plans to sequester some 8 million hectares of land across several African countries for tree plantations to offset its operational emissions, all while planning to increase its oil and gas production.[71] Similar examples of this carbon neo-colonialism abound. Critically, this is land already home to both communities of people and complex ecosystems. Consequently, offsetting schemes of various stripes over the years have been found to involve: the forcible expulsion of Indigenous communities from their homes; the razing of long-standing local communities to clear the way for 'conservation' and offset projects; the seizure of land occupied by subsistence farmers, devastating communities that had previously provided for themselves; and, ironically, deleterious effects on local ecosystems through the substitution of mono-species tree plantations for indigenous biodiversity.[72] In Chile, a hydroelectric dam registered for the sale of offsets has been the source of human rights violations as well as accelerated desertification in an already drought-stricken region, according to the Centre for International Environmental Law.[73]

As Adam Bumpus and Diana Liverman describe, the global carbon offset regime is a project of 'accumulation by decarbonisation' – a particularly devastating instantiation of David Harvey's 'accumulation by dispossession' – that combines: direct violence; land grabs and the erasure of livelihoods; new forms of commodification and financial speculation; and the enclosure of a wildly disproportionate share of the atmospheric carbon sink and terrestrial resources by powerful firms and the globally affluent.[74] It also forms the foundation of green capitalism by providing a justification (albeit false) for business as usual among the world's high-income and high-emitting countries, and enabling governments and firms to avoid engaging in the deep changes demanded by actual decarbonisation. Carbon offsetting is thus doubly harmful. In the technical sense, offsetting is, as climate scientist Kevin Anderson argues, 'worse than doing nothing', inasmuch as it 'triggers a rebound away from meaningful mitigation and towards the development of further high-carbon infrastructures', all while creating the veneer of action to placate both consumers and governments.[75] And in the human sense, it destroys livelihoods, communities and ways of life, rendering them casualties of the effort to resist dismantling the systems, distributions of wealth, and infrastructures at the root of ecological crisis.

Facing risk and radical uncertainty

Carbon pricing, markets and offsets can all be understood as efforts to rectify the 'market failure' of climate crisis, internalising the supposedly 'true cost' of carbon emissions into the market. A directly imposed carbon price, however, is not the only framework through which policymakers are seeking to reflect – at least in theory – this true cost in economic exchange. Indeed, second only to the framing of ecological crisis as a 'market failure' is its routine description by policymakers, the private sector, and even many civil society actors, in the language of 'systemic risk'. Economic and policy analyses of ecological crisis frequently centre on attempts to quantify the various risks it poses, and for no industry is this more true than finance, the vanguard industry of green capitalism.

Finance is, by its definition, preoccupied with risk. The risk of borrowers defaulting on their mortgages or credit card statements is fine-tuned to the rates they pay; insurers devote phenomenal resources to estimating risks of natural disasters or similar events affecting the assets they insure; investors' portfolios are allocated to achieve optimal risk/return profiles according to clients' appetite – the list goes on. When it comes to governing institutions' fixation on so-called 'climate risk', a very important question often goes unqueried: risk to what, and for whom? The answer, at least for those actors with considerable influence over the shape and direction of climate and ecological action, is that first and foremost, ecological crisis poses a risk to returns and, by extension, to the stability of financial firms.

Policymakers are increasingly fixated on the financial risks presented by a range of climatic and ecological phenomena, from the impacts of weather events (physical risk) to 'stranded asset risk', which describes assets whose value may be wiped off the ledger as the result of incoming climate legislation or the shift to alternative technologies (itself described as 'transition risk'). The Bank of England routinely publishes summaries of the extent to which the finance industry is at risk from accelerating climate crisis.[76] Larry Fink, CEO of mammoth investment firm BlackRock (discussed at length in the next chapter) and routine advisor of US government officials, argued in his annual public letter that 'climate risk is investment risk'. Legislators have proposed that banks conduct stress-tests to model the resilience of their balance sheets to climate shocks, while climate scenario modelling for financial portfolios is increasingly in vogue among investors and financial firms. Many within the NGO sector have also eagerly entered this fray, with several organisations devoted entirely to evaluating the financial risks posed to investors by ecological catastrophe.[77]

The financial sector has, over recent decades, become an outsized industry and influence in the global economy, but particularly within the US and UK. In line with this relentless rise, regulators, the private sector and civil society alike have seized on the fact that ecological crisis poses enormous risks to financial returns and profits to argue that through risk-based frameworks, financial markets can drive decarbonisation simply by acting in self-interest. As Larry Fink argues, attending to climate risk and pushing governments to mitigate it is not 'woke' – it is a straightforward path to maintaining profits.[78] In line with the idea that ecological crisis is a market failure caused by flawed or insufficient information, apparently all that's needed to correct the failure is proper information about the risks firms face. Indeed, according to Fink: 'because capital markets pull future risk forward', shifts in capital allocation driven by the markets are a sure-fire route to swift decarbonisation, and will soon occur 'more quickly than we see changes to the climate itself.'[79]

This logic underlies the booming 'sustainable finance', industry explored in depth in Chapter 4; it also provides the intellectual bedrock for the growing enthusiasm among regulators for new obligations on firms to 'disclose' their exposure to climate risks, providing financial markets with the intel they need to begin appropriately pricing the 'true risks' of investments and in doing so drive a 'tectonic shift' in capital allocation.[80] The result is that, alongside the advance of carbon pricing architectures, a central policy framework advancing under green capitalism is the reduction of ecological crisis to a quantification of financial risk, and a corresponding pivot in policy approach from regulation to incentive and financial market-based pursuits. The trouble is, despite the clever calculations of financial firms and scenario modellers, conventional frameworks for quantifying risk – however sophisticated they may be – are unable to capture the 'radical' uncertainty posed by the climate and ecological crises.

As the first chapter noted, from the economics profession to policy and public perception, the climate and ecological crises are often inappropriately conceived of as gradual processes wherein, for instance, sea levels and temperatures rise at a steady rate between now and 2100 (beyond which point we seem for some reason disinterested, despite its being comfortably within the lifetime of many children alive today). However, this characterisation is fundamentally unrepresentative of how climatic change and ecosystem collapse are likely to progress. A focus on the potentially smooth relationships between rising surface temperatures and agricultural yield neglects the fact that these crises are likely to be punctuated by sudden, radical and irreversible shifts, with potentially cascading and self-reinforcing impacts. The growing recognition of complex feedback loops and potentially irreversible 'tipping points' in the climatic system, as well as the delicate interactions of the natural world with social and political dynamics and upheavals, make ours a world of radical or 'Knightian' uncertainty.[81]

In the language of finance, 'risk' describes a scenario in which, although the outcomes are unknown, there is ultimately a finite set of possibilities and known parameters that affect their respective probabilities; we can therefore measure the likelihoods of given outcomes to varying degrees of precision depending on the quality of our data. When I throw a die, for example, I can't know what the outcome will be; what I do know is the full list of possible results, as well as their relative likelihoods. An intermediary situation of 'pure uncertainty' describes the context in which I may know the possible outcomes of a scenario but can't properly gauge the relative probabilities between them. At the extreme end is Knightian uncertainty, which applies to contexts – like the climate and nature crises – where we cannot even be sure of what the relevant parameters are. Financial markets are meant to handle risk; they are not, however, equipped to deal with uncertainty – particularly the Knightian or 'radical' uncertainty that defines Earth's biosphere and climate, as well as the interactions between them. Their inherent unknowability imbues the natural systems we inhabit with many of the qualities we value and at which we wonder; it also makes them dangerous and unpredictable in a way that far exceeds our capacities to anticipate. This does not mean that trying to understand the world we inhabit is a futile exercise; it just suggests that our approach should be one of humility, recognising all the possibilities we cannot fully know in advance. Rather than approaching ecological crisis with the belief that we can ever have sufficient information to minimise its risks, then, radical uncertainty implies that the only way to engage with the potential for catastrophe is by adhering to a 'precautionary principle' – taking all the steps we are capable of in recognition of the fact that even a small chance of a catastrophic outcome is not one worth taking.[82]

Prices as politics as power

Both carbon pricing and market-based risk frameworks are presented as apolitical, resting on the idea that all that is needed to solve the problem of excessive emissions and ecological degradation is more and better information. Applying a price to carbon provides an essential missing data point for which 'it's hard to overstate the virtues' and that, once applied, will provide a clear signal to the market to drive a change in behaviour.[83] A disclosure-based approach to mitigating financial risks, meanwhile, relies on financial markets' wisdom and rationality as well as the belief that information can be sufficient enough for firms to make decisions reflecting the true 'costs' implied by accelerating ecological crisis. In both cases, the fundamentally political nature of prices is omitted – namely, the countless subjective decisions underlying the determination of what is or is not deemed a cost worth counting, and how these costs should be evaluated. And as the frequently brutal reality of carbon offsetting regimes underscores, the sanitised economic presentation of the price mechanism in textbooks and in mainstream discourse wilfully ignores the political and often violent processes underlying these exchanges.[84]

Similarly, to believe that the 'true cost' of various scenarios and economic activities can be gleaned from corporate and financial disclosures is to ignore the fact that many impacts may be deemed irrelevant to corporations' concerns, including anything to which a dollar value can't readily be ascribed. Whether the routinely unwaged forms of labour such as childcare or the ecosystems that sustain life, anything for which the market cannot generate an exchange value is likely to be disregarded in the calculus of climate-related risks, and therefore in the design of actions and policies to mitigate them.[85] To borrow from economic historian Adam Tooze: 'Encoded in prices and wages are not just the value of money relative to goods and the balance of supply and demand, but the entire hierarchy of inequality, privilege and class.'[86]

In Economics 101, students learn that the price mechanism, mediated through the market, is the ultimate exercise in democracy: a balance of supply and demand that, unbiased, aggregates and reflects the preferences of all actors involved. Viewed in this way, carbon pricing, the offset market, risk-based financial frameworks, and the litany of other market-based solutions examined in subsequent chapters, are both fair and unassailable, providing a least-cost pathway for confronting ecological crisis unfolding between free and equal partners in exchange, based on the ultimate objective mediator: prices. In reality, participants in an exchange are rarely both freely and equally engaged; moreover, the impacts of changing price signals are felt in profoundly different ways depending on one's economic position. One only has to look at the patchy implementation of carbon pricing schemes around the world to understand how powerful market actors can leverage their position in their favour. The sheer lobbying power of the fossil fuel industry has enabled their evasion of materially impactful carbon taxes in virtually all cases.[87] Conversely, even a uniformly imposed price on carbon – imagining, for a moment, the ideal scenario envisioned by its advocates of an effective and uniform global carbon price – will have outcomes which reflect not democratic input over what society genuinely values and needs, but instead the ability of wealthy individuals and firms to pay an outsized amount to shape the economy in their interests. As Cedric Durand aptly summarises:

> Carbon pricing does not allow society to discriminate between spurious uses of carbon – such as sending billionaires into space – and vital uses such as building the infrastructure for a non-carbon economy. In a successful transition, the first would be made impossible, the second as cheap as possible. As such, a unique carbon price becomes a clear pathway to failure.[88]

Underscoring these essential problems is the fact that for carbon markets, rampant financial speculation has rendered the Holy Grail of the consistent price signal virtually meaningless. Unlike conventional forms of market, carbon markets are constructed with a particular policy outcome in mind: curbing emissions. The entire mechanism for doing so relies on the incentive provided by a clear and consistent price signal. However, in practice carbon markets have frequently been defined by substantial financial speculation, generating price volatility that undermines the idealised steady price signal. For example, one study found that over a five-year period from 2010 to 2015, derivatives accounted for 99% of all trades in the EU ETS.[89]

Derivatives describe financial products whose value is derived from the value of an underlying security or asset; in the case of carbon markets, derivatives are based on expected fluctuations in the price of carbon allowances. In principle, derivatives are meant to enable firms to 'hedge' against the risk of price movements; in practice they have been used at length by financial firms to make speculative gains, increasing volatility in carbon prices.[90] The 'strong and stable price signal' is meant to be the beating heart of carbon pricing, providing a clear signal to firms over time; in conditions of high volatility from financial speculation, this long-term signal is undermined.[91] More fundamentally, critics have argued that for markets in carbon, there can never be a clear price signal. As mathematician Nicholas Bouleau explains: 'The illegibility of prices today does not enable the world economy to take the right decisions. On the contrary, it confines decision-makers in a universe of meaningless prices, whose short-term variations no longer reflect anything but the mimetic anxiety of traders.'[92]

In his acceptance speech for the 2018 Nobel Memorial Prize in economics, William Nordhaus argued 'there is basically no alternative to the market solution'. Encapsulated within this brief statement is the mainstream economic perspective on the ecological crisis – a perspective that continues to dominate public debate as well as the approaches of most institutions, from governments to international financial institutions to NGOs, tasked with addressing it. Through adherence to the idea that market mechanisms are somehow inevitable, this perspective deliberately obscures the inherently political, social and human character of the ecological challenge we face. Ours is a finite world, for which the atmosphere sustaining life as we know it has a finite capacity to absorb our refuse. It is also a world in which the lion's share of these resources and sinks has been and continues to be claimed by a vanishingly small proportion of the global population, which wields outsized power over the global marketplace. Within this context, there is no even footing. Rational actors do not enter the market on equal terms, nor can they similarly consent to its outcomes. In the formal, legal terms of liberal sensibility, when a multinational corporation and a subsistence farmer enter into an offsetting agreement, they are equals. In practice, nothing could be further from the truth.

Fredric Jameson famously contended that it was easier to imagine the end of the world than the end of capitalism. The discipline and profession of mainstream economics and market-centric forms of governance have been essential to this decline in collective imagination, compressing the horizon for alternatives onto the head of a pin and rendering as natural, inevitable and inescapable a world dominated by market dynamics and governed by the price mechanism. Fortunately, contrary to the confident assertions of its advocates, nothing about the neoclassical economic position on the climate and nature crises, nor the market solutions adherent to it, are beyond contestation. Contesting it, however, requires us to reopen the chest of possible futures and alternatives ways of living, being and organising our societies, which in turn demands we confront the sites of influence and control that presently dominate the global economy. As the next chapter explores, this is, ultimately, a question of power, and who exercises it.

Titans: assets, power and the construction of green capitalism

Indifference operatives passively, but it operates. –Antonio Gramsci[1]

In the Maldives, a country of 1,000 islands – some 80% of which are barely 1 metre above sea level – the ocean has already begun its reclamation of the land. In response, the state has, since the 1990s, been pumping vast amounts of sand from the seafloor to construct the artificial island of Hulhumalé. They hope within the next few years to have rehomed some 250,000 residents to the island. But even this effort may not be enough. Eyeing down the Maldives is Thwaites Glacier, a snaking expanse of ice along the coast of Antarctica, often referred to, rather ominously, as the Doomsday Glacier. As the largest ice sheet on the Antarctic continent, Thwaites has served as an essential barometer for scientists of our climatic trajectory. Covering an area nearly the size of Great Britain, Thwaites comprises enough ice to single-handedly raise sea levels by two feet (0.6 metres), exposing major low-lying cities from New York to London to regular flooding, and making the harrowing images of water coursing through subway turnstiles and desperate commuters

99

wading through cloudy subterranean pools that populated the summer of 2021 a routine occurrence. For low-lying islands like the Maldives, the extent of sea level rise that has already transpired (in the realm of 8–9 inches) is proving enough to threaten their very existence.

Like a crack etching slowly across glass until it shatters, the gradual recession and crumbling of Thwaites into the Antarctic Ocean (already at a rate of 50 billion tonnes per year) could spur a catastrophic glacial collapse across the entire West Antarctic ice sheet, which would raise sea levels by an unimaginable 10 feet, inundating the world's major cities, causing widespread salination of agricultural land, and displacing hundreds of millions of people. What we do know, as glaciologist Ian Howat put it, is that 'if there is going to be a climate catastrophe, it's probably going to start at Thwaites.'[2] In short, the collapse of Thwaites is not likely to be an isolated event. Its 'doomsday' moniker stems from what the dissolution of the ice shelf could become.

More than two decades ago, the Intergovernmental Panel on Climate Change (IPCC) first introduced the concept of 'tipping points'. Officially termed 'large-scale discontinuities', these are potentially irreversible events, such as the collapse of major glaciers, permafrost thaw, or the slowing of ocean currents, thought to have the potential to set off catastrophic chain reactions toward a rapidly destabilised climate and environment. For years after the IPCC began sounding the alarm on tipping points, it maintained they were only likely in the case of global temperature rises in the extreme realm of 5 degrees Celsius. Recently, the IPCC revised its predictions based on new evidence, instead confirming that several critical tipping points could become likely between 1 and 2 degrees Celsius – in other words, the state of warming in which we currently find ourselves.

The irreversible collapse of Thwaites, and of major features of the cryosphere more broadly, is just one among many climatic tipping points that could permanently alter our climate and environment, delivering us into a radically unknown world. At 2 degrees Celsius of warming, an astonishing 99% of tropical reefs are expected to be lost – the product of feedback interactions between ocean acidification, warming and pollution.[3] The world's forests face irreversible destabilisation. Anthropogenic deforestation in the Amazon is testing the limits of its capacity to maintain the world's 'lungs' and its most abundant habitat. If deforestation reaches between 20% and 40% loss of the original forest cover, the Amazon rainforest could rapidly and catastrophically flip from carbon sink to net carbon source; as of the most recent estimates, total Amazon deforestation stands at 17%, and its annual rate continues to rise.[4]

Rather than hypothetical 'doomsday' projections in the computer models of scientists exploring a distant future, the tipping points about which experts have been raising the alarm for decades are, increasingly, upon us. The trouble is, the complexities of these events don't lend themselves to precise prediction of how or at what temperature threshold they may occur, nor do they vary smoothly with the impacts of our actions, like rising emissions. We can't know for certain when Thwaites will give itself over to the sea, nor which razed acre of Amazon rainforest could finally cause the planet's lungs to choke. What we do know is our actions are rapidly shrinking the distance between our present and a radically altered future.

Staring down this future of intense risk and uncertainty, it is salient that ours is an economy in which value is increasingly derived not from conventional production so much as from asset ownership and, as political economist Ivan Ascher argues, control over the capacities of 'prediction' – that is, the capacity to decide where investment will or will not be provided based on assessments of risk and possible future conditions.[5] As Ascher articulates: 'capital's relation to its own future (and hence everyone's relation to the future) is itself mediated by financial markets.'[6] Financial markets are preoccupied with risk, and with attempting to predict the future. At the moment, they are betting on climate change – not only through their allocation of investment to the firms and commodities fuelling it, but in a whole host of ways, including trading in new financial products whose pay-outs are tied to future climatic events, conditions and disasters.[7]

Under these conditions, those actors with privileged access to and influence over the crystal ball of financial risk analysis, prediction and allocation wield substantial economic power. And, as the preceding chapters argued, it is power, in the end, rather than neutral market forces that will determine the contours of our confrontation with deepening ecological crisis. This chapter is dedicated to understanding the sites and forms of power shaping the contours of green capitalism. Namely, it identifies within an increasingly finance-dominated global economy a critical and historically recent force: the asset management industry. Through a combination of explosive growth and intra-industry concentration, this chapter traces how a relatively small cohort of firms has come to form a new locus of economic power by two connected means: by amassing and concentrating ownership across the economy, and in the process of doing so fundamentally altering how capital is allocated and the future constructed. As this and subsequent chapters argue, this shifting architecture of control, prediction and influence has significant implications for the shape of the global response to and governance of the climate and nature emergencies.

The asset management industry is by no means a monolithic superpower that has supplanted all others in the global economy. It is also not the only sector concerned with risk analysis and attempts to predict the future, nor with influencing climate and environmental policy. It is, however, an industry whose fingerprints are particularly visible in the shape of the green capitalist programme. This chapter explores how the relentless growth of and concentration within the asset management industry, mediated through the rise of so-called 'passive' investing, has begun to fundamentally change how corporations are governed and investment is allocated, such that the line between guessing the shape of the future and sculpting it is increasingly blurred. By necessity, the chapter focuses primarily on the UK and US, first because the most powerful firms within the asset management industry are concentrated within these two countries, and secondly because the legal systems of New York State and England govern a majority of global finance and exchange.[8]

The titans of asset management are a cohort whose unique arrangement of incentives and power – exercised through ownership on an unprecedented scale within an asset-oriented economy – makes them critical actors in the struggle for a just and sustainable future. Propelled increasingly by the mechanics of passive allocation, the industry's growth and concentration are fundamentally altering how finance understands, responds to, and ultimately constructs the future. Despite this, in comparison to stalwarts such as the fossil fuel majors, it is an industry which features little in the public consciousness surrounding engagement on environmental policy. This chapter seeks to rectify this issue by delving into the shape, scale and function of the asset management industry, as well as the routes by which it is reshaping the logics governing the global economy. Ultimately, it argues that 'green capitalism' is a programme substantively shaped in their interest and image.

A short drop and a GameStop

The deeply uneven economic impacts of the COVID-19 pandemic offered an unlikely window of insight into how the shocks of ecological crisis are likely to unfurl across an economic model geared toward the interests of asset ownership. As the virus first began to course through the global economy, financial markets were briefly shaken. Key stock market indicators tumbled, and record amounts of capital flowed out of areas considered higher risk, including the so-called 'emerging markets' of lower-income countries, into the stability of Northern government bonds, particularly US Treasuries. However, the shock and the sudden drop were swiftly soothed. By the close of 2020, the S&P 500 had reached record highs amidst a peak of pandemic suffering. The value of the index doubled between March 2020, the bottom of its pandemic-induced shock, and August 2021, closing off the highest rate of growth since the Second World War.[9] Amid record unemployment, total economic shutdown, and absent clarity on when those conditions would change, a look at the financial markets would thus have given no indication that anything was amiss, let alone that a global pandemic was claiming hundreds of thousands of lives and bringing economies to a standstill. Coupled with audacious monetary easing, the performance of financial markets – so regularly gestured toward as an indicator of a booming 'real economy' – was utterly divorced from the experience of those living and struggling in the real world.

The disconnect was widened further when, in early 2021, a group of Redditors, with a user going by the name 'DeepFuckingValue' among those at the helm, decided to pile into shares of GameStop, a struggling video game retailer. Upon realising that a hedge fund had 'shorted' the stock (effectively betting on its share price declining), this band of internet vigilantes teamed up to instead send the company's share price soaring in an effort to topple the hedge fund. The spectacle prompted a torrent of responses in the media, ranging from scorn to triumph and, more often than not, mild confusion. One columnist for *Business Insider* wrote on Twitter: 'I know people think this is fun but — why do we have a stock market? So productive firms can raise capital to do useful things. Detaching stock price from fundamental value makes the markets serve the real economy worse.'[10]

Well intentioned as it might have been, this scolding ultimately rests on myth. In the succinct words of former trader Doug Henwood, 'the stock market has almost nothing to do with raising productive capital for investment.'[11] Stock prices are meant, in theory, to reflect investors' belief in a company's future profit-making prospects. However, they routinely have no relation to even the market's own indicators of 'fundamental value', let alone 'real world' conditions. This has been particularly true in the context of post-2008 quantitative easing programmes, which have firmly detached asset prices from conventional indicators of real economic performance, such as wage growth and productivity.[12] Critically, while the stock market may have a role in allowing companies to 'raise productive capital' for growth or investment in the things most of us would consider valuable, like decarbonisation or higher wages, this has long ceased to be its primary function. The ratio between new share issuances and share buybacks is heavily skewed, such that much more cash is funnelled out of companies to shareholders than shareholders put in.[13] While 'initial public offerings' (when companies first 'go public' and offer shares on the market) and the issuance of new stock by mature companies are the events that tend to grab headlines, the vast majority of activity on exchanges takes place not between investors and firms, but between the hands of traders.

Why, then, did several governments take such bold steps to stabilise financial markets, even as others in the economy suffered record unemployment, income loss and, for those who are private renters, housing insecurity? The clear decision to protect the interests of shareholders (and asset owners more broadly) throughout the pandemic left deep cracks in the apparently iron-clad justification for shareholders' legal privileges: that these actors bear the most risk. Indeed, shareholders' exorbitant entitlements are often justified by their status as 'residual claimants'. In theory, this implies shareholders are the primary risk takers of the corporation, with no guarantees of a return or even to hold on to their original investment. Were this actually the case, the havoc wrought on much of the global economy by the pandemic should have seen shareholders take on losses as firms buckled, whether in the form of diminished stock prices or drastically reduced pay-outs.[14] Instead, corporate bailouts were routinely doled out without any accompanying terms on firms' subsequent behaviour, meaning many continued to pay out enormous dividends, even while shedding employees. At the same time, central bank interventions coupled with a savings glut on the part of the rich meant that financial markets broke record after record throughout the pandemic, even as the world's majority endured profound suffering and economic hardship.

A deflationary coalition

The instinct on the part of many states to preserve the value of assets, both real and financial,[15] was neither neutral nor spontaneous; it represented the product of a decades-long shift toward the prioritisation of asset owners and asset-based rather than wage-based income in policymaking – a coalition of interests and actors that economic historian Yakov Feygin has termed the 'deflationary coalition'.[16] From the late 1960s, the political-economic agendas of capitalist economies – particularly the US – have been defined by the struggle over how to manage inflation. Though I will not recount its full history here, the essential result of this struggle has been to cement the interests of asset owners – particularly older homeowners – as 'the common sense of our economic policymakers and the policy they write.'[17] Critically, as this chapter explores, this shift in the common sense has shaped, and continues to shape, the approach of policymakers to the climate and nature crises.

In the simplest terms, the doctrine of the deflationary coalition manifests as a deflationary bias in the real economy, such as a preference for keeping wages down, and an inflationary bias in the world of assets, ensuring their rising values, from shares to real estate. This dual bias has permeated recent decades of economic policymaking, guiding the so-called 'Great Moderation' between the 1980s and the rupture of the 2008 Financial Crisis. Over this period, managing inflation became

the almost singular fixation of central banks; financial deregulation exploded and the extension of credit soared; and politicians became increasingly unwilling and unable to challenge
the wealth and interests of older homeowners, which was often
maintained at the expense of the young.[18] The outcome of this
deflationary assault can be seen in sharp relief in the significant
growth in the ratio of global wealth to income, which has doubled in so-called 'Western' economies since 1950.[19]

Though their connection to the management of the climate and nature crises may not be immediately apparent, the
imprints of the deflationary coalition – its constituents, their
interests and the actors helping advance those interests – are
ubiquitous in the resistance to and watering down of many
policy programmes predicated on mass investment and economic mobilisation to decarbonise the economy. This is in no
small part a reflection of the influence and effective lobbying of asset managers, with which this coalition is intimately
linked. For instance, on both sides of the Atlantic, Green New
Deal proposals continue to meet with ridicule and obstinate
resistance couched in the terms of their expansionary fiscal
proposals – in other words, commitment to a massive mobilisation of public investment, ownership and capacity. Coupled
with proposals such as a return of industries like transport and
energy to public control, wealth taxation, or a jobs guarantee,
certain more ambitious or justice-oriented Green New Deal
programmes also take direct aim at private assets and the interests of the deflationary coalition, prompting even more staunch
resistance. Instead, the deflationary/asset inflationary duality
underlies the escalating obsession among policymakers, from
the Biden administration to the European Union, with 'sustainable investing', financial 'innovations' in carbon and nature

markets, and private sector-led innovation and investment in lieu of a publicly coordinated programme of decarbonisation, all of which offer new opportunities for private investors to benefit from the response to ecological crisis. The reorientation of the economy toward assuring secure and consistently rising asset values, and the concomitant rearrangement of power in the economy toward those with assets and the managers who oversee them is thus essential for understanding the politics of managing ecological crisis in the years to come.

High noon of the asset manager

While 'too-big-to-fail' traditional banks have long been the gravitational centres of finance, when it comes to shaping the global response to ecological crisis, a different type of firm holds court. Though estimates vary, by 2016 the so-called 'shadow banking' sector (a somewhat nebulous term describing non-bank firms that provide credit, the traditional domain of banks) constituted over a third of global lending,[20] with capital markets providing a key source of this liquidity.[21] The scale of non-bank lending in the global economy has only continued to grow since.[22] The result, as *Financial Times* columnist Gillian Tett wrote in the context of COVID-19, is that 'while the banks played a starring role in the last big Financial Crisis, non-bank financial structures … matter much more now.'[23] Chief among these non-bank financial structures is the asset manager, primarily through the funds they manage. As their name suggests, asset managers oversee how the assets of different entities – whether a wealthy individual, a university endowment, or a multi-billion-pound pension fund – are invested, acting on behalf of these entities by allocating their assets to various forms of investment, from shares in publicly traded companies to corporate bonds and real estate. Their success as an industry rests largely on a belief that these firms, and the fund managers within them, have a monopoly on the expertise, insight and capacity required to be successful in the financial markets, enabling them to charge the substantial fees on which most of their revenues are based. While the term 'asset manager' can technically cover a range of different types of firm (hedge funds, private equity and so on), I focus here on those firms whose primary offering are mutual funds and exchange-traded funds (ETFs, defined in more detail below), through which most investment is directed.

Though it was not always the case, today asset managers dominate ownership of the global corporate economy as well as provide an integral source of credit for firms, traditionally the domain of banks. Half of all financial assets are now held by non-bank financial institutions, a substantial increase since the 2008 Financial Crisis.[24] Importantly, credit for corporations is also increasingly provided by non-bank institutions: according to the Bank of England, 'all of the net increase in UK corporate debt between the end of 2008 and the end of 2020 has come from market-based finance' – that is, forms of finance raised in financial markets, the domain of asset managers, rather than from direct bank lending.[25] For asset management in particular, rapid overall growth has occurred alongside a substantial concentration of assets *within* the industry itself. Today, just two firms, BlackRock and Vanguard, preside over a total asset pool of nearly US$20 trillion. To put that figure in context: it's enough to own all the shares in every corporation listed on the London Stock Exchange, more than three times over. These two firms' asset pools also constitute nearly a fifth of the

US$100 trillion now sloshing around the *global* asset manage-ment industry, which comprises thousands of firms represent-ing countless individuals around the world. And in certain key parts of the industry, such as the rapidly growing market for ETFs, just three firms (BlackRock, Vanguard and State Street) control close to 80% of the market.[26] It's a profound degree of concentration in an industry that is enormously influential. Nor are these trends on the wane: asset managers boasted a record year in the middle of the pandemic, with global assets growing 11% to soar past the US$100 trillion mark.[27]

The growth of and concentration within the asset manage-ment is not merely an academic curiosity. Rather, the solidi-fication of a small cohort of asset managers as the primary holders of both equity and debt assets represents a major shift in power in finance and, by extension, the global economy. In the process, their relentless rise has upended previous under-standings of the systems that govern our economy, from control over how corporations behave, to where investment is directed and who gains access to it. By occupying top shareholding positions throughout the global economy and wielding enor-mous allocative discretion at a scale that can single-handedly move markets, today's top asset managers and the coterie of firms associated with their industry, namely providers of the 'financial indices' we explore below, increasingly dominate both direct control of corporations and the power of predic-tion, mediated through growing control over capital allocation. Their sheer scale has also given a select cohort a steering role in political circles and in the policy programmes of governments from the US to the EU, particularly with respect to confront-ing ecological crisis. Through these myriad channels, they are increasingly shaping the world, and the future, in their image.

Corporate personhood

We live in a corporate economy. The corporation is a world-building force, equipped with a heady blend of legal rights and privileges that enable them to coordinate both capital and labour to tremendous effect.[28] Though often synonymous with private companies in general, corporations are a specific legal form, recognised with a form of legal 'personhood' and therefore entitled to many of the same rights in economic disputes as a person. For example, in the United States, the case of Citizens United vs. the Federal Electoral Commission determined that corporate donations to politicians' campaigns were protected under the First Amendment, as corporate 'personhood' endowed corporations with freedom of speech ('speech', in this case, rather generously interpreted as cash donations). In the private sector, it is the specific legal form of the corporation that dominates global economic activity, in contrast with much less common alternative forms like worker cooperatives. The systemic importance of the corporation is such that Hyun-Song Shin, Head of Research at the Bank for International Settlements (the central bank of central banks) argues the global economy is best understood not as a series of national economic 'islands' trading with one another, but as a matrix of interlocking corporate balance sheets.[29]

Ownership of financial assets such as shares generally brings various entitlements to the owner. These might take the form of interest or dividend payments and, in the case of equity, certain governance rights at the company in which you hold shares. With the invention of share capital, the corporation became able to capitalise the future, which is to say it became able to raise capital based on equity investors' expectations about the future growth and profitability of the firm (or at least about increases in its share price, which need not be related to the former). In buying a share, the shareholder becomes entitled to a portion of the corporation's future income, for instance when dividends are declared, as well as various governance rights.

The legal specificity of the corporate form has generated profound impacts for the climate, biosphere and human societies. Specifically, the combined power of the corporation's legal privileges (explored below) and the formal separation of ownership (shareholders) from control (management) and from capital itself (belonging to the corporate body, not shareholders) has enabled corporations to wreak profound ecological and social damage while insulating shareholders from responsibility for doing so.[30] The corporation's systemic importance as well as its structuring to insulate various parties, from shareholders to managers, from accountability, raises questions whose answers have significant implications for how the world grapples with the ecological crisis. For instance, who controls the corporation? Where is power located within it?

While day to day decisions about the functioning and strategy of the corporate body are executed by management, the corporation is ultimately owned by its shareholders, who have governance rights of their own, and to whom the managerial class is formally accountable.[31] However, when share ownership occurs via a financial intermediary, as is increasingly the case, these rights are bifurcated. Despite being the most prominent shareholders throughout most corporations in the global economy, asset managers do not, strictly speaking, own the assets they are buying. Their role as intermediaries means that although they may legally hold the stocks or bonds issued by a company, because these firms are investing other people's money, the income rights from assets remain vested with the entity who entrusted their money to a manager – that is, the pension-holder, endowment or individual saver (known as a beneficiary). Unlike income rights, however, it is the intermediary that becomes vested with the governance and control rights associated with a financial asset. Predominantly, this takes the form of voting rights at public corporations' 'Annual General Meetings' (AGMs), during which decisions are taken such as whether to reappoint or remove company directors, and shareholders file and vote on 'resolutions' related to corporate strategy and actions, like whether a company will set an emissions target, quit regressive lobbying groups, or eliminate companies implicated in human rights abuses from their supply chains.

Your risk, my reward

To justify their entitlement to both income and governance rights, shareholders are often cast as society's great 'risk takers', putting their money on the line to support productive enterprise with just as great a risk of losing out as seeing a return. However, when a corporation folds, and an investor loses the value of their original investment, that is the limit of their potential loss. Thanks to the advent of 'limited liability' – a legal protection that shields shareholders from liability related to decisions which the corporation takes on their behalf – a shareholder's losses are limited to the value of their shareholding, even if, for instance, they played a key role in the decision-making that led a company to insolvency. Unpaid debts or wages become the responsibility of the corporate body itself, not the shareholder or even, in many cases, management. The justification for this protection is, in the words of legal scholar Paddy Ireland, 'to induce wealthy shareholders to bear risk for the economy as a whole: the shareholders bear the first loss in exchange for being assured that that loss is limited, and reaping significant rewards if the corporation has profits instead of losses.'[32]

In practice, risk and loss are often distributed very differently. Whether a pandemic-induced downturn, financial crash precipitated by speculative mania, or looking toward a future of escalating climate and nature-related harms, in moments of crisis it is the public – not the shareholder – that ultimately bears the residual risk of the corporate economy. This might take the form of subsidising lost livelihoods through the welfare state; mitigating or repairing social harms when a company fails in a sector like electric utilities or social care; or preventing collapse in the first place through public bailouts. The response from many high-income governments to the pandemic-induced economic downturn demonstrated all three of the above in spectacular form, absorbing its impacts on corporations through wage subsidies, corporate bailouts, and enormous programmes of monetary easing, during which central banks bought up vast quantities of government bonds, and in some cases corporate bonds.

Certainly, the pandemic was an unprecedented shock that the average business could not have been expected to prepare for, and some of these interventions sought to minimise immediate harms for workers and the wider public. However, COVID-19 exploded onto a corporate economy already made fragile over decades in which the demands and interests of shareholders – articulated in the form of higher dividend payments, share buybacks, and other means of share price inflation, often financed through rising debt – have been prioritised at the expense of other needs, such as higher wages, protections for human rights and the environment, or stable balance sheets that don't leave workers and society on the line when shocks hit. In the FTSE350, a shorthand for the 350 largest corporations listed on the London Stock Exchange, twenty years of rising shareholder pay-outs were directly mirrored in declining productive investment,[33] all while debt soared. Nor were these trends unique to the UK: worldwide, corporate bond issuance averaged nearly US$2 trillion per year between 2008 and 2019, more than twice the amount issued between 2000 and 2007 in the run-up to the Financial Crisis.[34] And in 2021, major US corporations recorded their highest ever year of share buybacks as the COVID-19 pandemic continued to rage.[35]

In crisis after crisis over recent years, the prioritisation of the interests of the deflationary coalition has been made glaringly evident. From the Global Financial Crisis to COVID-19, systemic ruptures have been navigated in line with the interests of asset ownership. These actions presage the probable priorities of many governments in responding to the acute crises that will increasingly punctuate deepening environmental and climatic damage. As subsequent sections explore, the importance of ensuring this prioritisation has not passed the asset management industry – whose wealth and power are driven by rising asset bases and prices – idly by.

Living in the age of asset manager capitalism

The titans of asset management – BlackRock, Vanguard and a handful of their peers – are vast operators with global reach. Their investment portfolios are distributed across all industries, regions and asset classes (equity, corporate bonds, sovereign debt, real estate and beyond), making them truly 'universal owners'. They are also relatively 'strong' investors, in that they generally have significant stakes (5% of a company's shares, for instance) across this full range of asset classes. The combination of these distributional characteristics is, as political economist Benjamin Braun argues, without historical precedent.[36] According to Braun, the combination of concentration, relative strength and universality is constitutive of an entirely novel era of corporate governance and control which he calls, in a hat tip to Hyman Minsky, 'asset manager capitalism'.[37]

To understand the implications of this new regime, we have to begin with the distributions of ownership and control that defined previous decades, and the frameworks of economic governance that emerged from them. In both the UK and the United States, the twentieth century played host to two very different corporate governance regimes. During the decades leading up to and immediately following the Second World War, corporate shareholders were highly diffuse, made up largely of individuals with savings. For instance, following the war, US households directly owned 94% of all corporate equity.[38] Corporate managers thus exercised substantial control over the firm's governance, and feared the power of organised labour far more than dispersed and individually weak shareholders. In the decades following the Second World War, the pensions system swelled substantially, bringing countless workers into new forms of contact with the financial system. Over time, pensions supplanted individuals to become the foremost owners of corporate shares by the mid-1980s. Importantly, at the time of the neoliberal turn in governance, shareholders, including pension funds, remained relatively weak and dispersed. This structure of ownership lent empirical support to and provided the ideological bedrock for sweeping neoliberal policies, such as Margaret Thatcher's waves of privatisation in the UK – opening up state assets to private shareholders – and her corresponding vision of a 'shareholder democracy', according to which bureaucratic and inefficient state control would be supplanted by a genuinely 'democratic' structure of mass share ownership. While initially a popular and intuitively appealing idea, the plan was doomed from its inception.

Setting aside the substantial problem that, left uncorrected, extant patterns of economic inequality would decisively skew financial asset ownership and therefore 'democracy' in favour of the wealthy, the diffuse shareholder structure that marked preceding decades was not to last. Neoliberal reforms meant that the pensions base began to erode, wealth inequality swelled, and finance was unleashed from previous constraints. Thus, in the decades around the turn of the millennium, financial intermediaries such as asset managers supplanted pensions as direct owners of shares. Over time, the fund management segment of asset management became uniquely dominant, pooling together the wealth of asset owners from individuals to vast university endowments and, increasingly, pension funds themselves. Since the turn of the millennium – and particularly in the wake of the 2008 Financial Crisis – concentration within asset management itself has meant that today, regardless of who the largest shareholders previously were in any given country, the rankings are topped by a shrinking number of firms, with BlackRock and Vanguard chief among them.

BlackRock and Vanguard together control 10% of the total value of the FTSE350 (the index of the 350 largest companies on the London Stock Exchange), and together with State Street (another passive investing giant), an average of more than 20% in any given S&P 500 company, spanning all the US corporate giants from Exxon and Chevron to Facebook, Amazon and Pfizer. In practice, these combined stakes often creep even higher, because in many jurisdictions like the US, asset managers are required to vote at corporate annual general meetings, whereas other types of investor, such as individuals, are not (and may simply lack the will or resources to do so). A 20% or even 25% collective share of the votes in a corporation may not sound particularly vast at face value, but in practice it is often decisive. Although an imperfect comparison, it helps to imagine the corporation as a country, in which just two or three individuals out of thousands controlled a fifth or as much as one in every four votes. Now imagine that same handful of individuals had equivalently outsize power not just in one country, but in most, if not all, influential countries all over the world, and the picture becomes deeply undemocratic. It is this *combination* of factors – strength, concentration and universality – that makes 'asset manager capitalism' unprecedented. The era of corporate ownership and control which we now occupy is undeniably distinct from the conditions that came before it, and which are still used to justify the primacy of the shareholder in the corporation and, by extension, the wider economy.[39]

The extraordinary protections and privileges, such as limited liability and voting rights, which we grant to shareholders are thus based on an ownership regime whose characteristics and distributions of power are obsolete. In seeking maximum returns from the small basket of companies in which they were invested, the investors of the shareholder primacy imaginary were presumably acutely interested in the actions and performance of their few investments. Shareholders, construed as weak relative to 'insiders' such as management, and instrumental in preventing 'expropriation' of the corporation's

119

gains by these insiders, were cloaked in legal protections and given significant sway over the direction of a corporation, to the exclusion of other stakeholders like the company's workforce or wider societal interests. However, the current ownership regime has undermined the framework used to justify this system. Instead, today's behemoth management firms are interested in growing their pool of assets, both through new inflows and through aggregate growth in asset prices, rather than on the performance of any given company. These shifts, in combination with the seemingly relentless rise of a new form of 'passive' investing, have created an altogether different set of imperatives in the governance of the corporate sphere.

Passive revolution

The extreme concentration that now defines financial asset ownership really took off in the wake of the Financial Crisis. This is not a coincidence. The present arrangement of ownership was propelled by the growth of a financial innovation whose transformative implications we are only beginning to appreciate: the 'passive' or 'index-tracking' fund. Images of wolfish Wall Street masculinity and the roaring din of the trading floor tend to dominate public perception of the finance industry, but contrary to this image, today the shots are increasingly called by 'indices' – in effect, lists of securities that are assembled based on criteria such as a corporation's market capitalisation (size), industry, or geographic location. These indices form the basis of the ascendant passive segment of fund management.[40] For an index-tracking fund, rather than having its investment decisions made by ruthless asset managers trying to beat the market, the goal is simply to 'track' the performance of a given index by buying up the securities it contains (or a representative subset) to replicate its performance over time as closely as possible. For instance, a fund that 'tracks' the S&P 500 would simply aim to replicate the returns (or, at times, losses) of that basket of companies over time – not to outperform it by gambling on a handful of companies.

Passive investing is not a particularly recent innovation; it was originated in 1976 by Jack Bogle, former director of Vanguard (today an almost exclusively passive-investing asset management giant). The concept was slow to take off, initially meeting with resistance and even ridicule.[41] After 2008, however, the industry took off in a perfect storm of post-crash dynamics, not least the growing untenability of active mangers' much higher fees following a crisis in which the industry had demonstrated its capacity for irrationality and fallibility in spectacular colour. Above all, when examined over longer periods of time, it became clear that passive funds outperformed their active counterparts, leaving cracks in the idea that active managers had a particular grasp on predicting the future and picking winners. Post-crash, passives stolidly replicated the impressive growth in financial markets that followed, supported in no small way by the massive and market-spanning injection of liquidity provided by vast programmes of quantitative easing (QE) from multiple central banks.

In the words of a former economist at the Central Bank of Ireland, QE 'drove up asset prices and bailed out baby boomers' without kickstarting a commensurate recovery in wages, widening the gap between those with assets at the time the programme began and those without – the younger, poorer and less powerful.[42] But why should these post-crisis central bank interventions have been better for passive than active funds? The logic is fairly straightforward: by buying up large quantities of the market's 'safe' assets – sovereign debt as well as investment-grade corporate bonds, it pushed the 'yields' of those bonds down, driving investors elsewhere and generally inflating the values of other assets, from equities to real estate. QE thus drove up asset prices across the board, making it difficult for active managers placing industry or company-specific bets to compete with the strong, steady returns promised by the mainstream passive industry, which simply tracked the rising tide of asset prices as a whole.[43]

Investors have since poured money into passive funds; worldwide, assets invested in a passive strategy trebled between 2015 and 2020 alone.[44] In 2019, assets under management in passive funds surpassed a new landmark in the US, overtaking the total invested in active strategies and positively dwarfing the net inflows of new cash taken in by active funds, thereby cementing a new era of passive-dominated investment. Other economies are now following suit.[45] The explosive growth of index funds post-crisis has also drastically altered the landscape within the asset management industry, supporting the significant concentration within the Big 3 and a handful of other firms we see today. Since 2008, the Big 3's collective ownership stake in major public companies crested on the wave of passive investment from about 13.5% of the average S&P 500 company at the time of the crash to roughly 22% by the beginning of 2020.[46]

Inertia and amplification

All of this may seem like a (perhaps dull, perhaps interesting) detour into a technical component of the finance industry, but the redistribution of ownership and relocation of control over

capital allocation brought about by the rise of passive investment strategies has profound implications for addressing challenges from decarbonisation to ecological restoration – how
and whether we do it, on whose terms, and to whose benefit.
In part, this is a product of the technicalities of index-tracking
funds. In theory, shareholders have several pathways for influencing corporate decision-making, including the right to vote
at corporate annual general meetings. Often, however, asset
managers prefer to influence corporate behaviour through less
hostile or overt means through behind-closed-doors 'engagement' on various issues, access to which tends to be granted in
proportion to one's significance as a shareholder. Making both
these tools substantially more effective is the threat of 'exit'
(selling your position in a company). Large enough selloffs of
shares can apply significant downward pressure on share prices,
thereby 'disciplining' managers and increasing their cost of capital, while big public divestment statements can have material
effects on a company's public image.

By definition, index-tracking funds are meant to lack an 'exit
option' (industry terminology for the ability to 'liquidate' or
divest holdings in a particular investment at will). Because the
selling-point of an index-tracking fund is that its contents (and
correspondingly its performance) are set by 'objective' criteria
and beholden to tracking the performance of a known index, in
principle the asset managers offering these funds don't have the
option to divest their holdings at leisure. On the one hand, this
makes them, in theory, long-term shareholders whose interest in a company's performance will last as long as that firm
remains in the relevant indices. This bias toward smooth, long-
term consistency likely underlies the fact that the Big 3 overwhelmingly side with corporate management on key issues like

executive pay – decidedly more than their active counterparts.[47] However, it also means that, should a company not respond to shareholder pressure over – to name two salient and increasingly common examples – plans for decarbonising their business model or divesting from contentious assets like coal mines, there is not a lot of pressure the fund manager can apply by threatening to divest.[48]

The same principle served as justification for widespread exclusion of index-tracking assets from the commitments made by the 'Net Zero Asset Manager Alliance' at the COP26 climate summer in Glasgow, ultimately making the pledge to strive for 'net zero' portfolios ring hollow (among other reasons).[49] There are many campaigners and experts who, it should be noted, dispute that index-tracking funds have no ability to divest any of their holdings, emphasising that there isn't actually a legal requirement that stipulates the funds precisely track the index on which they're based; many funds already invest in only a subset of the index's securities, for example.[50] What matters is not necessarily exact replication of each constituent, but of index performance. Nonetheless, practices and norms within the industry are that passive funds should, by definition, not operate according to manager discretion on individual holdings as it risks introducing 'tracking error', and so selective divestment generally remains out of reach. Strikingly, in response to the conflict in Ukraine, BlackRock committed to suspend all purchases of Russian securities, including from its passive funds, making clear that, in circumstances they deem sufficiently extreme or politically salient, this option is in fact available.[51] However, whether the climate crisis will be considered a sufficiently politically fraught issue to divest from, say, the fossil fuel industry, remains unclear. Indeed, following the 2018

Marjory Stoneman Douglas High school shooting in Parkland, Florida, activists pointed out the big passive providers were among the largest investors in the major gun manufacturers, and demanded they take a stand. As a former BlackRock executive put it: 'Parkland was interesting. It was such a tough question for an organisation like BlackRock. Are you going to make a moral statement and sell those gunmakers, but introduce tracking error?'[52]

Perhaps more important is the extent to which passive funds have begun to change the way money flows in financial markets, from allocation based on informed predictions about a company or industry's movements to an altogether different mechanism. In mainstream economic theory, financial markets are considered efficient insofar as outcomes reflect the sum of the decisions of ostensibly rational actors like fund managers who might, for instance, bet on a stock they recognise as undervalued, or against one they consider overinflated. Setting aside the fact that this theoretical efficiency is highly disputed, the rise of index funds calls this function fundamentally into question.

Aside from providing a list of securities to track, an index also tells fund managers how much of each security should be bought, in relative terms. In most cases, these ratios are 'capitalisation-weighted', meaning that when the fund takes in new money, it allocates most of it to the highest value holdings – for stocks, the firms with the highest market capitalisation, or in the case of bond funds, the largest bond issuers.[53] In other words, when an index fund is buying from the S&P 500, it allocates much more of its value to Amazon and Apple than it does Ralph Lauren or Hasbro. The consequence is that as new money flows into passive funds, it tends to disproportionately accrue to firms that are already large, passing over the 'dynamic upstarts' that might be considered undervalued at a given point in time, and which feature prominently in the popular imagination of how financial markets work. In other words, as financial journalist Robin Wigglesworth documents, 'size can beget size': ten years ago, for every dollar going into Vanguard or State Street's S&P 500 fund, roughly 10 cents would have gone into just the five largest companies (in other words, 10% to the top 1% of firms). Today, this has crept over 20 cents, its highest ever.[54] The same applies to firms 'already on the up', amplifying existing trends and conditions and creating a 'self-fulfilling prophecy' of outperformance relative to the active management strategies these funds increasingly supplant.[55]

As the industry grows, this tendency in index investing toward self-fulfilling prophecy and the amplification of existing trends now materially changes how money is allocated in the economy. Indices began as a method for tracking market performance: they're designed to measure some subset of the market, based on observable data such as market capitalisation that is inherently backward-looking. Most index funds thus reflect existing or past market conditions. However, in their rapid growth, indices have come not just to reflect markets, but to move them.[56] The aggregate pool of assets invested in index-tracking funds is now so vast that even the prospect of a company's being added to a major index can materially inflate its share price before it has officially been added. Companies aren't the only ones affected, either. Each year, MSCI, one of the world's largest index-providers, effectively defines which countries are considered 'emerging markets' by including them in their indices, thereby meriting the inclusion of a country's debt in countless financial products and investment strategies. In 2018, MSCI decided to add Argentina – which had previously been relegated in the wake of its sovereign debt default – back into the category. Within a single day, the 'Merval' (Argentina's flagship stock market index of major corporations) had shot up 6%.[57]

Corporations, meanwhile, have begun to alter their behaviour in pursuit of inclusion in key indices. For instance, research suggests a relationship between the rise of indexing and the characteristics of corporate bonds, namely larger value and longer-duration issuances.[58] Considered in the context of the climate crisis, this could increase the already substantial pool of 'stranded assets' by driving longer-dated and larger bond issuances from, for instance, fossil fuel firms. In another troubling instance, Calgary-based oil firm Encana moved its headquarters to Colorado to benefit from the share price inflation that would result from its inclusion in new indices.[59] It has also been suggested that the shift of global assets into passive funds can amplify the negative impacts for emerging markets of major shocks, such as the pandemic or, critically, ecological crisis.[60]

Indices' ability to move markets is mirrored by their ability to create inertia within the financial system – the result of much of the index-tracking industry allocating its investments on the basis of inherently backward-looking data. Often, this occurs at the neglect of real-world conditions and incoming threats to certain companies' profitability or long-term viability, such as climate legislation. This limitation is inherent to the calculation of financial risk and opportunity, wherein reliance on data about previous events means 'the future is essentially conceptualised as a replication of the past.'[61] Campaigners have been quick to point out that this has kept fossil fuel companies firmly within mainstream indices, and risks making the passive fund industry 'holders of last resort' in these companies' securities, 'artificially' keeping their valuations high, and in the process enabling them to access additional finance more easily.[62]

Heisenberg's Index Fund Principle

All of this points to a relatively new and increasingly decisive gatekeeper in the global economy, moving in lockstep with the ascendance of asset manager capitalism: index providers. Indices, of course, don't emerge out of thin air; there is a reason their titles are adorned with brand names like S&P. The construction of financial indices is its own highly lucrative industry: providers sell a dizzying array of indices to asset managers from the mainstream ('global energy industry') to the ultra-niche (with themes like 'videogaming' or 'millennial'). Some funds track indices built in-house; however, brand reputation and the effort involved in constructing and maintaining them means much of the index fund industry sources its indices from these external firms. The index-providing industry is itself enormously concentrated. Just three companies – MSCI, S&P Dow Jones and FTSE Russell – each account for about 26% of the entire industry's revenues.[63] Moreover, they hold a near-monopoly on certain critical categorisation systems, such as whether or not a country gets to join the 'emerging markets' club, directly steering financial flows with potentially immense implications for low-income countries' access to and cost of capital. As political economists Jan Fichtner, Johannes Petry and Eelke Heemskerk argue, this gives index providers a newfound 'private authority' that increasingly rivals the World Bank and IMF in shaping whether and on what terms certain governments around the world can borrow.[64]

In quantum mechanics, the Heisenberg Uncertainty Principle describes the impossibility of knowing both the precise position and momentum of a particle, because in measuring the particle, you have necessarily 'disturbed' it, and changed its character. It's a helpful analogy for the index fund and its predictive paradox, applied at grand scale to the global economy. With the scale of assets following their decisions and the volume of activity they undertake on any given day, it is no longer possible for large indices to simply measure a given section or characteristic of the market. The very act of doing so changes the market, often reinforcing existing patterns. For the largest players, theirs is a life of both trying to predict the future and, in doing so, subtly moulding it in the image of that bet. As Wigglesworth writes, this means 'active managers are in effect competing against a rival who controls and influences the yardstick of success.'[65] This represents an immense shift in the nature of and control over financial 'prediction', yielding huge influence over the future to a new private authority.

A genie in a bottle

With respect to control over the means of prediction, BlackRock, in particular, has an additional trick up its sleeve: Aladdin. Shorthand for the considerably less punchy 'Asset Liability and Debt and Derivative Investment Network', Aladdin is the world's leading portfolio and risk management programme, playing host to at least $21 trillion in assets worldwide. Aladdin doesn't directly manage this $21 trillion (more than double BlackRock's assets under management); rather, these assets belong to or are managed by firms which pay for access to the Aladdin platform, and which use the platform's bespoke analytic software to make decisions about how to allocate their portfolios or manage segments of their company. Importantly, this figure is likely a significant underestimation, in part because the formal count doesn't include all the assets of the roughly 250 companies using the software, and in part because BlackRock stopped disclosing the total value in 2017 due to the negative press it garnered.[66]

Not all the firms using Aladdin are financial, either; for instance, the platform's first client was General Electric, which used Aladdin to price the assets on the balance sheet of a subsidiary company it was looking to offload. That was 1994. Since then – and particularly since the 2008 Financial Crisis – Aladdin has exploded in its reach, as well as the scope of its analysis, transitioning (in the expressive framing of BlackRock Chief Operating Officer Rob Goldstein) from X-ray to MRI machine.[67] BlackRock are keen to emphasise that Aladdin does not, explicitly, tell its users what to do with their money. Nonetheless, in its singularly expansive risk analysis of the world's financial assets, it has become the 'central nervous system' for many of the world's largest corporations, including: BlackRock's top competitors Vanguard and State Street; half of the world's biggest insurance firms; and three of the largest US corporations, Apple, Google and Microsoft, all of whom use the platform to allocate billions in corporate investment assets.[68]

Aladdin's core offering is its ostensibly superior methodology for risk modelling and management, enabling users to optimise their portfolios and protect themselves against potential shocks. In 2020, BlackRock announced the launch of 'Aladdin Climate', intended to offer integrated analysis of portfolios' climate risk. The product combines, in the words of a BlackRock executive, 'BlackRock's strength in financial modelling and risk management to set a standard for climate risk analytics'.[69] Here, it's worth returning to the discussion of risk and uncertainty from the previous chapter. Climate scenario-modelling and risk projections are, by definition, predictions about the probability of events in the future based on data about how events have transpired in the past. In the case of the climate and nature crises, then, Aladdin is, through its enormous influence over the actions of the world's largest corporations, building a future 'conceptualised as a replication of the past.'[70]

Aladdin's models and BlackRock's allocative decisions are not reflections of the radical uncertainty of potentially cata-strophic climatic and environmental events; rather, they are representations of various possible futures that embody varying levels of risk deemed subjectively acceptable to varying degrees for particular interests. As a product of their reliance on acces-sible data, as with economic models of ecological crisis more broadly, these tend to focus on gradual, smooth changes such as sea level rise, average temperatures or rainfall, while neglect-ing the very real, if difficult to model, tipping points resid-ing within our natural systems.[71] In the near term, this may bring climate-aware investors better returns. But in the longer term, an economy whose decisions are so strongly informed by a financial risk-based approach could be ruinous. A low-probability catastrophic event is, after all, still catastrophic. Neither the growth of Aladdin nor the asset management industry's rising concentration and turn toward passive invest-ing look set to reverse course in the near future; we are there-fore marching steadily into uncharted territory with respect to how decisions in the global economy are made, and who gets to make them. With this in mind, one question looms large: what do these firms want?

No exit: the view from East 52nd Street

As a small individual investor, you and I adhere to certain truths: we might be able to buy shares in a few companies, but not all of them; we might feel ethically averse to arms manufacturing, and choose accordingly; and our return on investment would be based on a rising share price and pay-outs (dividends or share buybacks, wherein a company buys back its own stock to inflate the share price). Overall, this combination of factors might make us very preoccupied with the actions taken by the companies we'd placed our bets on.

From BlackRock's glossy offices on East 52nd Street in New York, the view is very different. Their lifeblood is the size of the total asset pool they manage on behalf of clients. For the asset manager, then, the aggregate growth of their assets under management – whether by asset price inflation, inflows, or cornering market share – is all there is. Certainly, all investors are interested in growing their assets; however, unlike individual investors keen on the performance of a few carefully selected companies, universality makes these firms interested purely in the *aggregate* growth of their asset pool – in other words, of the economy as a whole. In a crowded industry flooded with thousands of similar products, asset managers are driven by the need to appear to provide the best (lowest cost, most reliable) one. To do so, some have even gone to the extremes of offering funds with zero fees to draw money away from competitors. In recent years, the way to garner the most cash from clients has been a low-fees index tracking fund, and, owing to their high level of liquidity and accessibility, an exchange-traded index tracker in particular.[72] With these imperatives in mind, it becomes easier to understand how today's asset management titans engage with the climate crisis – both in theory, and in practice.

First, the growing prominence of passive investing, as well as its contribution to the concentration of power and ownership within asset management, is altering both how capital is allocated, and how governance rights are executed within corporations. The reaction to a surging passive industry tends to raise intuitively negative responses and concerns, some of which were discussed above. Others, however, have pointed out that index funds have a democratising function, insofar as they make access to investing much more affordable when compared with the huge costs associated with the underperforming, high-fees stock pickers of days gone by.[73] By lowering the cost barrier of investing, they've opened up the opportunity to much more of the population and saved trillions of dollars in fees that, instead of lining the pockets of overpaid financiers, remain with those whose assets are being invested.[74] But when it comes to the climate and nature crises, the implication of the so-called 'rise of the financial machines' is complex.

On the one hand, the implicit lack of an exit option makes shareholder engagement relatively toothless. However, from the perspective of the climate and nature crises, a subversive potential also emerges when we imagine instead that there is, indeed, no exit. Namely, the inability to divest selectively from holdings (indeed, from entire baskets of companies, should they constitute a major index) should, in theory, make passive shareholders distinctly long-term in their investment horizons. In other words, because they can't speculate by constantly trading their holdings and trying to make a quick buck, passive shareholders should behave in line with long-term interests.

This 'long-termism', in the jargon of popular economic literature, is the holy grail of scholars and professionals hoping to reclaim capitalism from what they perceive as its worst tendencies. In this view, the problem with most corporations and investors today is their in-built indifference to or discounting of conditions even a handful of years into the future.[75] In theory, passive funds break from this mould by placing their bets based on relatively stable long-term criteria, rather than looking to speculate and cash in on brief oscillations in the market. Indeed, rather than the comparatively zero-sum game played by more speculative investors who might bank on one company succeeding at the direct expense of others, in general passive funds are built around the premise of stable aggregate returns across an entire industry or the whole market (the S&P 500, to return to our favourite example, spans everything from energy to pharmaceuticals to clothing, agriculture and Big Tech).

Because they lack the discretion to pick and choose companies as events transpire (indeed, when a company is added to an index it receives a significant immediate boost as funds are compelled to add it to their portfolios), these are investors in it for the long haul.[76] The constituents of indices change relatively infrequently, and when they do, the changes tend to constitute only a fraction of the index's total size and composition. Passive investment strategies, much more so than actively managed funds or alternative types of investors like hedge funds, are thus predicated on aggregate, economy-wide, long-term growth in asset prices – something runaway climatic and ecological catastrophe would severely jeopardise. In principle, this innate 'long-termism', in combination with many passive giants' universal exposure to the impacts of systemic ecological crisis, could be harnessed to create an investment system that allocates capital based on an interest in long-term stability and sustainability. What about in practice?

The promise and pitfalls of universal passive ownership

The aggregate portfolios of BlackRock and other 'universal' investors constitute a more or less representative sample and distribution of the global economy. While this has the advantage of distributing risk in their portfolios, it also generates a tricky contradiction: universal owners are by definition exposed to companies whose actions – while potentially profitable in the near-term – could have direct negative effects on other companies or assets they own. For instance, by continuing to scoop up new bonds from fossil fuel firms, asset managers directly contribute to putting other assets in their portfolio at risk by driving climate and ecological crisis, effectively stealing from one pocket to put in the other. This insight has generated a debate that, while admittedly insider-y and technical, cuts to the core of the tensions inherent to green capitalism, and informs one of its primary frontiers: 'sustainable investing'.

The details of this frontier are explored in depth in the next chapter, but in brief: recognising the financial sector's central role in the climate crisis, a significant movement has emerged spanning the finance industry, policymakers and a vocal segment of civil society, which seeks to leverage the peculiar features of 'universal' or 'common' ownership for good, particularly within the domain of shareholder activism. The prospect is a basic distillation of the market-centric belief system underlying green capitalism: the most efficient action to combat these crises will derive from the rational self-interest of market actors – in this case, universally exposed financial firms and asset owners like pension funds – who simply require better information to make optimal decisions.[77] Champions point to the 'successes' of shareholder campaigns that have, for example, compelled Shell to set emissions reduction targets, with a press release from a prominent coalition of activist investors extolling 'the power of collective global investor engagement.'[78] Combine this with the supposed 'long-termism' inherent to increasingly passive universal investors, and it's a striking proposition, with the implication that by leveraging these trends, green capitalist logics can save capitalism from itself.

To repeat a key point from above: for the most part, asset managers are not strictly 'owners' of the assets under their control; nonetheless, that their business model is predicated on the aggregate value of the assets in their portfolio brings their motivations in line with those described by universal ownership theory – namely the counterproductivity of investing in one asset whose impacts directly undermine another in your portfolio. By this definition, BlackRock is the world's foremost universal owner, yet it retains massive holdings across the fossil fuel industry (including in some of the most destructive and capital-intensive sectors, like tar sands and thermal coal), as well as large positions in several companies most implicated in global deforestation. Moreover, they (along with most other large universal managers) have, up to the time of writing, proven fairly disinterested in using their positions to demand and vote for radical changes in corporate behaviour on the climate and nature crises, preferring instead to pay lip service to the issues.[79] According to the logic of universal ownership, this is a clear violation – not just of ethical principles, but of the firms' own long-term self-interest. How to explain this apparent contradiction? In large part, it reflects the extent to which BlackRock's portfolio is allocated based on indices. However, the bifurcation of rights and entitlements that come with owning a financial asset under asset manager capitalism also creates differing incentives for the various parties involved, which often come into conflict. Many of these – such as cornering market share and undercutting rival managers – undermine the long-term, expansive perspective meant to guide the actions of universal owners.

But there is a more fundamental flaw with the idea. The early advocates of universal ownership's potential approached it from the perspective of widespread pension participation, arguing that it implied a world in which it was 'virtually inconceivable' that the interests of pensioners were not representative of those of society writ large.[80] Pensions are indeed the most widespread and frequently the sole means through which ordinary people acquire financial assets. Today, some 30 million individuals in the UK and a further 100 million in the United States have some level of pension saving. In combination with the shift toward defined contribution schemes (wherein your pension pot is ultimately tied to financial asset prices), this distribution has entangled record numbers of people in financial markets and aligned their interests with those of the 'deflationary coalition'. However, despite these absolute figures, the distribution of assets and interests in pensions and in financial assets more broadly offers a far from representative slice of society, neither with respect to chronology, wealth and income status, nor geography. It is therefore entirely possible – indeed, likely – that the interests of pension holders could be in direct conflict with those of society as a whole.

For example, imagine an economy in which corporations distribute the profits from their productivity primarily to shareholders while labour's share of income declines (a reasonable description of Anglo-American capitalist economies since the 1980s). In this case, the negative externalities of these corporations' behaviour for workers might well be considered a net positive impact for those in the upper echelons of income and wealth, who are enormously overrepresented as shareholders, both through pensions and in direct shareholding. Within the UK, for instance, half of all pension assets belong to the top 20% of the population by income.[81] In the US, the picture is even more unequal. According to a long-term analysis by the Federal Reserve, pensions have been marked by two troubling trends: declining overall participation and rising inequality, such that: 'the entire bottom half of the wealth distribution had a very small share of total retirement assets in 1989 – only about 7 percent – and that share fell to about 4 percent by 2016.'[82] And outside of pensions, in the United States, 38% of all corporate shares (whether directly or through investment funds) are owned by the wealthiest 1% of the population, while the bottom half of all Americans – some 165 million people – together own just 1% of all share wealth.[83] The same logic applies in our response to the accelerating degradation of our planetary systems, whether its speed, quality or ability to achieve justice in the distribution of both costs and benefits. A private sector-led transition to decarbonised energy in the United States that prioritises private firms' profits and stock prices over universal and affordable access to that clean energy would be both deeply unjust and entirely possible if only the interests of those financial asset owners were considered.

What if, however, this discrepancy was resolved by righting these intra-national inequalities in financial asset wealth, for instance by fully universalising inclusion in the pensions system? Even in this (unlikely) imaginary, pension trustees and asset managers would still face the dilemma of whose interests to prioritise at a given point in time – those of the near-retirees about to access their pensions and who therefore have the most entitlements (assets) represented in the pot? Or those of the youngest generation of workers who face a radically different world at the time they will retire? In certain instances, these interests may be aligned, but where it matters for the climate and nature crises, they are often in direct conflict, with nearer-term returns benefiting older pension holders while potentially directly contributing to environmental catastrophe down the line.

The insurmountable obstacle to the theoretical promise of universal ownership, however, is most painfully clear when examined at a global scale in recognition of the continued expansion of profound *global* inequalities in wealth, ownership and power. Not only are the world's leading asset managers based overwhelmingly in the Global North, but so too are their clientele disproportionately represented in the mid-to-upper echelons of high-income countries. Under these conditions, even the citizens of a country with a relatively equal domestic wealth distribution could financially benefit from actions that compromise the welfare of others around the world. There are many possible futures wherein the world's wealthy nations prioritise their interests to the exclusion of the global poor majority, whether this implies failing to meet more stringent temperature targets under the understanding that they are comparatively able to adapt, or pursuing a 'green economy', which effectively designates whole swathes of the world and its people as sacrifice zones for intensive extraction of key resources or carbon offset plantations.

Neither of these futures necessarily conflicts with the financial interests of the global wealthy, who are so disproportionately represented in financial asset ownership, nor the firms who manage their assets – even if that ownership is 'universal' in its exposure. Provided aggregate financial asset values continue to rise, BlackRock has little reason to care about erasing community livelihoods in the Atacama Desert to service the demand for lithium electric vehicle batteries among the global wealthy or the seizure of subsistence farmers' land for carbon offsets. This is particularly true in consideration of the fact that asset prices can be, and regularly are, detached from conditions facing the 'real economy'. As the performance of the financial markets throughout the pandemic demonstrated with stunning clarity, even in the extreme of circumstances, the backing power of the wealthy world's monetary toolkit can leave financial markets unscathed.

It is worth emphasising that, in theory, what's good for the planet is good for asset managers, too. After all, thriving ecosystems and a stable climate are the bread and butter of, well, life – which is, though we tend to forget it, what the economy is ultimately meant to serve. Severe drought, extreme storms, mass migrations – all of these prove detrimental to the interests of the asset manager, risking the valuations of their swelling real estate portfolios and placing at risk the viability of countless corporations. It is for this reason that the giants of the asset management industry, rather than seeking to obstruct and undermine, are at the helm of shaping the climate and ecological policy agendas, as we explore in the next chapter. The trouble is not so much a lack of recognition of their universal exposure to ecological crisis, but their influence over evaluating and shaping how this crisis will unfold, and the 'solutions' they propose for addressing it.

Universal owners, universal power: the politics and policies of asset manager capitalism

Ultimately, the way we respond to accelerating ecological duress comes down to a question of power – who has it, and to what ends it is exercised. At the root of power in the global economy is the structuring force of ownership. As we will see in subsequent chapters, among the world's powerful governments and institutions, 'leveraging private finance' and 'shifting the trillions' have become central slogans and pillars of plans for addressing the climate and environmental emergencies. This is not by chance. The rights and privileges endowed upon shareholders; the power of bondholders over borrowing costs; and the trends toward immense concentration of ownership over the past few decades, have generated a new molten core of power in the asset management industry and its adjoining sphere of index providers. These entities are of increasing systemic importance. Consequently, the most powerful asset managers are now leveraging that position with remarkable success to shape how politicians perceive and respond to the challenge of climate and ecological breakdown.

Many asset managers are presently succeeding in walking a tightrope, effectively branding themselves as champions in the climate fight while working to ensure that any legislation coming down the line protects their interests. Recognising the inevitability and necessity of action on carbon emissions and environmental degradation, certain titans of finance have proven very eager to shape the policy mindset of powerful global administrations and institutions – as well as very effective at doing so. Though the industry is, on the whole, eager to shape policymaking in its image, one firm, in no small part by dint of its size, stands out from the pack: BlackRock. The firm's impact on the politics of governing bodies, from the Biden administration to the European Commission, is undeniable, to the extent that commentators have often remarked that CEO Larry Fink is constructing a 'shadow government' comprised of US political insiders to maximise the firm's influence.[84] And the revolving door between BlackRock and government is, in a word, dizzying. Brian Deese, formerly senior advisor to President Obama before becoming Global Head of Sustainable Investing at BlackRock, is now chairman of Biden's National Economic Council, while Mike Pyle, former BlackRock chief investment strategist, was appointed chief economic advisor to Vice President Harris. The former UK Chancellor of the Exchequer, former chairman of the Swiss National Bank, former deputy governor of the Bank of Canada, and a former vice-chairman of the Fed – all have, at different points, been hired by BlackRock.

In Europe, BlackRock was also invited to advise on sustainable finance legislation and 'ESG integration' for the banking sector, giving them a direct hand in determining what would be considered compliant under the EU sustainable finance frameworks and, in effect, drafting the rules that would govern themselves and their peers. The contract – and the conflicts of interest inherent to it – were later investigated by the European Commission's Ombudsman. This was not the only time BlackRock has been called on to provide expertise and carry out contracts that could directly impact or benefit the firm. In the summer of 2019, the three ex-central bankers-cum-BlackRock employees identified above presented, alongside a fourth colleague, a paper at the Federal Reserve's annual Jackson Hole symposium, the Grand Prix of banking conferences. The paper, entitled 'Dealing with the next down-turn' argued that in the event of a crisis, central banks should respond with bold monetary easing and 'unprecedented policy coordination' between fiscal and monetary authorities.[85] Just a few months later, when the COVID-19 pandemic swept the globe, the Federal Reserve did just that, buying up $120 billion per month in Treasury bills, mortgage-backed securities (MBS), and corporate bonds to stabilise the markets. Who was at the helm of carrying out this Herculean task? BlackRock, of course, who, having been tasked with carrying out the massive corporate bond and MBS-buying scheme, bought up several of the firm's own corporate bond ETFs in the process.[86]

The extent to which BlackRock has penetrated the halls and functions of governance has led even insider financial press like Bloomberg to dub them the 'fourth branch of government'.[87] While Wall Street lobbying of government is ubiquitous, BlackRock's degree of influence seems increasingly singular, exercised through a range of channels from alumni perched directly within the administration's upper ranks to the soft power of Larry Fink's public speeches and private counselling sessions with Treasury and Federal Reserve officials.[88] The sweeping and coordinated pandemic response by the Fed and Treasury was only the start. It is arguable that the greatest influence wielded by entities like BlackRock is the power of their assumed monopoly on expertise, garnering them regular invites into the counsel of the most elite halls of governance in North America and beyond.

Thus, between the vast scale of their own assets, the extent of their political influence and perceived expertise, and their unrivalled status in providing predictive risk analysis for the global asset management industry, BlackRock has emerged as the leading voice of the vanguard industry of green capitalism. In doing so, as the next chapter explores, it is advancing a response to the climate and nature crises defined by three related pillars: using the state to minimise financial risk; generating new and ideally state-backed opportunities for private investors through climate and environmental policy; and ensuring the aggregate stability and growth of asset prices.

From governance of the world's climate-critical corporations to growing control of Global South sovereign government debt, the relentless rise of the asset management industry is cementing a new site of governing power within the glass towers of Wall Street and the City of London. The actions, interests and predictions of just a handful of titans now influence wider decision-making in the global economy, determining which companies and projects get access to investment, how much, and on what terms. They place bets on the future while contributing materially to the shape of it. With the rise of the index-tracking, universal and powerfully situated asset manager, the lines between measuring and reproducing the past, predicting the future, and creating it, are increasingly blurred. In the face of the grave threats posed by accelerating damage to our climate and environment, how can we understand the motivations of these actors, and what form their influence will take, if any, on these issues?

We cannot predict the future. Staring down the barrel of an unprecedented threat to returns and asset values, the new titans of finance are undertaking a profound effort to ensure global efforts to tackle ecological crisis align with their interests, and those whose wealth they manage. The fight for an ecologically stable economy and world could have radically egalitarian consequences. It could be that the world envisioned by this private, minority interest could, in creating security for asset values, also secure a safe, thriving future for the global majority. That world might exist – but as the next chapter explores, it seems unlikely that we live in it.

4

Alchemists: what's green is gold

Nature's first green is gold, her hardest hue to hold. –Robert Frost[1]

In the throes of Cold War tensions in 1960, the US military constructed a secretive base several metres below the surface at the centre of the Greenland ice sheet. Snaking across a labyrinthine, kilometres-long network of tunnels, Camp Century housed not only soldiers but also a chapel, shops and a cinema, all powered by the world's first mobile nuclear generator. While officially branded a research facility, the clandestine mini-city below the ice was built to gauge the feasibility of building a nuclear missile launch site close enough to strike at the Soviet Union directly. When the project was abandoned only a handful of years later, so was its nuclear refuse, which the military presumed would stay hidden forever, entombed beneath sheets of millennia-enduring ice. At the time, 'global warming' was not yet fully understood or even widely recognised.

Some fifty years later as I write in the summer of 2021, air temperatures within the Arctic Circle have reached as high as 38 degrees Celsius, and each summer brings new waves of suffocating heat. The Arctic is warming far faster than the global average temperature: in just under 50 years from 1971 to 2019, the Arctic warmed by 3 degrees Celsius – three times faster than the global average of 1.1 degrees. Its sobering fate is the outcome of a phenomenon called 'polar amplification'. As the sea-ice melts, its reflective surface gives way to the jet dark ocean below, trapping ever more heat and further melting the ice above in a feed-forward loop that is wreaking havoc on major ocean currents and the life that depends on them. Several years of record-breaking heatwaves have brought record-breaking devastation to the Arctic, unleashing forest fires across Siberia, which this past year spewed a toxic cocktail of ozone, benzene and dangerous particulates into the air so thick the event was described by officials as an 'airpocalypse'.[2] Many of these fires were 'zombies' – the echoes of previous years' fires which, never fully extinguished, smouldered on just beneath the surface awaiting more amenable conditions.[3] As the planet warms and fires rage, things that should have remained below are thrust increasingly to the surface. Throughout the region, permafrost has been thawing at accelerating rates, and out of the rapidly softening earth are unleashed bullet-like pockets of methane, as well as the carcasses of long-dead life. In 2016, during a particu-larly acute thaw, the body of a reindeer infected with anthrax – a contaminant not seen on the continent for 75 years – became exposed to the air, infecting 23 Siberian residents and killing a young child. Russian epidemiologists predict other horrors now lurk just out of view, from smallpox to ancient diseases pre-served in the bodies of mammoths.[4] With each passing summer, extreme thaw is entrenched as the Arctic's new normal – one the architects and stewards of Camp Century could not have envisioned. In 2019, a team of Danish researchers found that as the ice sheet recedes, Camp Century has begun to shift westward, toward the ocean, carrying its contents with it.[5]

Despite the Arctic's warnings, those riches and relics not already emerging from the thaw continue to be eyed by the world's extractive industries and investors. Among the last gasps of the Trump administration, the then-President pushed through a lease-sale in the Alaskan Arctic Wildlife Refuge to drill for oil and gas. His administration had mandated the sale in 2017, reversing decades of protection that had been hard-won by environmental activists and, crucially, the resistance of the Gwich'in and Iñupiat Indigenous people of the region. As the move prompted a wave of public outrage and backlash, there was a fleeting satisfaction to be had in the fact that at the first auction for leases to explore for fossil fuels on the land, almost no one came to the party. Ultimately, just three bidders sought leases on the land. Of the 16 bids placed, only 5 came from the private sector, which was supposedly so hungry for these new opportunities; 11 came from an Alaskan state authority whose function is to promote economic development, and which had no existing drilling capacity, expertise or equipment. Evaluating the combined risks to their reputations and the significant expense of Arctic exploration and extraction among record low oil prices, the vast majority of firms steered well clear of the auction, preferring instead the appeal of less divisive (if similarly destructive) investments elsewhere.[6]

Nonetheless, the riches to be extracted from beneath the delicate and rapidly deteriorating ecology of the Arctic have since proven too much to resist. For French oil major Total, the key to capitalising on the land within the Arctic Circle without also destroying their reputation has been the issuance of a financial product called a 'sustainability-linked bond' (SLB). The bonds operate in most senses like a conventional corporate bond, except that the cost of the bond, determined by the rate of interest paid on it, is linked to a particular sustainability-related target. In early 2021, Total announced that from thereon in, it would exclusively issue this form of bond, linked to emissions targets, which – should the firm fail to meet them – would mean higher rates of interest, costing the firm more and putting more in the pockets of the bondholders. One might assume this much-publicised new commitment would mean a marked change in the firm's plans for the future, such as a pivot away from fossil fuel production. By contrast, Total's published plans show it still directing a full 80% of its investments toward fossil fuel projects by 2030. Moreover, just under two years before their bond commitment, Total signed a binding contract for a stake in a major fossil gas development on the Gydan Peninsula, a remote region of the Siberian Arctic tundra, with production starting in 2023.[7]

How to square this circle? How is it possible that Total can, from this point forward, claim to be issuing exclusively 'sustainability-linked' bonds while remaining committed to Arctic extraction (let alone a fossil fuel-dominated portfolio of activities as a whole)? As ever, the devil is in the detail. Despite the implication by their label that these are products are intended to finance sustainable activities, an SLB, as described by financial analysts at S&P Global 'comes with *no restrictions on how the proceeds can be used*' (emphasis added).[8] The key sustainability marker to which the financial instrument commits the company – and upon which the cost of the bond 'coupon' will be based – is performance against Scope 1 and 2 emissions targets. This sounds reasonable enough at face value; however,

Scope 1 and 2 emissions represent only a tiny fraction of Total's impact on the climate and nature crises.

Scope 1 implies those emissions that result directly from the firm's activity, such as 'flaring' natural gas during production or operating combustion-engine vehicles, while Scope 2 covers those emissions the company creates indirectly through their use of services such as heat or electricity. Glaringly absent from the calculation are any of the emissions associated with the actual product itself: fossil fuel. These so-called 'Scope 3' emissions constitute between 90% and 95% of the average oil major's actual carbon footprint.[9] Nor does the ecological impact of extracting fossil fuels figure anywhere in the calculation, whether the direct pollution and environmental disturbance associated with producing fossil gas in a remote peninsula; the disruption by massive transport tankers of marine migratory paths in the Arctic Ocean; or the local impact of whatever the fuel's end use may be. In other words, while any and all proceeds from issuing the SLBs could in theory go directly to financing Arctic fossil gas extraction and the expansion of similar projects, so long as the company emits less carbon from its internal operations – perhaps installing some solar panels on its office roofs – the targets have been met. Bondholders receive their returns, the company cleanses its image, and a swathe of the world's remaining protected wilderness is, at long last, put to use for profit. Everybody wins. All the while, carbon accumulates in the atmosphere. In the case of Total, using SLBs to finance expanded fossil fuel production in remote and fragile wilderness would be an impressive sleight of hand. However, they are far from alone in their alchemical pursuit of turning 'green' into gold.

In recent decades, the default position of most carbon intensive industries, like coal mining firms or petrochemicals producers, has been to resist or to obstruct any transition toward an economy which might not risk the continued viability of the climate and ecosystems upon which we rely. Outright denial of the climate crisis – that is, the total refusal to acknowledge the scientific consensus on the relationship between carbon emissions, a warming climate and catastrophic consequences – was until relatively recently somewhat mainstream. Recently, there has been a palpable shift. ExxonMobil now takes pains to publicly cleanse its image on the climate crisis, celebrating its minute investment in 'algal biofuels' and theoretical support for a carbon price, while global banks are tripping over one another to make the biggest splash with their various 'net zero' commitments. What's changed?

In brief: money. The urgent need to transition to a carbon-free, ecologically sustainable economy has been recognised and seized upon as a potentially vast new frontier of profit and, on the other side of the coin, an enormous source of financial risk. Nowhere is this about-face more visible than in the financial sector, whose role in determining which initiatives and industries receive the financing they require to operate and expand gives them truly world-shaping power. Perceiving both the specific threats posed by ecological crisis and the opportunity to reorient our response to this threat toward new domains of profit-making, the finance industry, and in particular asset management, have dedicated enormous energy toward the prospects for and design of 'sustainable finance'. This decisive rebranding – from the outrageous scale of hype surrounding it ('Here's how you can save the world, and your portfolio'!)[10] to the commensurately negligible impact it is having – are the subject of this chapter.

151

Follow the money

In recent years, 'sustainable', 'green' or 'ethical' finance has become an explosively popular and profitable industry. In particular, funds marketed as ESG ('Environmental, Social and Governance) have boomed. At the time of writing, estimates of the total scale of assets invested in 'sustainable' strategies vary (it's challenging to find people who agree on a methodology for what counts as 'sustainable'), but as of late 2020, ESG fund products had surpassed the $1 trillion mark, while total global assets invested according to ESG criteria (not just funds) sat closer to $30 trillion.[11] Financial data giant Bloomberg anticipates ESG will represent a third of all global assets under management by 2025.[12] SLB issuance in 2021 reached $93 billion in 2021, a ten-fold increase from the previous year.[13] 'Green bonds', meanwhile (which differ from their peer the SLB insofar as they're meant to state explicitly in their terms that proceeds be used on green initiatives) topped a cumulative issuance of US$1 trillion by the end of 2020.

The 'sustainable finance' industry has grown so vast that both the for-profit private sector and civil society now have entire sub-sectors devoted to shaping the industry's agenda, from eco-bond certifiers to non-profits offering free transition risk analysis on investors' portfolios, to firms entirely dedicated to providing investors with data on companies' sustainability practices. The Task Force on Climate-Related Financial Disclosures, chaired by Mike Bloomberg, aims to provide standards for firms to disclose 'how they manage the financial risks and opportunities that climate change poses to their business',[14] and now claims hundreds of industry supporters with a combined $175 trillion in assets.[15] The idea of leveraging the private financial system's considerable power to combat climate breakdown by 'shifting the trillions' into 'green' investment also increasingly forms a central narrative for many governments and institutions, from the UK Presidency of the COP26 Conference, to the European Parliament and the United Nations.

At the COP26 conference in November 2021, a full day of the summit was devoted to the role that private finance should play in leading the charge on the climate crisis. Summarised in a sweeping speech from Mark Carney, former governor of the central banks of England and Canada, the pledges that emerged on 'Finance Day' were incredible – in the sense that they were in no way credible. Headlines splashed a stunning figure: $130 trillion pledged to fight the climate crisis. The sum immediately raised eyebrows; as Carney himself emphasised, the figure was substantially greater than the $100 trillion supposedly needed to bring the world in line with 'net zero' by 2050. It was also larger than the entire value of every company on every single stock exchange in the entire world ($120 trillion, at the time of writing), and one and a half times the value of *global* GDP in 2020. Casual observers were rightfully astounded that such triumphant success could come out of a conference that otherwise seemed to be on a steady path toward failure, and many in the media responded with confusion as to whether, in reaching such a vast sum, we had solved the problem that has eternally plagued climate and environmental action: finding the money.

However, the claims that stemmed from 'Finance Day' were at once wholly misleading and strongly representative of the finance industry's 'action' on and understanding of their role in ecological crisis. Foremost, the $130 trillion figure adorning many front pages had no clear relationship with money actually committed to climate adaptation or emissions mitigation. Instead, it was simply an estimate of the total assets under the control of the 450 or so financial firms who signed up to an entirely voluntary pledge to 'align their activities with the Paris Agreement'. Thus, from pension liabilities to home mortgages and credit card debt, the array of assets making up that tally was overwhelmingly unrelated to combating climate and environmental breakdown. Even within the rules of this already disingenuous estimate, figures were inflated.

The Net Zero Asset Manager Initiative – a sub-grouping of the larger Glasgow Financial Alliance on Net Zero (the industry is fond of ambitious-sounding and wordy coalition names) – stipulated that member firms cut the carbon impact of their portfolios by 20% by 2030, already substantially lower than the 50% emissions reductions worldwide called for by the Intergovernmental Panel on Climate Change over the same time frame. However, the fine print of the agreement contained an important caveat: signatory firms are free to choose which portion of their assets will be included in this 20% reduction. There is thus no requirement for the portion they choose to be representative of their portfolio as whole, and, by extension, the emissions associated with it. About 85% of the average financial portfolio's emissions are concentrated within just a tenth of its value. As the non-profit Universal Owner argued, a firm signed up to the pledge could therefore readily claim to have aligned 90% of their portfolio with the target while excluding the 10% in which virtually all the investments that actually matter to the climate are held.[16]

Without question, the figures were outrageous. However, they and the flurry of financial grand gestures stemming from COP26 offered a perfect distillation of the lens through which financial institutions and governing bodies view our accelerating ecological crisis and their position within it. This perspective was summarised tidily in the conference leadership's strategy document for private finance, which highlights four central pillars structuring finance's role in combating climate crisis: reporting, risk management, returns and 'mobilisation' – in that order. To break down the jargon, the document's authors see the essential tasks for the finance sector as: an increase in climate-related 'disclosure', which describes documentation of how the firm's activities and assets might be affected by the climate crisis; use of these disclosures to minimise financial losses and maximise the returns to be had from the energy transition; and finally, 'mobilisation', which implies the reorientation of financial flows toward investing in the enormous task of decarbonisation. Even here the fine print tells a slightly different story, as discussed below. In effect, the four commandments can be summarised as: make as much money as you're able from the climate crisis, reduce your exposure to impending losses as best you can.

The full text of the finance strategy's fourth pillar reads: 'mobilisation of private finance for investment in developing and emerging economies through new market structures and public-private partnerships.'[17] Though this may sound fairly innocuous, the framework – which perfectly distils the solidifying public policy position on finance's role in addressing the climate crisis – is a textbook example of what political economist Daniela Gabor has termed the 'Wall Street Consensus' (WSC).[18] As Gabor's work has documented – first within initiatives surrounding global development, and now in the enormous task of achieving global decarbonisation and ecological stability – public policy and capacity has been oriented squarely toward serving the interests of the private sector and guaranteeing their returns, rather than necessarily meeting vital objectives like emissions reductions or improved public health. The technocratic disciples of the Consensus have many tools in their kit. For example, the European Green Deal advocates 'financial innovations' like securitisation to draw in private finance, whereby undesirable loans are packaged into bundled financial products that investors consider less risky – incidentally, the very 'risk distributing' strategy for packaging together subprime mortgages that sent the dominos toppling in the 2008 Financial Crisis. Meanwhile, the public-private partnerships pushed by firms like BlackRock, and which cropped up in the Biden administration's infrastructure bill, offer a route for private interests to profit from often vital public services and infrastructures, such as health care institutions or decarbonised energy and transportation networks.[19]

At its core, the WSC is about states 'de-risking' investment opportunities for the private sector. As its name implies, de-risking is a process by which the risks of investments are reduced for the investors involved. In this case, it means having the public sector use its fiscal and monetary capacities and policy decisions to reduce risks for the private sector, with the idea that this will 'crowd in' private investment. Beyond the 'new market structures and public-private partnerships' outlined in the finance strategy document, de-risking also takes the form of loan guarantees and preferential access to credit to 'shepherd' private capital into new spaces or those previously deemed too high risk, particularly vital public services and projects in low-income economies.

Though the specific financial tools and policies may vary case by case (some are explored below), at its core the WSC is a project for leveraging the public sector's capacity to create new lucrative and low-risk opportunities for private investors, rather than using public funds to invest directly and holding these assets on public balance sheets. The argument is that this enables the most effective use of 'scarce' public resources, despite accumulating evidence to the contrary.[20] As Gabor documents: 'The distinguishing feature of the WSC is the introduction of mechanisms that allow global institutional investors to become critical actors in international development.'[21] As its corollary, the WSC also routinely entails packages of policy 'adjustment' to render the recipient developing economies more amenable to the flows and whims of globalised private finance, often to the detriment of outcomes for local populations.[22] Ultimately, the WSC is a project for socialising the risk of losses while allowing private capital to privatise the returns.

The mindset of the WSC can be found throughout the financial sector's emergent approach to thriving amidst deepening nature and climate crises, namely the twin tasks of generating new assets for investment and using the power of the state to 'de-risk' those investments. For the finance industry, acting on the climate crisis (or in the very least appearing to) was once a relatively niche aspect of their business aimed at environmentally-minded clients. Now, it is an effective requirement for mainstream participation as well as an indispensable marketing tool. The crisis of ecological collapse is increasingly recognised by industry leaders as an immense systemic risk and, to borrow from the COP26 private finance strategy, a source of 'enormous commercial opportunities'. Out of this heady combination of enormous risk and potentially more enormous return was birthed the now booming industry: ESG.

ESG: A star is born

ESG investing is a strategy according to which criteria related to companies' practices on everything from human rights to carbon emissions and boardroom gender balance should feed into the processes by which investors decide where to park their cash. In practice, the ESG approach splits broadly into two factions.[23] The first, acolytes of what we'll call the 'portfolio approach', strive to minimise exposure to ESG-related risks through the securities they choose to have in their portfolio. Risks can range from physical risk to assets like coastal real estate to 'transition risk' – the industry term for the potential hits to financial returns that could come from more ambitious action to combat the climate and nature crises. In practice, this might mean an investment fund enacts a blanket ban on holding shares in any companies in the fossil fuel industry, minimising their exposure to the risk of more stringent regulations on the industry and the potential for 'stranded assets' – those assets, like oil and gas reserves, that might become unexploitable due to overbearing costs in a future with tighter regulation or steep carbon pricing. Alternatively, the fund might simply 'tilt' a mainstream index like the FTSE100 (the index of the 100 largest firms on the London Stock Exchange) so that it reduces its exposure to various industries and assets by a certain amount relative to the primary index on which it's based. For example, funds marketed as climate-friendly often have portfolios that underweight or exclude investments in the highest-emitting companies in the index, while largely maintaining the same overall basket of investments.

At the other helm of ESG investing is the 'stewardship' approach mentioned in the previous chapter. Per this approach, the key to securing change in major corporations is to remain invested in them and to use one's position as a shareholder to demand changes to business practices, investment plans or board membership. Often, this takes the form of casting votes at corporations' annual general meetings, though many investment houses advertise themselves as expert in the art of closed-door engagement, wherein they meet with corporate management in private to negotiate change under the threat, implicit or explicit, of retaliatory action like divestment. As an approach to 'sustainable investing', stewardship has become tremendously popular, boasting multi-investor initiatives representing trillions in assets, the actions of visible asset owners like the Church of England, and the support of many civil society organisations and NGOs. However, despite its popularity and the intuitive logic of using one's leverage as a shareholder to demand change, in practice the threat of this shareholder democracy is not usually all that thrilling or impressive. Until very recently, the largest asset managers, such as BlackRock, Vanguard and State Street, have participated very little, and most votes are won in line with the preferences of corporate management. Moreover, the behind-closed-doors or 'tea and cookies' engagement popular with many investors[24] undermines both transparency and accountability – in the process undermining any semblance of a 'democratic' process unfolding in the current shareholder engagement regime.

For champions of the ESG approach, the logic (and sales pitch) is simple: you can do well by doing good. Shirking the image of the ruthless wolves of Wall Street, they are committed to the idea that growing your wealth need not be a zero-sum game played against the planet, labour or human rights. Advocates insist that for most people, it's no longer enough to simply park your money in Big Tobacco or arms manufacturers and watch it grow; studies suggest that today's average asset owner – particularly the young – wants to see their money contribute positively to the world in some way.[25] And, so the argument goes, this is an approach that pays off. The financial press is flush with articles and analyses showing ESG strategies outperform the mainstream counterparts on which they are based. In November 2019, consulting behemoth McKinsey published a report entitled 'Five Ways That ESG Creates Value', going on to argue that 'getting your environmental, social, and governance (ESG) proposition right links to higher value creation.'[26] BlackRock CEO Larry Fink used his annual letter to CEOs – now a major event in the industry – to emphasise that the key to maximised risk-adjusted returns is to invest 'with purpose.' At the start of 2020, ESG had been on a consistent and rapid ascent for several years, and the mantra of doing well by doing good rang more true with each passing day. Then, the pandemic shook the world, and the industry met its first test.

For the asset management industry as a whole, despite early jitters, the collective trauma of COVID-19 proved (in no small part thanks to central bank interventions) to be a boon – but ESG in particular soared. Ethical funds took in record inflows of new cash at a time of profound economic distress for the global economy.[27] At the same time, the valuations of the average ESG fund ballooned, outperforming other segments and strategies over the first year of the pandemic.[28] In the eyes of insider commentators and advocates, the time of ethical investing had come. The logic was simple: having seen first-hand the potential impact of the pandemic on their portfolios, investors were suddenly thinking with systemic risks like the climate crisis in mind. Moreover, early indications suggested it was paying off: ethical funds invested in 'ethical' companies seemed to be delivering higher returns. Not only could one do well by doing good, one could apparently do *better* than everyone else.

The Wild West

Unfortunately for its triumphant cheerleaders, the seemingly indelible runaway success of the 'ethical' investing industry has largely been smoke and mirrors. With respect to their performance during the pandemic, many ESG funds – rather than necessarily reflecting the merits of investing with a 'conscience' in ethically minded firms – got lucky. Owing to the environmental aspect of their investment criteria, fossil fuel firms – which fared very poorly in the early stages of the pandemic through the convergence of a massive demand shock and a price stand-off between Russia and Saudi Arabia – tend to be underrepresented in ESG funds. Moreover, as a result of 'underweighting' fossil fuel and other untoward firms, many ESG funds are proportionately more invested in the other key components of a mainstream index like the S&P 500, namely the tech giants. In Vanguard's flagship US ESG Fund, the top five holdings at the height of the ESG boom were all tech giants, with Tesla coming in sixth place. Together, these six holdings constituted an entire quarter of the fund's whole value. Impressively, and in large part the result of its extra tech-giant exposure, the fund returned 28% between its creation in 2018 and late 2020, compared to the 17% return enjoyed by those invested in its mainstream counterpart.[29] However, it would be difficult to argue this exceptional level of return is the product of investing according to stringent ethical criteria, embroiled as many major tech firms are in human rights abuses,[30] data breaches

161

and scandals, and tax avoidance.[31] One longitudinal study look-ing at the performance of ESG funds found that, over time, they tended to substantially *under*perform mainstream peers, casting doubt on the industry's glossy self-promotion.[32]

The picture is not much rosier for the stewardship and engagement approach. While some activist firms and hedge funds, often aided by the coordinating capacities and pressure of civil society groups, have scored a peppering of wins – for instance dislodging two board executives at ExxonMobil or forcing Shell to reconsider its membership of industry lobby groups – outcomes of coordinated shareholder efforts have, to date, been primarily limited to supporting climate-related dis-closures.[33] Importantly, under the conditions of contemporary asset manager capitalism, the titanic voting power of the largest asset managers is often decisive in shareholder votes, with the 'Big 3' effectively controlling up to 25% of the average public corporation's vote in the US – a combination of their enormous collective stakes, the SEC requirement that they participate in votes, and the frequent failure of many smaller investors to par-ticipate in most votes due to resource constraints or disinterest. An analysis of 100 climate-related shareholder resolutions over the span of a year by civil society organisation ShareAction found that in 17 votes, a vote in favour from just one of the Big 3 would have enabled the resolution to pass.[34]

According to their annual report, BlackRock participated in some 166,000 votes at 17,000 annual general meetings of over 13,000 companies in 2020–21 alone – an astonishing degree of participation in decisions at the corporations critical to the oper-ation of our economies. The other two firms making up the Big 3 are not far behind. Unfortunately, despite BlackRock's recent bid to mark itself as a climate leader, the record of the Big 3 on votes critical to the climate and nature crises is poor, to say the least. Overwhelmingly, they have tended to vote in line with management, propping up the status quo. For instance, in 2020 BlackRock voted in favour 90% of the time in 64,000 director elections.

BlackRock has been celebrated for dissenting more regularly on votes, for instance voting against directors at 255 companies in 2020–21 for climate-related issues (a significant jump from years prior); however, the numbers pale in comparison to the vast diversity of firms in which they are among the largest shareholders, and represent an even smaller fraction of the total votes in which they participate.[35] And, BlackRock voted against management based on 'climate risk concerns' at just 2% of companies.[36] Between 2012 and 2019, the Big 3 voted against or abstained on every resolution related to curtailing deforestation in the supply chains of their portfolio companies.[37] In 2021, BlackRock did vote in favour of a resolution at Procter & Gamble which called on the company 'to report on whether and how it could increase the scale, pace, and rigor of its efforts to eliminate deforestation.' However, beneath the word salad of the resolution is very little of impact; rather, the only requirement would be to report on whether the firm could up its efforts against deforestation – not to actually do so.

These are the basic realities of the ESG industry. Innumerable studies have emerged from civil society and activist groups exposing the rampant 'greenwashing' within the industry, as well as the total lack of regulation or cohesive rules for what counts as 'sustainable' or 'ethical'. To date, only the EU has made any real progress toward such a standard with its efforts toward a green 'taxonomy' of investments, but the process has been consistently obstructed by industrial lobbying and reticent governments with keen interests in perpetuating the fossil fuel industry. These obstructive efforts have proven so successful that in May of 2020 it emerged that the EU regulators' proposed definition of 'fossil fuels' for their sustainability disclosure requirements *excluded* oil and gas, sending any legitimacy the initiative might have held up in smoke;[38] as of mid-2021, a decision had yet to be reached on whether fossil gas would be considered 'green' within the framework. On the 'Social' side, mega-financial data and index provider MSCI gave UK fast fashion retailer Boohoo one of the highest possible ESG ratings just weeks before it emerged that the brand's supply-chain workers were paid just £3.50 per hour.[39]

Absent any regulation, claims of greenwashing are so abundant it seems there is a new 'Green funds miss the mark' report or editorial in the financial press every week. Countless analyses from watchdogs and campaign groups replicate these sorts of findings.[40] Insider press has even started to have its own cliches to deal with the mayhem: a quick search of the terms 'ESG' and 'Wild West' returns dozens of wry op-eds sounding the alarm on the total lawlessness of the industry. However, a peppering of fossil fuel firms in so-called 'green funds' is far from the only problem with the explosive growth of ESG investing, and certainly not the most significant. There are several more fundamental issues at hand – questions that raise serious red flags over the green finance industry's seemingly unstoppable ascent to forming a core component of governments' plans for the transition to a decarbonised economy, enabling them to point to the private sector's 'action' on the climate crisis and, in doing so, argue that more robust direct regulation isn't needed. The first problem: even if we reached a stage in which deceptive labelling and 'dirty' holdings were completely eliminated – what would the funds be selecting *for*? In other words, even if the entirety of the industry was rigorous in eliminating its investments in the fossil fuel industry, what 'investments' would take their place, and based on what criteria? To date, it's not all that clear that inclusion in an ethical or sustainable fund requires much of either trait on the part of the firms in question.

For instance, a study comparing ESG funds to the mainstream Russell 3000 index found the defining characteristic that explained how they differed from the primary index – by 'an order of magnitude 100 times higher than any other input' – was the number of companies in their portfolios which had no employees.[41] In other words: no employees, no labour issues to resolve. In my own research I've found that funds marketed under an explicitly climate-conscious theme are primarily filled with Big Tech and other financial firms (each at about 15% of the fund's total assets); the utilities and energy sectors, where we would expect to find the companies we'd think of as being part of the 'green' transition, were two of the sectors receiving the lowest asset allocation by these funds, at just 5% and 3% of assets, respectively.[42] The top five holdings of Vanguard's flagship ESG fund at the time of writing are Apple, Amazon, Microsoft, Facebook and Google. Thus, even setting aside the more egregious cases of 'fossil fuel free' funds invested in coal mines that tend to make headlines in the financial press, it remains difficult to convincingly argue the industry has much to do with directing investment toward building a decarbonised, ecologically stable, or human rights-respecting future economy. Convenient as it may be to assume as much, this isn't because everyone employed in the ethical finance industry is inherently evil or incompetent. Nor can this issue be resolved by rooting out 'greenwashing'. Rather, the fact that ESG funds have little interest in the economic activities that we might consider key components of a more just and sustainable future is a feature, not a bug, of its logic.

The efficient markets hypothesis and other fables

At its core – and despite what its champions might claim or even believe – ESG investing is not a framework whose purpose is to drive change in the real economy. It is a strategy based on reducing *financial* impacts, not material ones – that is, the actual impacts of economic activities on the climate and environment. Sometimes these two issues overlap, but this is by no means necessary, or even common. Rather, ESG offers a mechanism for investors to minimise 'exposure' to financial risks – whether incoming regulation to end fossil fuel extraction or an exposé on a clothing manufacturer's human rights violations – that could harm their portfolio's financial returns. In that sense, 'green' or 'ethical' investing can be far better understood as a means through which the wealthy and those with financial assets can bet on the likelihood of a greener economy, rather than contribute to bringing that economy into being. In other words, ask not what your portfolio can do for the climate crisis, but what the climate crisis will do to your portfolio.

This underlying logic explains why the bulk of activity surrounding ESG and ethical investing, whether from regulators, companies or investors themselves, surrounds the issue of disclosure.[43] In the UK, the Chancellor's much-anticipated plan for 'greening finance' through an 'ambitious' strategy effectively boiled down to mandating that companies disclose the climate and environmental risks to which they are exposed – not necessarily, it should be said, those to which they may directly contribute. There is nothing wrong with disclosure per se; having companies publish their activities evaluated through the lens of systemic risks can be a helpful exercise, and achieving greater mandated transparency within the corporate economy more broadly is also a useful tool for holding them accountable. However, a critical problem arises insofar as disclosure is currently the core – if not sole – ask that governments have of corporations and the financial industry when it comes to the climate and nature crises, with the assumption that disclosure in and of itself will spur the markets to drive a sustainable future. Unfortunately, there is little evidence to support this assumption.[44] In fact, a recent longitudinal study of ESG-themed funds found that while they tended toward companies with higher ESG-related disclosure ratings, their investments were also biased toward companies with higher carbon emissions or worse environmental and labour records than their industry peers.[45] While not claiming direct causality, the results suggest the disclosure-dominated agenda could be generating a regressive side-effect: by conflating real sustainability improvements with improvements in disclosure, disclosure-based approaches might simply be encouraging companies to publish better information on their activities and stop there, having accomplished the necessary task in the eyes of investors.

Entire cottage industries of non- and for-profit companies each have their own designations for what is considered ESG-compliant or 'sustainable', and virtually all are predicated on minimising risks to investors' returns, not minimising risks to the planet or its inhabitants. As we've already seen, disclosure and risk/return optimisations were the cornerstones of the private finance strategy documents and deliberations at the COP26 summit in Glasgow. Disclosure of how they plan to engage with net zero currently constitutes the only binding requirement related to the climate crisis for financial firms and listed corporations in the UK. In the view of world leaders and private finance champions, the critical task in the coming years is to optimise available information and, in doing so, reorient the money currently pouring into high emitting and environmentally devastating industries.

When it comes to the role of finance in either driving or mitigating environmental catastrophe, governments and regulators worldwide have thus far limited binding legislation to mandating disclosures from firms. The justification for this position rests on the 'efficient markets hypothesis', which posits that asset prices reflect the real underlying valuations of companies and expectations about their future revenues based on all available information. In other words, financial markets efficiently and optimally allocate capital via rational actors who base their decisions on a clear-eyed assessment of all available data. In the logic of the efficient markets hypothesis, then, a world of vastly improved and universal disclosure will free the invisible hand of the market to make the most efficient decisions regarding where to place investment. What presently obstructs the pursuit of a sustainable economy is insufficient information, which can be overcome through disclosure and corporate sustainability reports. Armed with this information, market actors will no longer be prevented from acting rationally, and respond accordingly to minimise the risk of catastrophe, inevitably rerouting investment from polluting sectors to green alternatives.

The trouble is, there's scant evidence this so-called 'transfer myth' – the assumption that money moving out of the 'dirty' sectors will be drawn, magnetically, into investing in the clean industries of the future – has any basis in reality.[46] There are

several reasons for this, but most come down to the fundamental trouble with a risk-based perspective on climate and
environmental action. Investors construct their portfolios based
on a fine-tuned balance of preferences with respect to appetite
for risk (that is, the possibility of making losses) and desired
prospective return. In deciding to exclude certain segments,
such as fossil fuel companies on the whole, the surest replacement would be alternative firms with comparable risk/return
profiles. However, the profiles of companies in the fossil fuel
industry differ enormously from a financial risk perspective
from those in, for instance, the renewable energy sector. The
high degree of consolidation in the fossil fuel industry, coupled
with its maturity and the implicit guarantee of government
support due to its central role in the functioning of the capitalist economy give it an entirely different degree of risk and
probable return than the highly diffuse and relatively young
renewables sector, let alone more nascent and rapidly changing
areas like alternative modes of transport or battery innovation.
Thus, even when money shifts out of dirty sectors, to believe
that it inevitably shifts into areas of the economy that urgently
need scaling up to secure a habitable future is to believe a myth.

At best, then, a financial risk-based approach could temper
the financial instability likely to result from the shocks of the
climate and nature crises by reducing firms' financial exposure
to these risks over time, rather than in a sudden and widespread crash. Coupled with proactive investment in greener
alternatives, the movement might also have some effect on
lowering the cost of capital for more sustainable firms. As it
stands, however, the outpouring of enthusiasm for ESG-based
approaches appears to be doing little of either – particularly
when it comes to channelling investment toward a sustainable

future. In the process, as former chief investment officer for sustainable investing at BlackRock Tariq Fancy argues, the mania surrounding ESG is directly compromising the prospects for genuine, stringent and universal regulation on what the financial sector can and cannot provide capital to, creating the veneer of industry-wide action where there is none. As he wrote in a confessional essay on his time in the industry, 'we can no longer afford to answer inconvenient truths with convenient fantasies.'[47] This veneer of action is also amenable to politicians who, rather than needing to undertake the challenging work of enacting effective and binding legislation, are much happier to provide non-binding guidance and support on an initiative which the finance industry itself is firmly behind.

Anyone who has lived through the Dotcom bubble or the 2008 Financial Crisis will understand intuitively how little the efficient markets hypothesis reflects reality. The 2008 Financial Crisis, however devastating, was just one indicator among many in recent history of how profoundly irrational the financial markets are and can be. More recently – and thankfully more trivially – the reddit r/WallStreetBets phenomenon that gripped the internet at the start of 2020 offered a 'teachable moment' with respect to the relationship between share prices, financial market irrationality, and the 'true underlying value' of companies. The imaginary world of rational actors and full information on which disclosure-based approaches like the UK government's Task Force on Climate-Related Financial Disclosures and GFANZ are predicated is just that – imaginary, particularly with respect to the dynamics of the climate and ecological systems. As explored in previous chapters, in their essence, these are profoundly complex systems which we do not fully understand; they do not operate according to the logics of the tidy models and risk estimates which underlie corporate reporting and financial prospectuses. Tipping points in the climatic system – with the potential to be both devastating and irreversible – are not fully knowable, even by the foremost experts in the field. Our planet's systems are defined by radical uncertainty, according to which we cannot even know the relevant parameters in order to evaluate the odds of an outcome. In practice, this means that with respect to addressing these threats, the safest approach is the precautionary one – that is, taking steps to prevent the worst possible impacts of challenges we know are coming down the line, rather than hoping for gradually improved information to shift the markets into better decision-making, at the risk of catastrophe.[48]

Building or betting?

The third and most important myth is the pervasive belief that sustainable invest*ing* necessarily translates to sustainable invest*ment*. This is not just semantic pedantry. The assumption of an unbreakable link between participation in financial markets and changes in the real economy is an essential narrative underpinning the destructive and unjustifiable ongoing power of these markets in shaping our world in their image, and must be dispelled. Much of what we typically think of as financial activity – trading in stocks and bonds – takes place over secondary exchanges, changing hands between investors rather than flowing in and out of companies and impacting their actions. Thus, investors' abilities to grow their pots need not have any reflection in the behaviour of actors in the real economy; sometimes, as in the case of a venture capital firm investing in a start-up, the relationship is strong. Much of the time, it is not. Much 'ESG' activity involves reordering asset ownership through pooled funds investing in conventional assets like stocks and bonds over secondary exchanges. By extension, much of ESG-related investing activity simply involves money changing hands between investors rather than being directly put to use in ESG-aligned actions or strategic changes on the part of the firms. While some of this activity – for instance, when new stocks or bonds are issued and bought in the first round – does directly channel funds toward the companies issuing them, this is a minority of the actual activity taking place on financial markets.[49] The bulk of the ESG industry – particularly that which is available to most 'ordinary' investors, pensioners and savers – is made up of funds holding shares in, or the bonds of large publicly listed firms trading on secondary markets, meaning 'ethical investing' is much more an opportunity for those with assets to invest to place their bets on the winners of the future economy than to help bring that world into being. At best, big swings in investment allocation driven by ESG considerations might change the cost of capital for these firms, but the ESG sector is neither large and cohesive enough, nor our time ample enough, for this to be material to the question of ecological crisis.[50]

The importance of minimising their portfolios' exposure to 'systemic risks' like environmental collapse no longer escapes investors – nor has the opportunity to win big by betting on green. To borrow from Larry Fink's 2020 letter to investors: 'The evidence on climate risk is compelling investors to reassess core assumptions about modern finance.'[51] This might be harmless – if irrelevant – for how the nature and climate crises are tackled, if it were limited to how private investors calculate their risk-return profiles. However, disclosure,

ESG frameworks, and leveraging 'green finance' feature with increasing frequency at the heart of governments' and international institutions' plans for delivering the enormous investment needed to address the climate and nature emergencies. As we saw previously, at the COP26 climate summit in Glasgow, the 'Private Finance Strategy' placed these logics front and centre, championing the importance of the three Rs: reporting, risks and returns, while moving to advance the WSC at every possible opportunity.

The unyielding emphasis on 'mobilising' private finance to support climate investment in low-income economies also leaves these economies vulnerable to the whims of private actors. At the onset of the COVID-19 pandemic, so-called 'emerging economies' experienced record outflows of foreign capital, unimpeded by capital controls, as financial markets panicked. The volatility sent costs for the poorest countries – of imports, of borrowing – soaring at the time when need was most urgent. As the next chapter explores in more depth, in a world defined by private foreign investment with unrestricted mobility as the climate and nature emergencies deepen, their punctuation with acute crises will leave those countries already most vulnerable to their impacts doubly vulnerable to the caprice of private investors. By hedging our bets on industries and logics of investment that, by their very design, cannot deliver, we not only accomplish very little of the deep, drastic and enduring changes to the nature of the economy that we desperately need. Worse still, we undermine the prospects for genuinely impactful actions in the process, by creating the impression of material progress where there is, in fact, none.

There are many possible futures which could be articulated as we fight to secure a habitable world, some of which will allow us to build justice, democratic principles and equality into their foundations. But there are many alternative futures in which the powerful will scramble to ensure security for a shrinking fraction of the world's population, to the necessary exclusion of its majority. It bears repeating that along our current trajectories of ecological degradation, material throughput, rising emissions and unabated biodiversity loss, these sorts of futures – of mass displacement, exploitation and designation of certain regions and people as less worthy of protecting and securing – are less far away than we might like to imagine. What's clear is that a future which brings justice for all will not bring a boon for BlackRock, and indeed is likely to directly undermine the fee-based, asset-maximising model on which the asset management industry is built. This reality has not passed BlackRock (nor the wider industry) by, which helps to explain why it is now going to incredible efforts to shape the future in its own image, and reap the benefits of the 'enormous commercial opportunities' of the transition to a decarbonised economy.

Alchemists: what's green is gold

Why is it that 'sustainable investing' has only recently begun to boom and, critically, to feature at the heart of the policy programmes of world leaders and international institutions? This is an important question, with a multifaceted answer. After all, science on the climate crisis has been settled for decades, and climate risk has always been financial risk. What has changed over recent years to bring this approach from the side-lines and squarely into the mainstream? In part, the industry is likely reacting to growing public concern and demand, as well as an understanding that deepening public support for climate action from governments will change the prospects for certain types of investment. But there are other recent structural changes in the financial system that have combined to propel sustainable investing into the mainstream and, crucially, to motivate finance to shape environmental policy in its interests.

The explosion of ESG reflects the conditions of asset manager capitalism and universally allocated investors. ESG frameworks are a matter of convenience and efficiency for the asset management industry, enabling them to distil the many thousands of shareholder votes and company 'engagements' that must be undertaken by an often remarkably small staff (as of 2020, BlackRock, for instance, employed just 45 individuals in its 'Stewardship' team among a total global workforce of 11,000) into easy-to-manage tick boxes and letter grades.[52] From BlackRock's lofty vantage, for instance, towering above the several thousand firms in their portfolios and nearly 170,000 decisions at corporate AGMs they make in a given year, it is simply an impossibility for BlackRock to traverse the ocean of data related to all the elements of environmental, social and corporate governance-related actions that each of these companies take to inform their decisions. Instead, ESG ratings offer a profoundly simplified means for them to apply a unified, one-size-fits-all framework of general principles.[53] They allow firms to superficially fulfil their fiduciary duties while also marketing themselves to clients as leaders in environmental and ethical investing.

A second factor is that the industry's acknowledgement that incoming climate and environmental action should be shaped in their interests has collided conveniently with a dearth of opportunities for investment. Having just spent much of this book trying to convince you of the enormous sums of cash swirling around the vortex of the financial markets, this might sound counterintuitive. Here again, though, the essential point is that invest*ing* and invest*ment* are not necessarily the same thing. Investment, as understood in business economics, implies a business allocating capital to a particular project or asset that will yield a return or growth for a company. That might mean expanding the workforce, research & development, or additional physical assets like factory equipment. When I speak of investing, by contrast, I'm referring to the activities of those with savings, who are looking to grow them, whether that's a young worker with a new pension or a regular occupant of the Sunday Times Rich List.

In today's high-income economies, 'investing' is incredibly widespread, as is capital to be put to work. However, investing doesn't necessarily have a direct relationship to what we consider investment in the physical world. Investing can be entirely speculative in form, with many investors trying to make a windfall by betting on the failure of a company or negative changes in the valuations of shares or currencies. Clearly, in these cases, the investors have done little to contribute to investment on the part of the entities involved; indeed, often they are eagerly anticipating their failure in order to cash in. I repeat this distinction here to try to underscore the fact that we are not short of money to invest in the things we need. To the contrary, capital is both 'superabundant'[54] (meaning there's plenty of wealth to go around) and cheap (meaning the cost of receiving it, such as interest payments, are comparatively low). Instead, what's missing in the economy are attractive or – to borrow from Larry Fink – 'appropriate' investments, meaning those that are both relatively high-yielding and relatively secure. Enter: the 'enormous commercial opportunities' presented by the explosive growth of new 'clean' industries, and the prospect of trillions of dollars of investment in frequently government-backstopped infrastructure projects, such as electrified transport and renewable energy systems. The growth of the ESG industry and steady advance of the WSC in major policy programmes, from the Biden administration's Bipartisan Infrastructure Bill, to the EU's Green Deal and COP26 finance frameworks are reflections of the extent to which private finance – searching for means to both minimise their exposure to risks and maximise new opportunities for investment – has turned the 'green' into gold.

When it comes to scouring the Earth for new investable opportunities, the imperatives of asset manager capitalism have firmly penetrated the policy mainstream. For instance, the $1 trillion Bipartisan Infrastructure Bill – a sum which might at face value sound vast – belies an investment package that plans to rely very little on the US government's outrageous fiscal and monetary privileges. Instead, the Bill's proposals envision using that firepower to crowd in private investors. The strategies for doing so include: 'asset recycling' (selling off existing public infrastructure assets to private actors to fund the construction of new ones), scaling up 'Public Private Partnerships' (effectively backstopping private profits by socialising the risk and privatising the profits from joint ventures), and 'private activity bonds' (a special class of tax-exempt bonds which governments of various size can issue on behalf of private actors for projects).[55]

For the titans of Wall Street, these are kingly gifts: a bonanza of publicly-backed assets, frequently with secure, consistent income streams and government guarantees. The Bill embodies the WSC, joining ranks with the European Union's much-vaunted Green Deal. Described by Ursula von der Leyen, president of the European Commission, as Europe's 'man on the moon moment', the Green Deal was presented as an unprecedented investment package in decarbonisation and the transition to a sustainable EU economy. However, the €1 trillion-over-10-years pledge boils down to virtually no new public finance. Of the projected figures – which are, it should be emphasised, *projections* – much is envisioned to come from 'crowded in' private investors, with just €7.5bn in new public budget commitments through the so-called 'Just Transition Fund', distributed over seven years.[56] For comparison, at the time the Deal was launched, the Commission was slated to spend €29 billion on fossil gas projects. The Deal envisions half of the total figure coming from the 'mobilisation' of private investment – neither guaranteed to arrive, nor likely to be justly distributed, with motivations based on risk/return profiles rather than need. Thus, across high-income countries, policy packages purportedly designed to deliver a rapid transition to a sustainable and decarbonised economy seem instead to have been designed with two different motivations at their core: the profits of the private sector, and the presumed 'efficiency' of private capital allocation over public planning and delivery.

As the opening chapter argued, this bias is the critical fault of a market-based transition to a decarbonised economy: taking the tenets of market advocates at face value, what markets are best at is efficiently allocating capital.[57] However, efficiency in terms of cost need not align with effectiveness in terms of material outcomes. There is a compelling reason, for example, why in the face of wartime mobilisation or the electrification of entire countries, governments acted as a coordinating force, meeting the necessary outcome rather than prioritising 'the most economical use of resources'.[58] When it comes to preserving the qualities of the planet – climatic stability, thriving ecosystems – that make human life and flourishing possible, it is indefensible that the efficiency of meeting this life or death target should be placed above our actual ability and likelihood of meeting it.

Efficiency has less still in common with effective outcomes that, in addition to being effective, are just. Indeed, efficient markets can and routinely do produce socially unacceptable results. For instance, as economist Joseph Stiglitz outlines in his book *Freefall*, in a competitive marketplace where wages are determined by supply and demand, the 'equilibrium' wage has no guarantee of being a liveable one.[59] Without the state to correct this injustice (however inadequately) by establishing a minimum wage, countless individuals might live in destitute poverty (even more, it should be noted, than already do as a consequence of the untenably low minimum wages in many of those countries that do have them). As a consequence, the politics of the Green Deal, of the Bipartisan Infrastructure Bill, and of much of the mainstream political and economic consensus are not based in the burning need for tangible impact – that is, rapidly curbing emissions, addressing inequality, reducing demand for materials and resources, and so on. Rather, the inherent bias of world leadership and our international institutions is toward an imagined market-led efficiency of capital allocation that will not be realised, and which has no likelihood of being effective at delivering on the immensely complex challenge of overhauling our economy's relationship with the natural systems that support it. In the process, plans like the Green Deal make their priority the creation and guarantee of new profitable areas for investors – not doing everything in their power to secure a habitable future or a just present.

Doing well by doing good?

The thorn in the side of the much-celebrated turn to 'sustainable' private investing is that it is – clever branding aside – indistinguishable in the way it operates from an investment industry that has proven incredibly effective at concentrating wealth and power, the bread and butter of climate and ecological breakdown. Indeed, when the pandemic presented much of the world's population with an immediate and stark hit to their personal finances, safety, housing security and more, the wealthy rode the wave of booming financial markets, in no small part powered by the actions of the Federal Reserve. Even as unemployment and inequality hit an eye-watering scale, inflows to exchange-traded funds over the course of 2020 surpassed an all-time record, with a remarkable $762 billion of new money pouring into the financial system (only to be surpassed the following year by a wide margin).[60] Thus, from the perspective of the asset management industry, wealth inequality both within and between nations is optimal, as it provides a constant stream of individuals with savings to maximise by betting on stocks, bonds and real estate. These same concentrations continue to drive completely untenable rates of resource consumption and waste, rising emissions, and the dispossession of the global poor – something that any approach to tackling the climate and ecological crisis cannot maintain, either morally or materially.

In a similar vein, the quest to maximise the growth of asset prices and the returns from 'sustainable' investing implies a trajectory toward decarbonisation predicated on massive growth of 'sustainable' investments like renewable energy, electric vehicles, major physical projects like large carbon capture and storage facilities, and an increasing amount of land cordoned off for carbon offset projects to sustain comparatively high emissions in the Global North. This same vision of a sustainable future economy – one in which our current systems are not reimagined to meet societal needs far better than they currently do, but in which we replace them, one for one, with 'decarbonised' versions – ultimately collides with the same fundamental moral and material imperative: the need to drastically redistribute resource consumption, waste and material throughput, and rapidly slow our currently unsustainable exploitation of natural riches in the service of the world's wealthy. The contrast between the fervent rejection of finance for Loss & Damage at the COP26 conference, and the glee with which investors greeted pledges for governments to crowd in private finance to new projects in the Global South, underscores where the priorities of this vision of decarbonisation lie: not in meeting the needs of humanity or helping those on the frontline grapple with and recover from already-occurring climate impacts, but in ensuring the creation of new markets and investable projects in decarbonised economies.

This enthusiasm for government-supported climate-related initiatives and projects in so-called 'emerging markets', as the industry deems them, is troubling for another reason. Today, much of the world's most ecologically vulnerable population live in countries trapped in endless cycles of public debt, siphoning incredibly high interest payments to Northern governments, multilateral development banks and private investors, rather than those funds going toward providing for the citizens of the countries in question. Moreover, the growing prominence of private lenders and index-tracking funds filled with sovereign bonds leaves the borrower nations vulnerable to the whims of the financial markets: at the onset of the pandemic, 'emerging markets' were crippled by a record outflow of capital, as investors spooked at the potential economic impacts. This enormous vacuum of investment left the costs of capital for the most vulnerable nations even higher in a moment of acute need. It is also a window into a future in which investment in decarbonisation, sustainable ecosystems and infrastructure is dominated by the private sector, whose flightiness may just as easily be triggered by the acute shocks that will punctuate deepening climate and ecological damage with growing frequency.

This vicious, self-perpetuating cycle is not new. It is the product of generations of wealth extraction – in terms of resources, interest payments, unjust international institutions and beyond – from South to North, which have ensured much of the world remains oriented toward supporting the world's wealthy populations with cheap labour, cheap resources and, increasingly, access to cheap nature in the form of enormous demand for land in service of carbon offsetting projects and other climate 'solutions' like biofuels.[61] It is a history that was ongoing when US soldiers began boring deep caverns into the Greenland glacier to build their hidden city below the surface, and it continues to advance some decades since that city was abandoned, forgotten – or so its architects thought – beneath layers of history and ice. As the next chapter examines, it is a history of violence whose imprints can be seen throughout our spectacularly unequal present, the resolution of which will shape the contours of our path toward a habitable world in the years to come.

5

Time travellers: escaping ecological debt

The debt is with the people, not the IMF. (Sign at a demonstration
at Plaza de Mayo, Buenos Aires, Argentina, August 2019)[1]
The time is out of joint. –Hamlet[2]

The history of the Earth is recorded in tree rings and ice cores.
Ring patterns in the timber beams of the Church of the Nativity
in Bethlehem place its age at 1500 years. The Haber Bosch
process through which we learned to synthesise artificial nitrog-
enous fertiliser and transformed agriculture can be tracked with
precision to the year of its invention in 1914 by the explosion
in the presence of a manmade nitrogen isotope in ice sheets.
Within its laminations ice holds the isotopic imprints of trag-
edies from Hiroshima to Chernobyl. Variations in CO_2 show
how the genocidal violence of American colonisation, during
which tens of millions of Indigenous people were slaughtered,
was so profound it drove the 'little ice age' of the 1600s.[3] The
ice and forests also recount with startling clarity the story of
the 'industrial flow of carbon' from deep within the earth and
into the atmosphere that began with the burning of fossil fuels.[4]
Through subtle changes in the space between rings and tiny

183

bubbles of gas or microscopic particulates trapped in folds of ice laid down over millennia we can trace how – over a breathtakingly brief fraction of the existence of life on Earth – industrial capitalist society has entirely reshaped our planet's natural systems, propelling us toward an increasingly uncertain future.

When it comes to the climate crisis, time is everything. The interval from now, at the time of writing, to the point at which we are meant to have stabilised global emissions at 'net zero', is 28 years. This is my entire lifetime, making it seem – at least to many young people – in some ways a large expanse. It is also, by the time these words will be published, greater than the number of years since the establishment of the United Nations Framework Convention on Climate Change in 1992, making it at once incredibly, paralysingly brief. In the deep geological time of life on Earth, it's equivalent to a blink.

Time is also at the heart of one of the most contentious issues shaping international climate politics: who ultimately bears responsibility for the ecological crisis in which we now find ourselves? When it comes to carbon in the atmosphere, the question of how to apportion responsibility – who put it there, and how much – and by extension, responsibility for mitigating its impacts, has been a defining issue of every international climate summit since they first began. The 1997 Kyoto Protocol was ostensibly meant to address fairness by securing a framework of 'common but differentiated responsibility', with so-called Annex I and Annex II countries being bound to different degrees of commitment based on their level of economic development. Even this simple division was resisted by major emitters such as the United States, who – after lobbying aggressively for international carbon markets in the treaty – eventually refused to sign it, citing concerns over domestic economic impacts. The Paris Agreement tried to resolve this resistance by instead making all commitments voluntary, but still fell short of explicitly addressing countries' wildly different historical contributions to global emissions. Rather, in asking for different levels of commitment from various states, the text simply notes their 'different national circumstances.'[5]

An intimately related and perhaps even more divisive question than the apportioning of emissions themselves is its corollary: who should pay for climate and environmental action? From where will and should investment come? In advance of COP26, representatives of lower-income or vulnerable nations were rightfully outraged by the failure of the world's wealthy nations to meet their commitment, first agreed more than a decade prior, of $100 billion in international climate finance per year by 2020 to the poorest countries to help mitigate and adapt to advancing climate crisis. The 2020 deadline came and went, and still by the estimates of the International Monetary Fund (IMF), more than 40 of the world's wealthiest states had only managed to scrape together $79.6 billion in 2019 (the most recent date for which data is available). A big number, certainly. But to put it in context: the total $100 billion, to be collectively provided by the world's wealthiest nations, represents less than 1% of global GDP in 2021. Moreover, while the majority of finance committed thus far is publicly derived, either through bilateral government-to-government agreements or from multilateral banks such as the Asian Development Bank, a substantial portion of the $80-odd billion is attributed to 'mobilised private finance',[6] meaning private investments that are deemed unlikely to have happened without 'inducements' by the public sector, like loan guarantees.

The idea of wealthy governments providing finance to the poorest nations tends to carry the image of charity or aid, representing a transfer of wealth from the Global North to South. Reality is something very different. Of the total climate finance figure of nearly $80 billion delivered by the last tally, close to 80% came in the form of loans, including some 71% of the public climate finance commitments (that is, commitments made by governments and public institutions rather than private financial firms). Worse still, 40% of this public finance took the form of 'non-concessional lending', meaning loans offered at or above the often-exorbitant market rates, or with short grace periods in instances of default or delayed payment.[7] Grants, which would most closely resemble the common sense understanding of 'foreign aid' or charity, constituted less than a third of the public total.

This is a far cry from the sense of noble generosity in which world leaders tend to portray their role in these programmes. In advance of the COP26 summit, UK Prime Minister Boris Johnson described the agreement as 'an historic commitment to the world's poorest' from the world's wealthiest states.[8] Canadian Prime Minister, Justin Trudeau, similarly, described Canada's contribution as 'historic' and indicative of Canada's commitment to 'helping the poorest and most vulnerable countries in the world.'[9] Perhaps unintentionally, it was President Biden who provided the most honest appraisal of what the $100 billion commitment actually represents: 'a chance for each of our countries to invest in ourselves and our own future.'[10] Though it may run counter to collective understandings of these sorts of commitments, by taking the form of loans to be paid back with interest, particularly at or above market rates, this program represents a direct transfer of wealth not from the wealthy North to South, as world leaders describe, but the reverse. In this sense, as this chapter will explore, it is perfectly in keeping with the functioning of the global economy over generations.

What do we owe?

What does the wealthy world owe poorer nations in the context of ecological emergency? This question motivates unending and contentious debate in international governance of ecological crisis. Proposals such as the beleaguered Loss & Damage framework campaigned for in the context of the Paris Agreement are founded on the argument that responsibility must reflect historical contributions to global emissions, in no small part because these historical emissions fuelled the engines of imperialism and industry that generated the unequal division of wealth that defines the contemporary global economy. According to analysis from Carbon Brief, by the end of 2021 enough carbon will have been emitted to consume nearly 90% of the global carbon budget for a two-thirds chance of remaining within 1.5 degrees Celsius of warming. Who is responsible for this avid consumption of carbon? Based on the combination of fossil fuel use, forestry, and land use changes since 1850, the United States comfortably holds the top spot, having been responsible for a full fifth of all emissions. China places a distant second, at 11%, with the top five rounded out by Brazil, India and Indonesia. In fairness, however, these countries are among the world's most populous. Indeed, while Indonesia, India, Brazil and China are host to some 42% of the global population, they account for less than a quarter of cumulative emissions. By contrast, the remaining occupants of the Top 10 emitters list – Russia, Germany, the UK, Japan and Canada – account for nearly 40% of cumulative emissions, despite collectively being home to just 10% of the world's population.[11] Looking instead at cumulative *per capita* emissions, the list changes significantly, with the top five spots occupied by New Zealand, Canada, Australia, the United States and Argentina.

But while Carbon Brief's analysis is as robust as they come, there are significant disagreements with respect to where to draw the boundaries or responsibility for climate and environmental damage. Namely, when can we begin to hold people responsible for their role in catastrophe? Does it all start, as much environmental scholarship suggests, with the Industrial Revolution, when the first coal furnaces set us on a course toward climatic instability?[12] Some, like ecological historian Jason W. Moore, argue even this is not a comprehensive enough view. Instead, he and others place the boundary at which parts of humanity entered a radically different relationship with the planet in the era of Columbus and American colonisation, when a combination of exposure to new disease, enslavement and genocide caused population loss in the millions, a minimum in atmospheric CO_2, and a miniature ice age.[13]

On the other hand, some 90% of all anthropogenic carbon has been emitted within the average lifespan of a British resident (81 years), and the skew has only become more extreme with time: half of all emissions are the product of the last 30 years alone.[14] Moreover, many argue it isn't fair or reasonable to hold people accountable for emissions if they didn't know their effects. At the ill-fated Copenhagen UN Climate Summit in 2009, Todd Stern, the US State Department's lead negotiator, pre-emptively rejected the case for historical accountability in any agreement, stating: 'I actually completely reject the notion of a debt or reparations or anything of the like. For most of the 200 years since the Industrial Revolution, people were blissfully ignorant of the fact that emissions caused a green-house effect. It's a relatively recent phenomenon.'[15] If we were to take his argument seriously, where then would we draw the line? When global heating became a scientifically established phenomenon and entered the political mainstream, say some time in the 1980s? Or what about when this science, and its urgent implications, were first affirmed by the global political community, for instance at the establishment of the United Nations Framework Convention on Climate Change in 1992?

Still others, including many figures in politics and the media, ask whether even these most recent historical contributions are relevant. The spectre of 'Loss & Damage' payments based on historical responsibility haunted rich nations at the COP26 summit, with the US in particular drawing a 'red line' against the inclusion of its historical climate debt in the final text.[16] Detractors of a historical responsibility approach argue it is a distraction – an exercise in finger-pointing, which deters action now. Instead, the argument is made that pragmatism demands we focus on the largest emitters today, because it is their activities that require the steepest transformation. By the same logic, per capita emissions are also unhelpful, as all that matters is turning off the carbon tap, not how few people are generating the flow. The ongoing scapegoating of and 'whataboutery' surrounding countries like India, including by officials at the COP26 conference in Glasgow, marks this as a common mind-set in mainstream circles.[17] Admittedly, there is some intuitive power in the argument that historical emissions are irrelevant to the actions we take today, making it a popular one among the climate negotiators of countries whose historical contribu-tion to the climate crisis would place them at the forefront of culpability. After all, recognising that the US is by far the greatest cumulative emitter in the world does not change the growth rate of annual global emissions today. However, by refusing to look anywhere but forward – in other words, only asking who is most at fault today – we cannot arrive at a representative view of how to proceed.

This is neither a matter of charity nor an exclusively moral stance. Certainly, justice demands that those with the greatest responsibility for, and capacity to act to avert, ecological crisis undertake proportionately more action. Justice alone should be enough to make this happen. But for those less interested in or willing to pursue climate justice, doing so is also – contrary to the claims of US negotiators – the pragmatic position. It is in the immediate interest of the comparatively powerful nations of the Global North to ensure that everyone around the world is able to rapidly decarbonise their economies and adapt to an inevitably (and already) changing world while preserving and restoring ecosystems on a significant scale. Our ability to do so hinges on what for many Northern politicians is an uncomfortable truth: there must be a major redistribution of wealth, consumption and resource use both between and within the countries of the world. Indeed, almost as stark as the differences in emissions and resource demands between the populations of different countries are those within them, with the richest responsible for emissions several times greater than those in lower income groups; moreover, emissions among the wealthy tend to derive primarily from luxuries such as air travel, while poorer households' emissions are often the product of basic needs, for which less carbon-intensive alternatives are inaccessible.[18] As a recent review in *Nature* highlighted: 'consumption of affluent households worldwide is by far the strongest determinant and the strongest accelerator of increases of global environmental and social impacts', concluding that only by pursuing radical changes in the distribution of global consumption, particularly the excessive overconsumption of the highly affluent, can we remain within the boundaries of a stable climate and environment.[19]

Rather than engage with this fact and its implications, most politicians and many prominent voices on climate action, like Bill Gates, lean on the possibilities of innovation and technological solutions as quasi-'get out of jail free cards' for addressing economic inequality and resulting social and ecological injustice. It is perhaps telling that Gates' recent book, while acknowledging techno-fixes aren't *all* that's needed, contains over 90 mentions of the word 'innovation' – and not one of 'inequality'.[20] Unfortunately for the techno-optimists, as per the same review in *Nature*, 'the overwhelming evidence … is that globally, burgeoning consumption has diminished or cancelled out any gains brought about by technological change aimed at reducing environmental impact.'[21] Importantly, this finding holds true both in global aggregate and at the level of individual countries. Compounding this, and reviewed in the next chapter, is that evidence of our ability to absolutely decouple economic activity from carbon emissions, let alone material throughput, is scant. Together, these material facts offer harsh clarity on the urgency of confronting global inequality (both within and between countries) to avert devastating ecological and social implications.

Yet the institutions and practices that structure the global economy and define the economic relations between countries are designed to do just the opposite. They are also structurally deterred from operating within the time frames demanded by climate and environmental justice, and so far incapable of making the same connections between our present and future that our 'industrial flow of carbon' is so adept at.[22] In part, this is a forward-looking phenomenon. The average 'business cycle' lasts just over five years. Presidents and Parliaments last four or five, if they're lucky. Corporations are beholden to annual reports, with 'long-term' strategies that typically average just a handful of years. Financial traders might have horizons for their returns that span from mere seconds to weeks. The average holding duration for equity investments has plummeted, with advances in the financial system, from roughly four years on average at the end of the Second World War, to a record low of just over five months in 2020 as speculators sought to cash in on volatility at the height of the pandemic.[23]

Many of our failures to act on the climate and nature emergencies have been pinned on this inherent 'short-termism' – an ostensibly in-built incapacity among key actors in economics and politics to think with the necessary horizons to make rational decisions about the long-term future. Mainstream media discussion of the climate and nature crises is similarly embroiled in the war over time, in particular how to 'fairly' distribute the cost of action between generations. Over and over, fiscally conservative economists, commentators and politicians rail against the generationally 'unjust' implications of investing adequately now to stop catastrophic climate change and environmental degradation, claiming (incorrectly and often disingenuously, as we'll discuss below) that higher borrowing now to secure a habitable planetary future is effectively robbing from future generations, burdening them with debt for supposed flights of eco-warrior fancy.

But critically – and more often overlooked – is that this inability to grapple with time in the context of ecological disaster also applies in the reverse. It is no coincidence that the countries which have contributed most to the climate and ecological instability we now face are also those best equipped to adapt to its growing impacts. To the contrary, it is a direct relationship: the affluent, largely white world owes its relative safety in the face of environmental catastrophe to generations of enslavement, exploitation and economic extraction from other places and people.[24] This asymmetry continues today, facilitated by the institutions and rules of global finance and exchange, enabling historical blindness to fuel the continued expansion of inequality in the global economy. This chapter explores these institutions and the nature of their design, arguing they have served two essential functions: to transfer wealth from poorer to wealthier economies, and to ensure that private capital is uninhibited in scouring the globe for returns. Through their design, these institutions have cemented a sort of rear-view distortion. This chapter aims to make clear that the object in this mirror – that is, the debt owed by the wealthy to the world's poor majority – is much, much larger than it appears.

Debt in reverse

In his now seminal *How Europe Underdeveloped Africa*, Walter Rodney first contested the framing of 'developed' and 'developing' economies, used to distinguish between wealthy, industrialised economies located primarily in North America and Europe and the many states within which the world's poor majority live.[25] Rather than lagging in the process of economic development due to some inherent backwardness, economic failing, or other crude (and more often than not racist) generalisation, Rodney argued that the world's poorest countries had been actively 'underdeveloped' by colonial powers through the centuries-long, systematic exploitation of their labour and natural resources. Rodney's empirical analysis focused on the underdevelopment of the African continent by European colonialism, but he also showed how the same logics and systems had driven the underdevelopment of much of Asia and Latin America for the benefit of wealthier state powers. Writing some 50 years ago, Rodney argued: 'foreign investment ensures that the natural resources and the labour of Africa produce economic value which is lost to the continent.'[26] Little has changed since.[27]

The direct financial transfer of wealth through systems of debt, tax avoidance and other mechanisms has served, over recent decades, as a powerful siphon of wealth from South to North.[28] Among the most counter-intuitive mechanisms in this regard is the world of 'foreign aid'. Growing up in Canada, I was repeatedly reminded of the benevolence and generosity of countries like my own in providing billions in 'foreign aid' to countries in need. According to the Organisation for Economic Co-operation and Development, in 2019, rich countries provided some $153 billion in 'development assistance' to low- and middle-income countries (0.3% of their collective gross national income).[29] However, these sorts of headline figures, in giving the impression this represents a direct transfer of funds, are often misleading. For example, according to a report for the United States Congress, just 4% of the country's annual 'foreign aid' budget goes to foreign governments for public sector allocation; indeed, half of all spending is allocated to US companies doing work abroad, both non- and for-profit.[30]

To designate funds doled out to profit-making firms as 'aid' may sound scandalous, but it is instead a marker of a foreign aid system working just as designed. To borrow from a particularly honest appraisal of US foreign aid spending from the Rand Corporation: 'Why does the United States send foreign countries American taxpayer money? The answer, in short, is because it serves U.S. self-interest to do so.'[31] It is no accident, for instance, that of the 50 top buyers of US agricultural products, 43 have at one time received US foreign aid. This story is repeated in many of the world's wealthy 'donor' countries. In the summer of 2020, for instance, the UK government announced a new £6.8 billion 'aid' fund aimed at improving conditions for workers in low-income economies who worked for major UK corporations like retailer Primark and grocery chain Morrisons. In an almost admirable turn of transparency, the UK's trade secretary made little effort to conceal the true intention of this foreign aid: ensuring UK consumers 'can continue to buy affordable, high-quality goods from around the world.'[32] In effect, the fund proposed using UK public money to subsidise UK corporations reliant on exploitative employment practices in their supply chains. But the officially designated system of aid transfers represents a comparatively small part of the problem when it comes to the systematic transfer of wealth in reverse. Indeed, the entirety of the structures of international finance and exchange are designed to facilitate this one-directional transfer.

Finance, globalised

Finance is a world-making force. Throughout its history, from generations of colonial expansion and early industrial capitalism to the 2008 Financial Crisis, uneven access to and control of finance has enabled expropriation at spectacular rates for a select few, to the detriment of the rest. At the same time, the ability to pool resources and risk can also support collective effort and innovation, with the potential to vastly improve life for many. Essentially, finance – money – is a contract of trust between two parties: trust that one will repay the other. Economist Ann Pettifor argues that the formalisation of this faith into sound, rules-based monetary systems has in many ways facilitated enormous societal advance, insofar as it has enabled strategic mobilisation of resources to pursue necessary and important goals.[33] These systems have also, however, facilitated enormous violence and, left to metastasise at an extraordinary scale, have created a present defined by crushing indebtedness that compromises human and ecological wellbeing.[34] Moreover, finance has consistently exhibited a remarkable tendency toward speculative mania and, consequently, periodic crashes. Throughout history, many attempts have been made, to varying effect, to rein in finance's worst excesses.[35] Internationally, these efforts first took the form of the Bretton Woods system which, negotiated in the aftermath of the Second World War, sought to keep a system of fixed exchange rates stable by imposing strict controls on the cross-border movement of finance and currency, and setting the interconvertibility of US dollars into gold at a fixed rate.[36] Domestically, the Bretton Woods Agreement mandated firm regulation of countries' financial sectors, for instance bringing in caps on interest rates.

Despite its many flaws – the inevitable product of negotiating a 'global' system for transaction by a small club of powerful Northern governments, particularly a nascent US hegemon[37] – the Bretton Woods system did engender a period of relative financial stability. It was not to last. Financial sector resistance to the Bretton Woods arrangements coalesced with factors such as the Vietnam War into the significant deregulation of credit creation and financial flows, particularly among the governments of the world's financial hubs in London and New York. The system's death blow was dealt almost unilaterally by the United States in 1971, when President Nixon abandoned the fixed conversion of US dollars to gold. Within the vacuum left by Bretton Woods, a new and radically different architecture was built in the image of the neoliberal consensus, such that the increasingly globalised economic sphere could be insulated from interference by democratic demands.[38]

Indeed, the need to rein in democracy was a chief concern at this time, perceived as a threat to political and economic stability. Saliently, in 1975, the Trilateral Commission – a coalition of representatives including politicians, bankers, government advisers, academics and lawyers, among others, from the world's foremost capitalist democracies at the time (namely the US, Western Europe and Japan) – published its first and only report concerned with overcoming the 'excess of democracy' of the previous decade. In it, the authors note that while former President Truman 'had been able to govern the country with the cooperation of a relatively small number of Wall Street lawyers and bankers', by the time of the report's publication 'the sources of power in society had diversified tremendously, and this was no longer possible.'[39]

For the architects and policymakers of the neoliberal consensus, an essential task in building a market-ruled world insulated from excessive democratic demands was global financial integration, or 'financial globalisation'. The theoretical arguments in favour of financial globalisation – that is, the increase of financial linkages established as a result of cross-border financial flows – are often framed in terms of efficiency. Wielding loaded phrases like 'the forces of openness versus those of closure', globalisation's stalwart advocates (in this case, former Goldman Sachs CEO Henry Paulson in a *Financial Times* opinion piece entitled 'Save globalisation to secure the future') pit resistance to uninhibited financial prerogatives against the very ideas of freedom and progress.[40] In the view of its enthusiasts, financial globalisation allows capital to be optimally allocated by the market, not only domestically, but around the world, helping to redistribute capital from wealthy to developing economies, delivering growth for those economies while sharing risks between countries in the process. Arguments for strengthening capital controls to reduce finance's privilege to freely cross borders (a privilege, it should be emphasised, granted to capital but not people) have therefore often been denigrated as inefficient market distortions, or an unjust impediment to new sources of investment for developing economies from around the world. For instance, a 2005 paper by the National Bureau of Economic Research argued that capital controls were 'no free lunch', as they 'distort decision-making', 'reduce the supply of capital', and create a 'more inefficient allocation of capital and resources.'[41]

But while financial globalisation has certainly increased the cross-border flow of finance from Northern financial centres to the Global South, the promise of universal prosperity has rung hollow. Instead, globalised finance has created new vulnerabilities while enabling financial markets to 'discipline' the governments of poorer debtor nations. A major 2015 review by the National Bureau of Economic Research (the same Bureau that had argued dismissively against restrictions on capital mobility just a decade prior) found little evidence that lower-income nations had enjoyed the promised benefits, whether in the form of growth or better risk-sharing between economies, with a summary of the report affirming it was 'hard to find robust support for large quantifiable benefits of international financial integration.'[42] To the contrary: research by the UN Conference on Trade and Development (UNCTAD) found global financial integration has not only left poorer countries more vulnerable to periods of financial volatility in the developed economic centres, such as the 2008 crash, but has also facilitated a significant transfer of wealth from low to high-income economies. And, by limiting and stigmatising the use of capital controls in the global economy, financial interests and institutions have significantly increased the extent to which the world's lower-income economies depend on foreign rather than domestic investment.

Between 2000 and 2018, some $440 billion *per year* flowed from just 16 low-income countries to wealthy Northern economies.[43] This flow stands in stark opposition to the central premise of financial globalisation: that liberalised finance and mobile capital will redistribute wealth around the world, benefitting the poorest with productive investment. As UNCTAD argues, financial globalisation has enabled this vast net transfer of wealth from South to North because the returns which poor countries can make on new assets are substantially lower than the foreign liabilities which they come to owe through the process of 'investment' and 'development'.[44] Even the IMF, a central architect of financial liberalisation and integration, has recently started to come around to admitting (albeit tepidly) that these processes have not necessarily delivered for poorer economies, and that capital controls can have substantial benefits.[45]

Structural adjustment

Faced with this dearth of evidence in its favour, how is it that the tenets of financial globalisation – carrying within them all the interests and ideology of the neoliberal consensus – have been so effectively universalised and maintained? Much of this process has been the work of the Bretton Woods institutions (so named for their establishment within the context of the Bretton Woods agreement described above): the IMF and World Bank. In principle, these twin institutions were designed as fulcra for rebuilding the post-war global economy and promoting stable international economic cooperation. While the World Bank focused on 'development' lending to lower-income countries, the IMF was to serve as the great fixer of the global economy, keeping the monetary system (the system of exchange rates and international payments) stable. Often, this entailed lending to governments facing a 'balance of payments' crisis, meaning they risked being unable to pay for imports or service their debts. From the 1980s onwards, however, the IMF and World Bank took on a new role. Through their distribution of finance to primarily lower-income countries, these institutions began to engage in a systematic project of liberalising and integrating the global economy through the use of 'structural adjustment' packages.

These packages come attached as conditionalities to loans distributed by the IMF and World Bank and are typically made up of binding agreements to undertake various economic reforms. Since dubbed 'the Washington Consensus', the list of reforms demanded by structural adjustment terms significantly expanded on the original stated aim of the loans in question and their originating institutions, whether poverty alleviation or stabilising countries' public finances, hijacking the process as a vehicle for liberalised trade and finance and market-led growth. In concrete terms, adjustment packages regularly called for lowering or eliminating restrictions on capital mobility; the privatisation of public sector assets and industries; and widespread deregulation; in addition to restrictions on fiscal deficits. Presented as necessary interventions to bring supposedly 'backward' or protectionist economies into the modern globalised world while dealing with 'balance of payments' crises, the ultimate effect of these 'structural adjustments' was to open developing economies to (primarily) Northern private capital.[46]

Their impacts have often been as devastating as they are varied, including but not limited to: negative effects on child and maternal health;[47] elevated deforestation, often to clear land for export-driven crops like soy for animal feed;[48] widening inequality in recipient countries;[49] and elevated poverty.[50] Moreover, reviews suggest the programmes did not deliver on even their narrow goals of growth and macroeconomic stability, with outcomes on both these indicators underwhelming at best.[51] In lieu of rising prosperity or universal improvement in living standards, the world's less wealthy nations – overwhelmingly made so, it should be emphasised, by legacies of colonialism – have been locked into cyclic indebtedness. Pakistan, for instance, received loans from the IMF for 29 of the 40 years between 1970 and 2010, underscoring the inherent irrationality of the IMF approach: dealing with debt crises by providing bailout loans that leave countries with even more debt, while mandating economic readjustments that undermine economic and social prosperity.[52] Indeed, one study undertaken at the height of structural adjustment concluded that IMF-imposed policies were the 'primary impediment to economic expansion in the Third World.'[53] In the context of mitigating and adapting to the deepening ecological emergency – of which many of the world's poorest or most indebted countries are on the frontline – this cyclical debt generates a profound and unjust obstacle to the vital investment urgently needed to both mitigate and adapt to crisis.

The people of countries bearing the impacts of structural adjustment have, since the programme's earliest days, put up tremendous resistance to the brutal combination of 'deterioration in their standards of living, reduced access to public services, devastated environments, and plummeting employment prospects' – efforts that continue today.[54] However, as the next sections explore, the disciplining power of globalised finance and international financial institutions is such that these efforts have been overwhelmingly, and ruthlessly, crushed.

Monetary sovereignty

Underlying the cycle of indebtedness for many poorer nations is the question of the exorbitant privilege of 'monetary sovereignty'. While an exhaustive discussion of monetary sovereignty and its role in the unequal dynamics of the global economy is beyond the scope of this chapter, in the simplest sense it implies two essential elements. The first is that a country issues its own fiat currency, which is any currency whose value is based not on its being attached to some specific commodity like gold, but because the government issuing the currency guarantees its value. The second is that the country in question is largely able to borrow in its own currency, rather than someone else's. Monetary sovereignty is not a binary; rather, certain countries enjoy relatively more or less of it depending primarily on their ability to borrow in their own currency. Countries like the US, UK, Canada and Japan are fortunate to be at the highest end of the spectrum, largely borrowing in their own currency (often from their own central banks) and, as a result, generally enjoying more autonomy over policy and economic governance within their borders.[55] You might notice a trend: countries with the greatest monetary sovereignty are broadly situated in the Global North, with the exception of the Eurozone (the monetary union of the EU), within which countries have given up their national currencies to join the Euro, with monetary decisions therefore residing with the institutions of the Union.

On the other hand, poorer nations tend toward the lower end of the scale of monetary sovereignty, meaning they must borrow the currency of other, richer, more powerful countries in order to access and import the things they need. In broad terms, so-called 'developing economies' – overwhelmingly as the enduring legacy of a colonial history – tend to export lower-value basic commodities and labour while needing to import many higher-tech and higher-value goods and services from wealthier economies.[56] However, because wealthier countries and Northern firms largely refuse to accept payment for key imports in the local currency of poorer countries, developing economies are left with no choice but to borrow the currency of foreign states – primarily US dollars.[57] This imbalance tends to generate what's called the 'secular deterioration of the terms of trade', meaning that in order to acquire the same level of essential imports over time, poorer countries must export more and more over time.[58] It also leaves poorer countries vulnerable to fluctuations in currency valuations and to the whims of global investors who – while they may happily speculate on currency fluctuations – are much less inclined toward committing to durable, stable and productive investment. There are many examples in which speculative excitement from Northern investors who pour cash into a country or region have temporarily driven up the currency – before rapidly withdrawing that cash at the first sign of trouble. In the process, they often leave the local currency in freefall in a moment of crisis, to potentially devastating effect for local people who might suddenly find themselves unable to buy even basic goods.[59]

From monetary sovereignty to monetary triage

The privilege of monetary sovereignty was demonstrated with painful clarity during the pandemic, when the central banks of countries like the UK and US 'printed money' by buying up enormous quantities of their respective governments' bonds and supporting their suddenly elevated spending. While metaphors like the 'magic money tree' circulating in the media were intended to trivialise and ridicule perceived government largesse, they did contain an unintended kernel of truth: in this period of crisis, for governments with substantial monetary sovereignty, there was no shortage of money to finance the things they needed. In this sense, lack was a political choice, rather than a practical limitation. Much of the global population, however, does not live in a society that enjoys this privilege; consequently, when the pandemic hit, they had far fewer tools at their disposal to soften its blow.

The pandemic also exposed a second routine and pervasive injustice facilitated by the international financial and monetary systems: the supremacy of the US dollar and its master, the Federal Reserve. The US dollar is the world's reserve currency: 90% of all currency trading involves US dollars,[60] and the US dollar makes up 60% of the foreign currency reserves held by central banks around the world (a drop, it should be noted, from its high of over 70% prior to the creation of the Euro).[61] A significant portion (some 40%) of international trade is also transacted in dollars – even though the US is involved in just 10% of global trade and even, in many transactions, when neither trading party is US-based.[62] Consequently, the central banks of governments around the world need to keep stores of dollars on hand to ensure payments can be made and they can keep their currencies stable. At the onset of the pandemic, widespread panic drove a spike in demand for dollars, leaving many governments around the world facing dollar reserve shortages; in response, the Federal Reserve opened up exclusive channels for providing dollars to other governments. Called 'swap lines', this mechanism enables the Fed to swap US dollars with the currency of a foreign central bank under the agreement that they'll be swapped back (with interest) when the crisis is no longer so acute.[63]

The trouble was, this privilege was restricted to a select club of allies, including Canada, the UK, Switzerland, the EU and Japan, among others. In the midst of a deadly crisis, the United States Federal Reserve had the power to decide which governments around the world would have to scramble desperately for US dollars or simply accept an inability to cover necessary payments – and which did not. The effects were predictable. Currencies in countries given this access stabilised faster than those that weren't. In 2021, though it is a crude measure, the average per capita rate of growth in the lowest-income economies was just a mere tenth of those of high-income countries.[64] Critically, this 'monetary triage', to borrow a term from David Adler and Andrés Arauz, did not reflect some inherent limit to the amount of dollars available to the global economy. As a monetary sovereign and purveyor of the world's currency, the Fed's decision to extend swaps to an exclusive cohort of strategic friends was purely a function of political interest. As Adler and Arauz write: 'The injustice of the swap line system is obvious. No single country – no matter how exceptional – should have the right to decide who lives and who dies in the face of a pandemic.'[65] This exorbitant and unequal exercise of power scarcely raised eyebrows – indeed, the technicalities of 'swap lines' don't tend to penetrate the public debate over policy responses to the pandemic. Yet this was not the only injustice inflicted through debt and dollar dominance on the countries of the Global South in a time of urgent need. Looking toward a future punctuated by acute ecological crises, it is certain not to be the last.

Double standards

For the decade or so following the 2008 Financial Crisis, the central bank interventions that kept bond yields low consequently pushed many investors to 'reach for yield' – in other words, to look for higher returns in new places. As a result, enormous sums of money poured into so-called 'emerging market (EM) economies'. At the time of writing, over the past decade, foreign equity investment in emerging markets has doubled, while investment through emerging market bond funds has quadrupled.[66] The proportion of emerging market bonds issued in local currencies rather than, for instance, dollars or Euros, has also risen to 90%, partly driven by investor demand for higher-yielding assets.[67] However, rather than liberating these economies from dollar dependency, this shift has simply generated a new form of vulnerability: 'the acute sensitivity of EM bond markets to the global dollar cycle', such that any appreciation in the value of the US dollar prompts massive sell-off of these local currency bonds.[68]

The pandemic brought this vulnerability into stark relief: as the virus brought economies to enforced standstills, investors panicked. Absent controls to keep foreign money grounded to a particular location, instead those low- and middle-income nations were hit by record outflows of investments in both equities and bonds, totalling $100 billion in the months of March and April 2020 alone.[69] Devalued currencies sent the cost of vital imports from medicines and PPE to daily necessities soaring in a period of acute need. At the same time, investor hesitance and downgrades of countries' debtor status by credit ratings agencies[70] drove up the cost of public borrowing just as more was needed to cover crisis spending.[71] The long-term aftermath is yet to unfold, but it's likely the cruelty and volatility of the international financial system, coupled with injustices in vaccine distribution that are prolonging the virus's impact in many poor countries, will leave the world's poorest nations facing record debts and soaring interest rates following the pandemic as they turn to the immediate threat of adapting to deepening climate and ecological impacts, through no fault of their own.

Exceptional as the pandemic was, this type of volatility in poorer countries' ability to finance their needs is in many ways the norm rather than the exception. It is a cycle of escalating debt that has held back vital initiatives which would not only improve the basic standard of living for billions, from universal electrification to public health care services, but has also compromised urgent progress on adapting to and mitigating the climate and nature emergencies for communities on the frontline of their impacts. Worse still, as we enter an unknown era of ecological volatility, the acute crises that will punctuate them – from floods to drought and wildfire – will only exacerbate these punitive financial fluctuations in the moments when stable, long-term and affordable finance is most needed. Without significant changes to the privileges currently afforded to global finance at the expense of the world's poor majority, the impacts of deepening ecological crisis risk replicating the experience of the pandemic, over and over.

Recognising the unsustainability of the debt burden faced by many of the poorest economies amidst immense fiscal pressure to sustain elevated pandemic-related spending, the G20 (the group of the world's 20 largest economies) agreed in April 2020 to negotiate a temporary debt payment suspension for 73 of the world's poorest nations. In theory, this should have freed up money that would otherwise have been spent paying back interest to lenders for vital needs like medical capacity and other essential supplies. However, the negotiation applied exclusively to debt owed to other governments in what is termed 'bilateral' lending. Notably excluded were debts owed to multilateral banks such as the World Bank, which together accounted for 26% of the eligible debt payments, and those owed to private financial firms, which collectively accounted for over 34% (the largest share of any group).[72] The exclusion of these two groups – in combination with the fact that all suspended payments would need to be paid in full down the line – meant that of the more than 70 eligible countries, only 43 applied for suspension, and just 23% of their eligible debt payments were suspended.[73]

The architects of the scheme called on participating states to seek comparable relief from their other creditors, particularly private firms, and encouraged private firms to accept. Unwilling to take a firm stand, however, no country required private firms within their purview to do so, instead simply offering gentle encouragement, and in the end just 0.2% of privately held debt was suspended. Moreover, by suspending only public bilateral lending, debt savings ended up being directly siphoned to private firms. As the Jubilee Debt Campaign writes: 'Suspending payments to other governments has enabled private lenders to keep being paid – meaning that public money intended to help lower income countries has instead gone to banks, hedge funds and oil traders.'[74] In total, private lenders received nearly $15 billion in debt repayment over the first year of the debt suspension initiative – more than any other group, and more than the $10 billion total that was suspended under the mechanism.[75]

The hostility and double standards faced by low-income countries throughout the pandemic to date are emblematic of the globalised financial system and the injustices it embeds: US dollar supremacy; unsustainable and unjust debt burdens for the poorest; privileges extended among a club of powerful peers; and the prioritisation of private interests. In the same way that they have defined the differential experience of the pandemic for the world's wealthy and poor nations, this structural inequality is already defining – and will continue to define – how different parts of the world experience and respond to the climate and nature crises. At the same time, the escalating impacts of the climate crisis and perceptions of risk among lenders and investors this creates are raising the cost of capital for the poorest and most affected nations and straining public finances to pay for debts.[76] It is no exaggeration to say, in the wake of COVID-19, that the global financial system prioritises some lives over others; without radical changes to its operation, we will further cement this two-tier designation amid an escalating state of chronic emergency.

The default position

Amid the fiscal strain created by the urgent public health and social demands of the pandemic, why is it that the world's poor governments did not simply refuse to service their debts? Surely, in the context of acute human suffering and crisis, private creditors (largely but not exclusively located in the Global North) would be unwilling to demand or unable to enforce repayment. In other words: why did borrowers not simply default? This is a question that gets to the heart of the efficacy with which international financial institutions, law and common sense systematically protect the interests of private capital – even over human life. What are the mechanisms of enforcement that prevent borrowers from simply refusing to make payments? Based on a detailed historical survey, historian Jerome Roos has documented how, until relatively recently, sovereign default was in fact exceptionally common, considered part and parcel of lending to foreign governments.[77] Moreover, in many cases defaults were 'acknowledged, accepted, and eventually negotiated on terms favourable to the debtors.'[78]

By contrast, data on global defaults show how by the 1980s, a new common sense was cemented, according to which the unilateral decision to suspend debt payments became a strict taboo. Over the past few decades, the share of public debt in default has continued to plummet, from about 5% worldwide in the mid-1980s to below 1% beginning in the 2010s.[79] Somewhat counter-intuitively, this period of record-low and consistently declining public debt in default took place over four decades in which the global economy was highly tumultuous, and financial crises occurred at a historic rate. At the height of the Eurozone crisis of 2009–11, for instance, worldwide sovereign debt in default remained at a historic low of just 0.1%.[80] Absence of default has remained widespread even as many of the world's poorest countries have seen their debt burdens double relative to total government spending over the last decade.[81] Worse still, those debts deemed 'distressed' or at risk of default are often sold off by lenders on the secondary market at significantly reduced rates, only to be bought up by 'vulture' funds who have subsequently sued (successfully) to collect the full amount.[82] That the demands for payment by the private finance industry have been almost universally met even as that same industry has routinely wrought havoc on the real economy tells us a great deal about whose interests international economic institutions and practices are designed to serve and protect.

In the absence of a world government or enforcement body, how has this adherence been maintained, even at the punitive, unjust and inhumane cost of compromised public expenditure on vital tasks, including mitigating and adapting to climate and environmental change? The literature on this question is both expansive and unsettled; in short, there is no single factor ensuring compliance. Rather, the absence of sovereign default is the product of several institutions and economic dynamics, as well as conflicts of power, both domestic and international.[83] Their combined potency ensures the global economy functions with stunning efficacy to protect the interests of private capital over sovereign governments.

Of increasing relevance are the dynamics of asset manager capitalism and the growth of index investing, discussed in Chapter 3. While I specifically focused on the recent proliferation of and concentration within asset management as a result of their prominence in shaping the green capitalist programme, it's vital to point out that across the financial system, holdings in Global South sovereign debt are now markedly concentrated among a cohort of enormous financial institutions. Lending has become gradually concentrated among a few banks, while the share of sovereign debt in the form of bonds owned by large private investors has risen.[84] These conditions stand in stark contrast to earlier eras of lending, which were defined by dispersed and comparatively small investors 'who found it exceedingly difficult to coordinate collective action and exert the requisite leverage.'[85] Today's investors and lenders are comparatively powerful and able to exert substantial market discipline over even sovereign governments.

The IMF has long played (and continues to play) a central disciplining function by protecting the interests and stability of global capital markets, as well as through the longer-term effects of structural adjustment packages, the conditionalities of which are designed explicitly to prioritise the repayment of debts both public and private. Indeed, the role of the prescriptions contained within structural adjustment packages was the generation of hard currency to pay these debts, rather than efforts to build the infrastructures for recipients to become monetarily sovereign.[86] However, in the age of passive investing, index providers serve an increasingly powerful gatekeeping function for sovereigns' cost of and access to capital, with index inclusion bringing both more and lower-cost investment and, on the flip-side, exclusion inducing the reverse.[87] The impact can be enormous: in 2019, an index reclassification of 'emerging' economies led to a 'seismic shift' in fund flows (both passive and active), which reached $120 billion.[88]

Critically, for both governments and corporations, both the availability and cost of borrowing through the issuance of bonds are significantly shaped by a cohort of private firms: credit ratings agencies. Some of their names – such as S&P – you will recognise from Chapters 3 and 4 as the providers of many of the indices tracked by passive funds. Others, such as Moody's and Fitch, are more specialised bond raters, analysing both corporations and sovereign governments. Ratings agencies are private companies whose function is to investigate and aggregate information on firms or sovereign borrowers related to the risk of lending to the entity in question. Based on the degree of perceived risk, the agencies assign a rating to a corporation or a sovereign's debt, generally in the form of a letter grade where AAA represents the highest possible rating, and anything falling below a BBB is deemed non-investment grade or 'speculative' in quality, meaning the bond is high risk (though potentially high yield). Within the industry, the other term generally used to describe non-investment grade bonds is 'junk'.

Where concentration among index providers is, as Chapter 3 noted, high, the credit rating industry sets a new standard of excellence: 95% of all rating activity is conducted by just three firms, with Moody's and S&P each controlling about 40% of the market, and Fitch a further 15%.[89] All three are headquartered in New York.[90] Ratings agencies are meant, in theory, to provide robust and unbiased analysis of the risk of default to investors so that they can make sound decisions about where to place their cash based on their appetites for risk and return. However, by its own standards, the industry has a chequered history. Like any oligopoly, the industry is susceptible to corruption or collusion between providers. For the credit rating industry in particular, its business model is virtually founded on a conflict of interest: ratings agencies are paid by debt issuers to rate their debt, with these fees constituting the overwhelming majority of the agencies' income. This conflict – of 'trading reputation for profit', as *The Economist* rather succinctly put it – has been at the heart of financial turmoil from the Dotcom bubble at the turn of the millennium to the catastrophic subprime mortgage collapse of the 2008 Financial crisis,[91] during which ratings agencies systematically allocated AAA ratings to junk.[92]

While there are certain checks and balances in place to govern agencies' operations, these firms have proven to be deeply fallible on multiple occasions since the industry began to proliferate in the 1960s, with ratings ultimately reliant on substantial subjectivity on the part of agency employees. As firms whose function is ostensibly to support a functioning and efficient 'free market', it is remarkable that just three firms monopolise such a significant site of influence over how capital is allocated. As Mark Carl Rom articulates, these firms are at once private (with respect to their ownership and authority) and public (insofar as they effectively provide a major public function). That they have such immense power over the cost and availability of capital for the world's low- and middle-income countries is thus – in combination with substantial concentration within the industry – a significant vesting of power over inherently public issues with a private, subjective and fallible authority.

This authority is not merely symbolic. Ratings aren't just a rubber stamp of approval; they materially determine how much capital goes where. Moreover, they are continually under review: once given, ratings can readily be 'downgraded' by agencies. In response to calls by Global South governments during the pandemic for debt relief and cancellation, for instance, critics of the demands responded with warnings about the risks to those countries of losing the 'gains' many have made in the ratings game over recent years.[93] Fear of rating retaliation was also cited as a reason for numerous eligible governments declining to seek temporary debt payment relief as part of the G20's Debt Suspension programme, even though this was a formalised, internationally sanctioned programme specifically devised to respond to exceptional global circumstances. The threat of downgrading thus materially hindered the response of many governments to COVID-19, diverting huge sums of precious public funds to paying out to bond-holders rather than providing support for vital health and social initiatives. This is a pattern that, absent drastic changes in the functioning of global finance, will be replicated to devastating effect as the climate and nature crises advance. Already, the countries experiencing the harshest impacts of these crises are among the world's poorest, from cyclones in Mozambique to drought and famine in Madagascar.[94] The credit ratings agencies make no effort to deny these links. A 2014 report from S&P noted that 'lower-rated sovereigns tend on average to be more vulnerable [to climate risk] than higher-rated sovereigns', before continuing with the insight that 'sovereigns will probably be unevenly affected by climate change, with poorer and lower rated sovereigns typically hit hardest, which could contribute to rising global rating inequality.'[95] Faced with increasingly frequent and severe natural disasters, governments will be confronted with the trade-off between responding to crisis and meeting urgent humanitarian needs and risking a downgrading of their credit rating – initiating a downward spiral of costlier and more scarce credit. The industry is set up to give the impression that indices are purely objective and based on 'hard, quantitative measures'; however, as Robin Wigglesworth admits, 'an element of human discretion is inevitably and unavoidably part of the process', including in the decision as to what data are considered and what measures used.[96] This 'myth of objectivity' has established a system within which we hand the potential to enormously impact the sovereignty of many governments – and by extension countless lives – to some analysts at Moody's. It is a system that, to put it lightly, is irrational, unjust and indefensible.

Legal leviathans

All of this takes place against the backdrop of legal systems and protections designed in the interests of private capital. There is no globally unified legal code within which investors and corporations operate, making the international system of trade and investment, in theory, anarchic. However, as legal scholar Katharina Pistor argues, a universal legal framework has proven unnecessary for maintaining capital's interests. Instead, these are sustained by the global power of just two domestic legal systems, England and New York State, with the additional support of 'an extensive network of bilateral trade and investment regimes.'[97] As the hubs of global finance, the rules dictating what private firms and investors can and cannot do in these jurisdictions have become extended throughout the global economy through the terms negotiated between the entities involved in a foreign transaction in so-called 'conflict-of-law' rules. Under these rules, the parties to a contract or investment deal can choose the laws by which their agreement will be governed (overwhelmingly those of England or New York).[98] Regional or bilateral investment treaties negotiated between governments, meanwhile, set the terms of exchange through negotiation between parties who are often on very different footing when it comes to negotiating power.

Crucially, most international exchange is governed by treaties that contain a specific measure for protecting capital's interests: the Investor-State Dispute Settlement mechanism (ISDS). Among the more sinister acronyms in international systems of exchange, ISDS describes a private courts system that allows foreign investors to sue the governments of the countries hosting their investments for perceived infractions of their rights, as set out in trade and investment agreements. The reverse action – states bringing cases against investors – is *not* covered within ISDS, making the arrangement highly asymmetrical. When it comes to bringing ISDS disputes, the energy sector is uniquely prolific, having initiated dozens of disputes claiming perceived discrimination or a compromise of their investment, often related to environmental or climate regulations. The legal terms setting out these mechanisms are generally vague enough to permit these actions, opening up the possibility of damages for violating often legally ambiguous conditions.

Negotiated in the 1990s under the auspices of improving global cooperation on investment in energy, one such agreement, the Energy Charter Treaty (ECT), has been regularly invoked to protect the interests of fossil fuel investments in the face of government decisions – including on climate policy.[99] Its ambiguous clauses mandating 'free and equitable treatment', 'stable and favourable' conditions, and against 'expropriation' are often liberally interpreted to include any state action which might significantly impact an investment's returns. For instance, in 2019 German energy producer RWE sued the Dutch government under the ECT for compensation based on its proposed 2030 coal phaseout commitment,[100] while in 2017 UK-based firm Rockhopper sued the Italian government after it banned new oil and gas projects in an earthquake prone area, despite Italy having left the treaty the previous year.[101]

Even the prospect of a dispute can change a government's plans: in 2017, Canadian oil and gas producer Vermillion threatened to lodge an ECT complaint against the French environment minister's support for a law that would see fossil fuel extraction in France phased out by 2040 and immediately ban new drilling permits and renewals. Following the complaint, the law was significantly softened, leaving companies space to renew permits up to 2040.[102] The ECT is also far from the only tool for compromising states' ability to act on climate and environmental issues. The North American Free Trade Agreement and its successor the US-Mexico-Canada Agreement have also routinely been invoked in ISDS disputes: for instance, Westmoreland Coal Company has brought two disputes against the government of Canadian province Alberta for plans to phase out coal power production by 2030. Northern states such as Canada, France and the Netherlands often have a reasonable chance of success in their defence against companies – the combined effect of their comparatively powerful bargaining positions in drafting the treaties and robust legal representation – limiting the impacts of disputes to legislative delay and (often significant) legal costs. Many poorer countries don't enjoy these luxuries.

The ISDS mechanism has been defended as a means not only to protect the rights of foreign investors and thereby encourage international economic activity, but also as a route to improving governance practices and standards in host countries. The latter argument is as rich in neo-colonial undertones as it is lacking in empirical support.[103] To the contrary, evidence suggests the proliferation of global investment treaties has encouraged countries to create protective 'enclaves' for foreign investors, within which they are effectively subject to a different set of laws than operates in the country as a whole.[104] Indeed, it is far more likely that these treaties and the dispute mechanisms enshrined within them actively discourage certain types of positive legislation and policymaking on the part of host states. For instance, as legal scholar Dominic Dagbanja has documented, the countless investment treaties negotiated on the African continent since the 1960s have overwhelmingly denied the inclusion of exceptions to the agreements' terms based on public interest, such as environmental protection or – of singular importance in the context of many African countries' substantial mining industries – human rights.[105]

This combined power – of investment treaties, conflict-of-law agreements, and the implicit threats in reaction to sovereign debt default – significantly restricts the ability of many of the world's poorer countries to govern freely in their interests. Under these conditions, the notion of national sovereignty that the 'democratic leaders' of the Global North routinely champion is, in many senses, a myth. Pitted against the power of Northern investors and constrained by the volatility inherent to financial globalisation, the governments of the so-called 'developing world' are often left with little space in which to exercise genuine sovereignty, particularly as it concerns questions of human rights, environmental protection and climate action. As Katharina Pistor writes: 'What is good for effective law and democratic self-governance is not necessarily good for capital.'[106]

Our world is thus one governed by the prerogatives of corporate and financial interests, overwhelmingly situated in the Global North. From foreign investment to trade and public finances, the Global South is confined within a straitjacket of economic threats – some explicit, as in the case of ISDS arbitration or credit rating downgrades, and others more implicit, including the looming threat of capital flight. However, although this violation of the sovereignty of Southern countries and their people is perhaps more systematic than ever in history, it is not new. Rather, over the past few generations, formal systems of enslavement and colonialism have given way to new mechanisms for maintaining this immense and systematic siphoning of wealth, which has seen the Global South effectively develop the North, becoming its benevolent creditor.

Ecologically unequal exchange

Misleading accounting of financial flows and even more overt financial extraction make up only a small part of the force Walter Rodney first described as 'underdevelopment'. The incorporeal siphoning of wealth via financial means from South to North has been matched in kind through a much more physical form of extraction: what's called 'unequal ecological exchange'. In response to the explosion of international trade and establishment of the World Trade Organization in the 1990s, an expansive literature using 'materials flow analysis', which measures the flow not just of money but of material resources and goods, began to demonstrate how systems of international economic exchange ensure both 'energy and materials disproportionately flow from the Global South to the Global North'.[107] Although global trade is formally presented as the willing exchange of goods and services between wealthy nations rather than explicit extraction, participants in this exchange do not come to the table as equals in power. As noted above, exports from poorer countries tend to be primary commodities such as low-cost agricultural products or minerals. Critically, these products remain low-cost only because their prices fail to reflect the significant and negative ecological and human impacts they embody.[108] This asymmetry generates an 'ecological debt' on the part of wealthy Northern countries, who by contrast primarily export expensive services and manufactured products with substantially less ecological and social exploitation involved in their production. Through this asymmetrical exchange, wealthy countries exploit low-income economies as under-remunerated sources of the raw materials and cheap labour they demand, as well as 'sinks' for their waste and the environmental impacts of primary commodity production and extraction.

As ecological economists Ulrich Brand and Markus Wissen formulate, this unequal exchange facilitates an 'imperial mode of living' among the comparatively affluent global population (largely but not exclusively located in Northern metropolitan centres), whose everyday existence requires an increasingly untenable exploitation of the resources and labour of unseen 'elsewheres'.[109] These often invisible sites of exploitation might be domestic, such as in the routine misery faced by underpaid (often undocumented) slaughterhouse or factory workers, or shifted abroad in the under-compensated consumption of natural resources; horrors faced by workers in mining and extractive sectors; and monopolisation of natural 'sinks' to support consumption, such as forests claimed to offset the carbon emissions of wealthy economies. What makes them 'elsewhere' is not geography so much as their near-invisibility in sustaining the mode of living of those living in capitalist centres, in the process making the routine consumption, waste and violence of that life seemingly natural or inevitable. As Brand and Wissen document, by providing a measure of security and material comfort to the majority of the population within capitalist centres such as Europe and North America, the 'imperial mode' is the basis by which the working and middle classes in those centres remain in a compromise with capital – in effect, broadly accepting the vast inequalities that define our economies in exchange for a moderate baseline of comfort and consumption. In the process, the physical consequences of this elevated and increasingly universalised consumption are 'externalised' to elsewhere, from the fringes of affluent economies to the people and ecologies of the Global South.

While throughout this book I have, for expedience and clarity, used the framing of Global North and South to distinguish between two broad groupings of economies defined by higher or lower incomes and degrees of economic and geopolitical power, the concept of the 'imperial mode' is a valuable framing for deconstructing the impression of monolithic national islands, within which everyone endures or enjoys the same conditions. To the contrary, the ecological crisis is and will continue to be felt differently not only between countries but among the populations within them, cleaving along lines of class, gender and race. This is an essential challenge for the first pillar of green capitalism – the effort to minimise disruption of the structures and distributions of wealth and power that presently define the global economy. Indeed, the green capitalist programmes emanating from the US, UK and EU are increasingly confronted with the dilemma of ensuring the base consumption and comfort of enough of their populations in the face of an unprecedented threat to growth and advancing constraints on resources, particularly as economic 'development' increases consumption among previously poorer communities and challenges the North's unjust enclosure of a vastly disproportionate fraction of the resource pie.

Demand for energy, resources, land and sinks for our carbon and material waste among Northern economies has long been unsustainable. Now, as the chickens come home to roost, capital and its emissaries are seeking a path to maintaining the systems that support their interests in the context of looming climatic and ecological disaster. From voluntary alliances of the world's largest financial institutions helmed by Mike Bloomberg[110] to the enshrining of carbon markets at COP26; from the European Green Deal to 'nature-based solutions', capital is clearly no longer willing to deny these challenges. Neither is it short of proposals for addressing them. The thread running through these proposals is an unwillingness to engage with the deep roots of these crises in inequalities of wealth, power and consumption. Rather than financial debts owed by South to North, the world's wealthy economies owe an exorbitant human and ecological debt to the people and places that have produced our wealth and absorbed our waste.

Out of the recognition of this debt has stemmed a growing call for climate-related reparations – in short, payments to 'former colonies and marginalised developing countries' from which wealth has been extracted, and who are the most vulnerable to climate and ecological breakdown. In many cases, these are directly related: in the Caribbean, for instance, the legacies of colonialism have directly increased countries' vulnerability by reorienting many countries' economies toward industries acutely vulnerable to climatic change, namely primary resource, agricultural and tourism-related sectors.[111] As Leon Sealey-Huggins argues, the orientation of many Caribbean nations toward these sectors 'is not merely a feature of geography, but a condition with historical antecedents inseparable from contemporary social relations.[112] Moreover, histories of having been colonised are reflected in increased sovereign indebtedness in the present, further heightening the stress these countries face as ecological crisis continues to unfurl.[113] These direct contributions to vulnerability coalesce with the outsized cumulative contribution to global emissions and ecological degradation on the part of many wealthier nations in a spiral of heightened risk, poverty and vulnerability.

The mechanics of reparations are complex. Proposals have been made for a 'Global Climate Stabilization Fund' through which former colonising states can contribute funds in the form of cash transfers, not loans. In the immediate term, tools and mechanisms exist to begin this redistributive process; however, they are at present being consistently and unjustly thwarted. The first is the continued prioritisation of intellectual property (IP) at the cost of human lives. The refusal on the part of rich nations to waive IP protections for COVID-19 vaccines was a stark example of the callousness with which these rules can be enforced – a callousness that must be reversed in sharing technologies to mitigate and adapt to ecological crisis. A second is the continued stymying by, most saliently, the United States, of terms for 'Loss & Damage' payments under the Paris Agreement, whereby rich countries would contribute payments to those countries suffering disproportionate climatic impacts.[114] The essential task is the return and redistribution of extracted and concentrated wealth, both to support justice and to foster the greater economic equality needed to mitigate unsustainable ecological exploitation. However, the clear preference emerging from the emissaries and vanguard industries of the green capitalist project is to decarbonise things as they currently exist, rather than admit that something different (and, dare we dream, better) is not only possible but necessary. The nascent green capitalism we now confront is thus predicated on exclusion. As this chapter has argued, this exclusion is distinctly temporal. Carbon dioxide in the atmosphere is not ephemeral; it stays suspended for up to 1,000 years, warming the planet's surface for the duration of its tenure. Even if we were to turn off the carbon taps tomorrow in one decisive twist, the Earth would continue to warm, and our climate to change. Indeed, like drawing a bath, turning off the tap does not empty the atmospheric tub. Every molecule of carbon dioxide in the atmosphere is thus a communication with the past, a molecular footprint of the razing and growing and digging and burning of our ancestors and our earlier selves. The state of warming in which we now live is the cumulative history of industrial capitalism. The fires that fuelled it transformed carbon that, under the weight of millions of years had become coal and oil, and compressed those years into seconds of flame, leaving a mark that will endure centuries into the future. The air, in the words of Andreas Malm, is 'heavy with time.'[115]

The infrastructures and solutions of green capitalism are ill-equipped to grapple with the reality of this temporal exclusion, instead preferring to push ahead with Panglossian advocacy of 'sustainable development' and 'green growth'. Unfortunately, as the next chapter explores, despite the claims made by advocates of economic 'decoupling', decarbonisation does not occur in a vacuum. The process of overhauling our systems of energy, production and consumption is intensely physical, demanding the exploitation of both labour and nature at each turn. This exclusion is thus also inherently spatial. Walls are erected and barbed-wire fences extended to exclude certain people from the future that green capitalism envisions. Swathes of the planet are designated as the necessary sacrifice zones of achieving that future. Where the boundaries of these exclusions will ultimately be drawn is uncertain. What is clear, with every upward revision of projections for the pace,[116] sensitivity[117] and severity[118] of climate and environmental breakdown, is that the future is arriving faster than we thought.

Ghosts: valuing a disappearing world

They are always there, spectres, even if they do not exist, even
if they are no longer, even if they are not yet. –Jacques Derrida[1]
We will coup whoever we want! Deal with it. –Elon Musk,
discussing access to Bolivian lithium[2]

Over recent decades, the coastal regions of North Carolina
have become home to an ecologically unique expanse of forest.
Despite its protected status, much of the coastline has been
transformed to a ghost landscape, haunted by the bleached,
bone white trunks and levelled trees that suggest there was
once a forest. It's an anthropogenic graveyard, but the eerie
landscape is neither the result of industrial deforestation nor a
wayward fire. The Carolinian coast is low-lying, and human-
made changes to the landscape, including agricultural drain-
age ditches and channels, have left the land poorly protected
from an advancing ocean whose intrusions routinely soak the
earth with salt, choking the trees.[3] Since 1985, a third of this
protected refuge has been lost, either reclaimed by the sea,
swallowed by the advancing saline marshes or, in the case of
some 10,000 hectares, converted to 'ghost forest' – a distinct
type of land cover populated by the ashen trunks of washed out

forest, marking what was once a kaleidoscope of red maple, cypress and pine.

Most forests aren't left as spectres dotting an eerie landscape; instead, they're simply removed at an astonishing rate. In 2019, the world lost a football pitch of tropical rainforest every six seconds, totalling more than 36 million acres over the year – an area larger than England.[4] The next year, despite a global pandemic and unprecedented economic shock, global rates of deforestation surged a further 50%, and enough primary tropical rainforest to cover the Netherlands was lost. In the first ten months of 2021, the rate increased by an additional third,[5] while the rate of Amazon deforestation reached its highest in 15 years. The vastness and density of the Amazon rainforest is such that the myriad forms of life it may house have never been fully documented.[6] When we lose it to the insatiable machines of industrial agriculture and big-name brands, we mourn not only a world we've known, but worlds we have not yet discovered.

The planet's ledger is increasingly populated by both ghosts and by new forms of fossil – an enduring physical record of consumption and exploitation. Amid the sixth mass extinction, we are producing more and longer-lasting waste than ever in history. There is now more plastic in the oceans by mass than there were whales before commercial whaling devastated their populations.[7] In a year, a single open-cast mine can produce 40 times more solid waste than the average Latin American mega-city, churning endless tonnes of material from beneath the surface and leaving a scarred landscape as the only epitaph of the ecosystems and communities that may once have lived there.[8] Since 1950, bleaching and other disturbances have killed half of all coral reef cover, leaving ghostly miles of grey cityscape in miniature on the seafloor. Despite representing a fraction of a percent of life on earth by biomass, humans have driven the loss of 83% of all wild mammals; today, some 70% of all birds on Earth are farmed poultry, while 60% of all mammals are livestock.[9] And as Arctic permafrost thaws, microbes that were laid to rest tens of thousands of years ago are returning to stalk the Arctic's current inhabitants.

With numbing regularity, reports are published examining the extent to which the biosphere is being pushed toward a point of no return. Despite these warnings, the global policy and indeed general public discourse surrounding our ecological crisis, from NGOs, to popular books, to global youth movements, has in recent years tended to fixate on the question of carbon, often to the neglect of other urgent crises, from biodiversity loss to the destabilisation of ecosystems. The COP26 climate summit was the subject of constant mainstream media coverage, while its sister conference on biological diversity remains comparatively invisible. Major outlets like Bloomberg and the UK's Sky News now have (long overdue) segments and publications dedicated specifically to the climate crisis, while a study of media coverage found the climate crisis received eight times more media attention than biodiversity or other ecological issues.[10] Often the result is that the two become viewed as separate rather than indissoluble challenges, with one taking clear precedence over the other.

Oil companies publish 1.5 degree 'pathways', which advocate expansion of fossil fuels for decades to come, writing off the emissions to hypothetical carbon removal technologies and 'nature-based solutions' demanding areas of land the size of Brazil. The International Energy Agency constructs a decarbonised future that will see 230 million electric vehicles on the road by 2030 (a 23-fold expansion in just ten years from the

10 million on the road as of the end of 2020), glossing over the profound pressures this scenario implies for the ecosystems and communities from which lithium and other minerals are mined.[11] Analyses suggest that to be impactful in curbing emissions, mass rollout of 'BECCS' (Bioenergy Carbon Capture and Storage, in which biomass is burned and coupled with carbon capture to create a net carbon negative fuel source) would require a land mass the size of India for fuel, ultimately increasing global deforestation and species loss.[12]

The impossibly enormous numbers these projections contain are frequently taken at face value, so long as they line up with chosen pathways for eliminating carbon. In this sense, carbon has become an increasingly disembodied enemy – a spectral atmospheric menace that appears only as a figure on a spreadsheet. Replacing our combustion engine cars with electric vehicles (EVs) 'cuts carbon'. Biofuels 'curb emissions'. Offsetting our flights will help us reach 'net zero'. Eliminating carbon from our economic systems has, for many governments, institutions and private companies, become an incorporeal calculation, to be solved by replacing, one-to-one, the infrastructures and systems of our current mode of living with their 'decarbonised' equivalents. Where carbon can't be fully eliminated, meanwhile, an offset can helpfully round out the atmospheric balance sheet. The trouble is how quickly this abstract carbon accounting collides with the embodied reality of the biosphere: in the inescapable links between climatic and ecological breakdown; in the untenable pursuit of global eco-modernisation and unrestrained aggregate 'green' growth decoupled from material constraints; and in the accelerating commodification and financialisation of the environment as a site of accumulation, control and deepening inequity.

This chapter explores the increasing prominence with which 'nature' – from mineral resources to biodiversity – features at the core of green capitalism.[13] Having side-lined nature for decades, treating it as simply an input to the discrete and bounded unit of 'the economy', market-centric economics is now confronting the profound physical consequences of that neglect. The extent to which unabated consumption and exploitation of resources in service of the enormous economic growth that defined the twentieth and early twenty-first centuries have generated an untenable deterioration in the stability of ecosystems, biodiversity and beyond is not lost on advocates of green capitalist frameworks. To the contrary, this decisive challenge is understood as both a critical threat to be managed and an opportunity to create and seize.

First: a threat. As this book has argued, a central pillar of green capitalism is the reassertion of existing economic systems and corresponding relations of power and consumption – in short, preserving capitalism while taming those elements deemed a threat to the system's own reproduction. Green capitalism is therefore necessarily wedded to the principle of 'green growth' – that is, aggregate economic growth decoupled from material and ecological constraints – and the accompanying task of eco-modernisation, which describes the replacement of our existing economy and forms of consumption with decarbonised alternatives. However, as this chapter examines, in response to these frameworks a natural world pushed to its limits is rearing its head, straining against ecological pressures and setting the grounds for an increasingly violent contest over the finite capacity of the planet to provide the resources and sinks to sustain the green capitalist project. We are more than capable of sustaining a decent life for all – and for the long term – with the space, resources and natural 'sinks' this

231

planet generously offers.[14] Collective abundance is in large part a social, rather than a purely physical, question. However, current distributions of accumulation, production and consumption risk foreclosing this possibility.[15]

Second: an opportunity. Green capitalism is a response to the collision of the accumulative drive of capitalist economies with the profound threat to returns, asset values, and accumulation posed by deepening ecological crisis,[16] alongside the implicit need to scale down those parts of the global economy that are socially unnecessary, ecologically destructive, and, for the time being, highly profitable. Here, the threat of a deteriorating natural world is transformed to a new frontier for accumulation, based on its commodification and conversion into tradable assets, including new financial products from which speculative income can be derived. Within the same market-led logics that underlie carbon pricing, the frameworks for valuing 'natural capital' and 'ecosystem services' that feature with growing prevalence in the plans of governing institutions are presented as both a necessary and a pragmatic strategy for 'saving' nature based on the rationality of prices, markets and capital. Meanwhile, asset managers and other investors are circling the prospects of new products based on nature's conversion into financial assets, ideally backstopped and de-risked by the state.

The first half of this chapter is devoted to the question of ecological modernisation and green growth, asking whether and how they might be possible – and, even if they were, whether they would be desirable. Specifically, it examines the rush for resources and land demanded by the project of decarbonising the global economy as it currently operates. The second half examines proposals for 'conserving' nature by giving it a price, such that its destruction can be internalised to the market and its preservation handed over to financial markets. Many advocates of the natural capital approach acknowledge certain of its risk and limitations, but nonetheless affirm that economically valuing nature is a matter of pragmatism, realism and necessity. This chapter is in many ways the converse of these arguments. It acknowledges certain subversive potentials and proposals for the idea of natural capital to be harnessed for good. However, it also finds the inherent methodological limitations facing the approach alongside the practical and ethical problems already marring its real-world application make the idea that pricing, commodifying and trading nature can resolve ecological crisis on a global scale illusive. Critically, it argues that in attempting to make this happen, the advance of this accumulative frontier risks becoming a path to profound injustice and ecological loss.

A tale of two mines

Tiehm's buckwheat is a rare plant species whose entire global population lives within a 10-acre stretch of land in Esmerelda County, Nevada. In recent years, its fate has become a source of contentious debate at a frontier of the energy transition, with some campaigners describing it as no less than 'a symbol of our times.'[17] The plant's habitat, and by extension its future as a species, is threatened by proposals for a lithium mine on the site. After years of back and forth alongside various legal challenges and new requirements for environmental impact assessment, in 2021 the Biden administration submitted a proposal for Tiehm's buckwheat to be protected under the Endangered Species Act, thereby preventing the mine from going ahead.

Lithium is an essential component of many low-carbon technologies, from EV batteries to the grid energy storage needed to support renewable electricity sources. So integral is its role to 'clean' energy technologies that the International Energy Agency predicts demand for lithium to increase more than 40-fold by 2040 relative to existing demand, which in 2020 stood at nearly 75 thousand tonnes per year.[18] The process of extracting lithium can be immensely destructive. It is in part for this reason that the green capitalist rush to electrify our lives and infrastructures as they currently operate is so problematic and untenable. Within this context, the legal protection of Tiehm's buckwheat and the area it inhabits might be considered a triumph, pulling a plant back from the brink of extinction. Conservationists, including the more than 100 scientists and conservation organisations who signed an urgent letter calling on the administration to do so, certainly celebrated.

Thousands of miles away in Chile's Atacama desert, local people and ecologies have not been so fortunate. The Atacama is one of the driest places on Earth, bested only by certain regions of the Antarctic. It receives less than half an inch of rain each year, with a 'meaningful' rainfall of 1.5 inches or more quenching the dry earth just once per century.[19] It is also host, beneath the vast and austere beauty of salt flats, to more than half of the world's known lithium reserves.[20] Currently, Chile supplies nearly a quarter of global lithium demand, second only to Australia.[21] Doing so has come at a heavy cost. There are two primary methods for extracting lithium. The first involves relatively conventional mining techniques, scouring lithium ore from the earth and separating out the metal through complex physical and chemical processes. The second involves pumping vast quantities of underground water to the surface, creating pools of briny liquid which then evaporate, with the lithium separated out of the salt left behind after evaporation. In both cases, impacts on local areas and communities are often profound, but in the driest inhabited region on Earth, the toll of syphoning enormous amounts of water out of the local supply – roughly 2 million litres per tonne of lithium carbonate extracted – and into mining operations is placing both the Indigenous communities and the ecosystems sustained by this water under severe threat.[22] To make matters worse, the region is acutely vulnerable to the effects of the climate crisis, with drought and rising heat augmenting an already extreme climate.

Despite this, the mining firms operating on the sites show no sign of slowing. US-based chemicals giant, Albemarle, which operates in over 75 countries, is a chief presence in the Atacama. In 2016, the Chilean government gave the firm approval to increase its production from the salt flat, provided it could prove that its known reserves could sustain the rising output; minimising the implications for the surrounding environment and communities did not feature as a binding requirement. Both Albemarle and its competitor, SQM, have been accused of extracting more than their legal quotas of water,[23] while the Council of Atacameño Peoples, which represents 18 Indigenous groups in the area, has filed a lawsuit on the grounds that communities did not offer fully free, prior and informed consent for the projects, and has called for the revocation of SQM's licence, which currently extends until 2030.[24] According to the Global Campus of Human Rights, despite Chile's ratification of the International Labour Organisation Convention 169 into domestic law, which specifies protections for tribal groups, no current extractive operators have carried out the requisite consultations with Indigenous peoples in the area.[25] Now, similar operations are expanding into neighbouring regions in

Argentina and Bolivia – extending across the so-called 'Lithium Triangle' – and often leaving similar devastation.

Many of the firms involved assert that they put money back into the communities directly and to the national government's coffers via royalties; however, investigations show their record for doing so is patchy at best.[26] The Chilean government opened arbitration with Albermarle in February 2021, for instance, over its alleged failure to pay millions in royalties to the government. In Argentina, meanwhile, for a joint Canadian-Chilean venture projected to generate $250 million per year in sales, in exchange for rights to land and water in their area, surrounding communities were promised an annual payment between $9,000 and $60,000.[27] When asked about their treatment of local communities and their livelihoods, several firms pointed to their commitment to local economic development. One such initiative was an experiment into whether the area could be used to grow quinoa.[28]

The contrast with the plight of Tiehm's buckwheat in Nevada is stark. It is not, however, surprising. As articulated by Markus Wissen and Ulrich Brand, the maintenance of the enormous demands for materials and environmental sinks for wastes made by the globally affluent has always been predicated on the exploitation of 'elsewheres' – people and regions rendered invisible in global economic production.[29] In the exuberant rush to replace the world's vast vehicle fleet with EVs and its electricity demand with renewables, new elsewheres are being created, expanded and deepened. Critically, these regions and people need not be located across the world from the people whose consumptive demand they support; what matters is not geography, but the assurance of invisibility. While the proposed mine in the region inhabited by Tiehm's buckwheat has been routinely and even permanently stalled by conservationists' staunch and vocal defence of the plant, just a few hours' drive North at Nevada's Thacker Pass, the Paiute and Shoshone tribes' efforts to block a similar lithium mine on their ancestral land have been crushed by the courts.[30] The creation of these domestic 'elsewheres' is neither a new nor an uncommon phenomenon, from the disproportionate placement of toxic heavy industry near Black communities in the United States[31] to children living in poverty in London's Tower Hamlets borough, growing up with lungs 10% smaller than the national average as a result of exposure to concentrated air pollution from adjacent highways.[32] While not new, however, the process is certainly escalating, as demands for resources and sinks become greater and more challenging to meet, amidst the advance of a decarbonisation programme shaped by green capitalism.

As Thea Riofrancos documents, in response to China's 'dense ecosystems of green technology manufacturing and innovation, and its access to the world's raw materials', the United States and the EU have begun to embrace the idea of 'onshoring' the production of the minerals critical to decarbonisation, particularly lithium.[33] However, simply relocating this production does not resolve the issue of unjust or unsustainable extraction. Rather, as Riofrancos argues, 'the United States and EU aren't monoliths. Their populations do not equally benefit from unequal exchange with the Global South – or equally pay the environmental cost of Global North onshoring.'[34] Indeed in 2021, a report found that 79% of lithium reserves and resources in the United States are located within 35 miles of Indigenous reservations.[35] Onshoring this production does not, in and of itself, eliminate environmental harms; at the same time, suddenly abandoning areas whose economies have been reoriented around the mining industry without alternative sources of income risks creating new harms. Rather, as Riofrancos argues, the essential task is creating just and ecologically viable systems of mineral use in a different model altogether. This means ensuring mining practices protect human rights and local ecosystems while, crucially, limiting extraction to supporting those decarbonised infrastructures necessary for collective wellbeing – not exorbitant private consumption.

The proliferation of EVs is a symbol of the green capitalist vision for the future, while the phenomenal demand for mineral resources implied by the growth projections of entities like the International Energy Agency is emblematic of the irresolvable contradictions within it. The invisibility of these social and ecological sites of exploitation is the necessary condition for the rising consumption of the resources, products and sinks they provide. It is also necessary for maintaining the wilful consent for these systems of production by those of us living in more affluent centres. Like the explosion of 'food from nowhere' that defines contemporary globalised agricultural production – rendering invisible the exploitation of migrant workers, horrific cruelty, pesticide pollution of water tables in impoverished communities, or destruction of Ecuadorian mangrove forest to farm shrimp for North American consumption behind the food we buy – so too does ecological modernisation, an essential task of green capitalism, demand the separation of its products from the exploitation underlying them.[36]

The first commandment of green capitalism: maintain

As has been argued throughout this book, at the heart of green capitalism is an effort to defend and minimise disruption to existing economic systems, broad distributions of wealth and power, and institutions amidst the profound challenge posed by ecological crisis. This effort necessarily implies a programme of 'ecological modernisation': decarbonising our profoundly unequal present while preserving, to the best extent possible, the governing logics, structures and infrastructures that sustain it. It also relies on a belief in the enduring prospects of 'green growth'. To use the definition from the Organisation for Economic Co-operation and Development (OECD): green growth is defined by the combined project of improving efficiency while 'stimulating demand for green technologies, goods, and services.'[37] The implications of this vision – replacing rather than reducing private car ownership, maintaining or indeed growing primary energy demand, and beyond – rest on the implicit belief that accumulation and growth can be 'decoupled' not only from carbon emissions, but from material resource demands such as the consumption of lithium.

Support for the possibility of 'green' aggregate economic growth has been in no small part sustained by the fact that, in some high-income economies like the UK, there has been, to an extent, an absolute decoupling of carbon emissions from GDP growth (emissions cease to grow while GDP continues to do so) – rather than just a relative decoupling (emissions grow more slowly than does GDP). Some of this apparent decoupling is the result of 'offshoring' emissions: under certain carbon accounting methods, emissions are attributed to the jurisdiction in which they are produced. The result is that for those countries whose higher emitting industries have largely moved overseas, the emissions associated with products they now import remain off their ledger, even though their citizens create the demand for and consume them. Critically, however, offshoring does not fully negate the partial decoupling observed – suggesting that, to a degree, emissions can be separated in an absolute sense from the engine of expanding GDP.[38] So far, so good for the green capitalist vision of growth divorced from material constraints. Unfortunately, this is where the luck runs out.

A systematic meta-review of hundreds of studies into both relative and absolute decoupling of carbon dioxide emissions from production and consumption confirmed that while select post-industrial economies like the UK showed some small absolute decoupling, even when accounting for emissions from imports, these instances were rare and decoupling effects were weak.[39] Rates of emissions decoupling, even in absolute terms, are slow enough to preclude the possibility for GDP growth to continue at pace while remaining within climate targets.[40] At the global level, evidence of absolute decoupling is absent: between 2000 and 2014, both carbon dioxide emissions and global GDP grew at an average rate of 2.8% per year, in almost perfect lockstep. Even more pronounced is a lack of decoupling from resource and materials use. On a country-by-country basis, evidence shows that GDP growth is the single most important driver of resource consumption; indeed, absolute decreases in resource consumption in recent decades have been demonstrated only during periods of extremely low (near zero) economic growth, or recession.[41] As the global economy has expanded rapidly, so has consumption of materials. Globally, meta-analyses show that material extraction increased by 53% in just over a decade between 2002 and 2015; astonishingly, this means that a third of all materials extraction since 1900 fell within that same brief period.[42] As the European Environmental Bureau writes, when it comes to aggregate materials use, 'the evidence is clear and uncontroversial. There has been no absolute decoupling of resource use from economic growth.'[43]

Against the weight of evidence, several governing bodies including the European Union and major international institutions such as the OECD, World Bank and United Nations Environment Programme remain committed to the possibility – or, more appropriately in some cases, the inevitability – of green growth. Confronted with the threat of firm material limits to expansion, concentrated wealth and accumulation, the concept of green growth has become a necessary tool in the policy effort to minimise disruption to our existing economic model in the face of accelerating climate and ecological damage. Even progressive proposals such as the Green New Deal resolution endorsed by US Representative Ocasio-Cortez are not immune to these risks of injustice – advocating a massive roll-out of renewable energy across the United States while glossing over the potential material implications of this process.[44] Conceptually, the possibility for the existence of genuinely 'green growth', decoupled in absolute terms from both carbon emissions and other material demands and impacts, allows politicians and governing bodies aligned with the interests of capital (a reasonable description of most Northern governments as well as international institutions like the World Bank) to 'obfuscate fundamental tensions among the goals of poverty alleviation, environmental sustainability, and profitable enterprise.'[45] In doing so, it enables them to rhetorically – if not materially – reconcile these potentially competing imperatives.

In short, no governing body or political figure who wishes to remain within the core circles of political influence would openly state (or indeed, may not recognise or admit) their willingness to commit a majority of the world's population to poverty, or else to sacrifice poorer, less developed regions of the world to immiseration and to externalised ecological destruction. However, in committing to addressing ecological crisis through green growth in affluent centres while failing to address global inequalities in wealth, control and the distribution of rights to both consumption and natural 'sinks', this is what they commit to.

A shared inheritance

The tremendous growth in global GDP in recent decades has been accompanied by similarly tremendous ecological devastation. Confronted with this reality, economists have, in the same vein as with carbon, called repeatedly for nature to be economically valued (in other words, to have a price tag), such that damage to it can be internalised to the market. Doing so requires the construction of new frameworks through which to arrive at a dollar value for 'nature'.

Stemming from this demand, the concept of 'natural capital' has been popularised to articulate nature as a source of capital – that is, something which can be put to work for a return. Specifically, natural capital describes the monetary value of 'capital stocks', from mineral resources, to water, soil and species. Some of these, like minerals, are finite and are depleted with use, while others, in theory, are renewable, like fish populations or forests. 'Ecosystem services', meanwhile, describe those services the environment provides to humanity, albeit viewed through the narrow prism of their role in supporting the economy in a way that can be formally quantified and priced. These include a broad range of activities, such as providing fresh air and water, climatic regulation, pest and disease resistance, genetic diversity, nutrient recycling or recreation.

These frameworks are popular already within the private sector, with some $40 billion in transactions for ecosystem services in 2018.[46] Correspondingly, formalising systems for quantifying these values has become a major project in green capitalist governance: the World Bank has been developing and advocating natural capital accounting frameworks virtually since the concept's inception; the UN recently celebrated the adoption of its 'landmark' natural capital accounting framework in its system for economic reporting; the EU has been cementing its own accounting standards for several years; and the UK government has made natural capital accounting a centrepiece of its 25 Year Environment Plan.[47] Before examining the risks of and problems with the natural capital approach, it's worth engaging with the arguments among certain advocates who view natural capital accounting as a necessary framework for achieving a sustainable economy and, perhaps more importantly, for ensuring intergenerational justice.

Among prominent advocates of natural capital accounting is Dieter Helm, whose book on the subject details the need for natural capital accounting in ensuring long-term economic sustainability. In making this case, staunch green capitalists might find Helm to be a strange bedfellow on certain critical points, namely his uncompromising aversion to using GDP growth as a measure for prosperity and an economic objective. For Helm, the essential and insurmountable problem with GDP growth as a central economic indicator is its complete omission of how the 'assets' on the planetary balance sheet – that is, 'natural capital' – are being used and (more often than not) depleted in service of that growth. Because it is focused on a transient flow of income, GDP offers no information as to how we can ensure those living in the future can be as well or better off. As Helm puts it: 'We could have a giant party by depleting the Earth's resources as fast as possible. GDP would correspondingly look very impressive. But then would come the day of reckoning.'[48] For Helm, natural capital accounting is the only solution to this problem. Specifically, he advocates that total natural capital is maintained in the aggregate, meaning 'for every new bit of damage, there has to be a compensating increase in renewable natural capital elsewhere',[49] such as forest cover, with the goal of ensuring a stable supply for future generations.

Elsewhere, researchers Rahul Basu and Scott Pegg have made the case that for finite resources in particular, natural capital accounting can ensure that these supplies are treated as a 'shared inheritance' among current and future generations.[50] Similarly to Helm, the authors argue that GDP-based accounting treats the exploitation of a finite resource, such as a mineral deposit, as a net positive, without correspondingly marking down the value of the depleted asset on the (hypothetical) balance sheet. In this sense, they argue a natural capital accounting framework would eliminate the extraction of finite resources as a productive contribution to GDP. By instead treating it as the liquidation of an asset, they argue, implementing a natural capital framework could help distribute resource use more fairly between generations.

It is in the question of how to ensure distributional justice over time – reflecting both past exploitation and responsibility to future generations – that natural capital accounting has the potential to be used for more radical ends. As Patrick Bond and Rahul Basu describe, natural capital accounts applied to non-renewable resources – including fossil fuels – could better reflect the injustice of 'unequal ecological exchange', both geographically and intergenerationally. In other words, the extent to which the exploitation of fossil fuel resources by preceding generations and wealthier economies represents the exhaustion of a finite resource as well as an ecological 'debt' in the form of climate change could be accounted for through a natural capital framework, such that resources could be shared and stewarded more justly and sustainably, including minerals demanded by decarbonisation.[51]

Both these cases (a necessarily small sample of a larger ecosystem of proposals) hinge on the idea that natural capital accounting can provide the architecture for a better stewardship of our common gifts, particularly between generations, by allowing us to properly 'value' nature and its resources, as well as to internalise the cost of its use or degradation to the market and our accounts. Underlying both is the implicit assumption that – regardless of one's position on the merits of market-based solutions – within existing constraints, doing so is the pragmatic solution to resource stewardship: it provides the most efficient route for conservation, while providing the opportunity to formalise a justice-based approach that will facilitate fair outcomes. Indeed, ecological economist Herman Daly recognised this 'subversive potential' in natural capital accounting more than 25 years ago during his tenure at the World Bank. Daly, like Helm, advocated for the exploitation of natural capital stocks to no longer be tallied as income without also logging a corresponding debit on the balance sheet to represent capital depletion. For Daly, doing so implied a necessary transition away from the neoliberal 'ideology of global economic integration by free trade, free capital mobility, and export-led growth.'[52]

Effectively and fairly stewarding nature and resources while counter-acting the harmful impacts of economic globalisation are goals with which I am, unsurprisingly, closely aligned. Furthermore, in resolving the question of how to determine the scope of climate and ecological reparations or Loss & Damage, or in certain specific cases such as management of finite mineral resources as Basu and Pegg propose, properly accounting for these resources' unsustainable depletion through a natural capital framework may prove useful or necessary. However, in their use thus far, the subversive potential Daly and others have identified has quickly fallen apart in confrontation with the realities of financialised global capitalism – its accumulative drive, its ruthless innovativeness in finding new means for externalising costs, the immediate prospects for securitisation and speculative activity invited by new assets and forms of capital – and, critically, with the profound complexity of our planet's natural systems and their integration with social values. Helm is fond of referring to many variants of ecological activist – particularly those within the burgeoning 'de-growth' movement – as 'utopian', in contrast to the ostensible pragmatism of the natural capital approach.[53] However, by his own definition, as the sections that follow argue, attempting to collapse nature into discrete units of monetary value is the utopia: 'at best a distraction, and at worst an excuse for not engaging with the world as it is.'[54]

The second commandment: accumulate

If the first objective of green capitalism – that of broadly preserving existing structures, systems and distributions in the transition to a decarbonised economy – requires the consistently escalating appropriation not only of the labour but also the land, resources and nature of 'elsewheres', the second – the pursuit of new domains for accumulation – risks doing so even more acutely. As the second chapter explored, carbon markets are reliant on capturing land and ecologies such as forests and wetlands to service the demand for emissions in the form of an 'offset'. The premise of the transaction is, as discussed, ecologically problematic. But beyond this, a fundamental and irreconcilable contradiction underlying the idea is capitalism's fundamental drive to create externalities, with profit-seeking firms reliant on ever more inventive means of externalising the true costs of their activities. Consequently, in seeking to 'internalise' carbon emissions currently unpriced by the market, carbon markets are generating a cascade of new externalities through the appropriation of land, nature and livelihoods.

The problem capitalism now faces is that it is running out of people, places and ecosystems on which to offload these externalities. Of all habitable land on Earth, 40% has been diverted to raising livestock.[55] Since 1970, there has been a 70% decline in average populations of wild mammals, birds, reptiles and amphibians, with a quarter of all plant and animal species now facing extinction.[56] Widespread tree planting programmes baked in to existing net zero targets could subject up to 40 million more people to chronic hunger by 2050.[57] In recent years, the urgent reality of ecological decline has begun to feature on the horizons of green capitalist actors, from the private sector to governing institutions: in 2020, insurance firm Swiss Re published a report showing that a fifth of countries are at risk of teetering into ecosystem collapse, threatening the $42 trillion in global GDP they estimated to be dependent on thriving biodiversity and ecosystems.[58]

Like carbon before it, within these profound environmental pressures lies both a threat to be minimised, as well as a new opportunity for accumulation. As per Swiss Re, which created an index of biodiversity for the market: 'using Swiss Re Institute's BES Index as a basis for decision-making in underwriting and asset management will make businesses and investments more resilient ... and will create a new business segment for insurance.'[59] Creating this new arena for profit-making, however, requires several transformations, novel methodologies and conceptual shifts to enable the market to penetrate the unknowable complexity of the natural world and segment it into units whose value can be appraised and, critically, exchanged.[60]

The idea of applying market mechanisms to conservation is not new: under George H.W. Bush, markets were established to trade in wetland conservation credits under a newly minted principle of 'No Net Loss'.[61] At the 1992 Rio Earth Summit, the Convention on Biological Diversity opened the door to market-based approaches to conservation, while so-called 'debt-for-nature' swaps, in which debtor states agreed to conservation efforts in exchange for debt relief, began as early as 1987. In 1997, economists published a now seminal figure for the value of global nature, estimated at roughly $33 trillion per year based on the various ways in which 'nature' supported the functioning of the economy (defined as 'natural capital' and 'ecosystem services').[62] Looming above all these efforts has been the need to agree on a unified framework for quantifying the economic value offered by the biosphere. From these processes, the twin pillars of natural capital and ecosystem services have emerged.

Not unlike the argument for a price on carbon, many advocates of the natural capital approach rightfully denounce a lack of political will to conserve or restore natural systems, as well as the failure for ecologically destructive economic activity to be penalised. Prominent economists today admit that treating the economy as a closed entity distinct from the environment, wherein nature features only as an input, has created the conditions for its increasingly unsustainable exploitation and unimpeded negative externalities.[63] Up to this point, I am in close agreement with these advocates. Where we diverge is in the commitment to the idea that by internalising the costs of ecological damage, the market is where the solution to ecological crisis will be found. I should note that some of the foremost figures within this developing programme willingly admit that the distillation of the complexity of biodiversity and ecosystems into discrete services and capital may feel intuitively strange, or neglect some of the emotional and spiritual connection many of us have with it. In his landmark 600-page review on the economics of biodiversity, for example, prominent economist Partha Dasgupta argues 'Nature is more than a mere economic good. Nature nurtures and nourishes us, so we will think of assets as durable entities that not only have use value, but *may also have intrinsic worth*' (emphasis added).[64]

Primarily, however, the representation of nature and ecosystems in the terms of natural capital and ecosystem services is presented as a politically neutral, pragmatic shift: because nature does not have a price, we fail to value it. To 'save' nature, then, it must have a price. Better still, the price mechanism offers the most efficient route to doing so. As Neil Smith articulates, the construction of nature and its various benefits – biodiversity, thriving ecosystems, clean air and water – as exchangeable commodities addresses the fundamental demands of the neoliberal perspective: its faux depoliticisation; its 'substitution of private market economic measurement for social calculation;

and its insistence that anything of social worth must be tradable in the global market.'[65] However, contrary to these apolitical representations, the adoption of the natural capital and eco-system services frame is a profound conceptual and ideological shift. Ostensibly 'neutral' calculations of the dollar values of fresh water, biodiversity or forests obscure the countless political decisions and assumptions required to parse the complexity of the biosphere to a list of services it can provide the economy, and erases all those values deemed irrelevant to the calculus.

Non-fungible natures

Through this conceptual shift – the creation of natural 'assets' and ecosystem 'services' – new opportunities for profit making are created under the heading of 'conservation'. In this sense, the widespread take-up of natural capital and ecosystem service frameworks by numerous governing institutions is a major ideological victory for the advance of green capitalism. It represents a decisive shift from the mere domination and exploitation of nature – a tendency which, unchecked, increasingly threatened capitalism's ability to reproduce itself – to the 'production' of nature.[66] To put it another way, by breaking ecosystems and the surrounding environment into discrete, costed units, it has become possible to remake 'nature' on an unprecedented scale by concretising a system for directing our efforts to 'conserve' or 'restore' it toward the highest yielding assets and services, to the neglect of the rest. From a democratic perspective, this is deeply problematic, insofar as socially and politically fraught decisions about what to protect and restore are insulated from democratically articulated values, and are transferred instead to the will of the market's invisible hand. From an ecological perspective, it is a nonsense, setting us on a path toward a possible future of pristine mono-species forests– a sanitised idyll worthy of a theme park, and devoid of the ability to sustain diverse life.

To square the circle of converting complex ecosystems to quantifiable assets and services requires a set of abstractions, assumptions and willing avoidance of ecological fact. Ecologists will be the first to admit that the constituents and dynamics of many ecological systems are poorly and incompletely understood; indeed, estimates for the number of unique species on the planet range from 5.3 million to 1 trillion – an astonishing degree of uncertainty.[67] The prevailing estimate is closer to 8.7 million; to date, we have identified and named just over 1.6 million of these, leaving roughly 80% unknown.[68] To borrow from Eric Neumayer: 'our knowledge about the extent and the likely consequences of large scale biodiversity destruction resembles more a situation of ignorance than of uncertainty.'[69]

Our ignorance is even more evident when it comes to efforts to restore and regenerate damaged ecosystems, for which evidence suggests that conserving intact ecosystems, rather than damaging and later attempting to repair them, is far more effective.[70] Despite this, the natural accounting approach advances four basic assumptions in order to separate and quantify the capital and services the biosphere offers: fungibility, substitutability, rivalry and excludability. To be considered fungible, the units of a particular good, such as two redwoods in a forest, must be readily interchangeable. Substitutability, by contrast, implies that two or more entities can be substituted for one another, insofar as they have certain comparable traits. Rivalry in the economic sense implies that the use or consumption of an entity removes the ability for another to do so, while excludability implies the possibility of limiting others' access to the good or service.[71] Through combinations of these assumed traits, the biosphere can be readily segmented and 'unbundled' into discrete units which can subsequently be individually valued, speculated upon, and exchanged, abstracted entirely from the specifics of time and place.[72]

However, while deconstructing ecosystems into their constituent services and capital stocks may enable better accounting, if the purported goal is to sustain and indeed restore an increasingly threatened biosphere, this is an exercise (likely difficult and labour-intensive) in futility. As the experience of German forestry science recounted in Chapter 1 made clear, when it comes to natural systems, desirable traits or constituent elements cannot be readily abstracted from the ecological whole of which they are part. To borrow from James C. Scott, while the severity with which the variables not of immediate interest to the forest scientists were 'bracketed' out is what gave the experiment its supposed rigour, ultimately 'a whole world lying "outside the brackets" return[ed] to haunt this technical vision.'[73] Efforts to quantify discrete elements of the biosphere for their conversion into priced units suffer from this same inescapable limitation. As Sian Sullivan argues, market-based approaches to conserving and restoring ecosystems 'sanction habitat loss through development transformations by decoupling the distinctiveness of nonhuman natures from the geographical locales in which they occur' – in other words, by artificially separating out elements of an often-indivisible whole.[74]

It should come as no surprise, based on the inappropriateness of these methods, that the track record of conservation mechanisms based upon them is difficult to defend. One such 'innovations' is 'biodiversity offsetting', though the divisiveness of the term has meant that it now operates under many pseudonyms, including the increasingly popular umbrella of 'nature-based solutions'. Biodiversity offsetting – in practice if not always in name – has been a relatively common practice for several years, allowing developers and firms who claim that their proposed projects cannot avoid the partial or full destruction of an ecosystem to 'offset' this damage. Frameworks for doing so have generally taken the approach of asking developers to first try to avoid or minimise this damage; however, for those residual harms that cannot be avoided, a biodiversity offset allows for the creation of a new 'equivalent' habitat for the species under threat to replace the ecosystem damaged by the project.

To date, these processes have also tended to involve requirements regarding proximity to the original site and the date of destruction, obviating the need for detailed natural capital and ecosystem services accounting. As such, their use has, until recently, been relatively piecemeal, mandating corporations to pay developers to plant a stand of the same species of trees nearby to a forest they just razed, rather than a global strategy for preserving the biosphere. Nonetheless, where they have been implemented, their record of success has been almost impressively poor. In Australia, a review of biodiversity offsetting by the NGO Nature Conservation Council found that in six out of eight cases, offsets resulted in 'Poor' or 'Disastrous' outcomes for wildlife and bushland, while just two resulted in 'Adequate' outcomes. None resulted in 'Good' outcomes.[75] An even more damning evaluation of over 500 offset projects by the Nordic Council of Ministers (an intergovernmental forum of the Nordic states) found that offsetting resulted in a 99% loss of habitat in areas under study.[76]

Despite this track record, political support for, and implementation of, these mechanisms is on the rise. Moreover, within this increasingly popular agenda, the advent of natural capital and ecosystem service accounting frameworks has been seized on to transform the comparatively basic (albeit flawed) form of biodiversity offsetting outlined above into a machine of commodification and financial speculation. Within the European Union, over the past decade the concept of 'habitat banking' has been advanced by several member states as a solution to ecological decline. Unlike the biodiversity offset projects described in the preceding paragraph, which required like-for-like compensation of lost habitat within as close temporal and geographical proximity as feasible, within the banking framework, using natural capital and ecosystem services accounting, offsets can be either like-for-like or like-for-better, defined not in terms of ecological but of monetary equivalence. The concept relies, in other words, on strict adherence to the idea that different ecosystems or species are substitutable, provided the services and capital they provide are equivalent in monetary value.

While the adoption of the framework within the EU has been routinely stalled by resistance based on its total lack of grounding in science and its consequent certainty of severely exacerbating ecosystem loss, the proposal has by no means been abandoned, and has also been picked up elsewhere. In the summer of 2021, the UK government awarded a grant to a habitat banking scheme whose proprietors celebrated their unleashed potential to 'enable habitats to be created or restored before any biodiversity loss is caused by developments.'[77] According to the scheme's proprietors, this approach is 'much better news for nature' – though any clarity or evidence as to why this is the case was not offered. As the abject failure of existing biodiversity offset schemes demonstrate with devastating clarity, offsetting is rarely, if ever, good news for nature.

Indeed, the ability to 'bank' the creation of new ecosystems prior to development proposals bears the considerable risk of encouraging demand for offsets that may otherwise have been avoided.

Financialised nature

The idea that ecosystems and biodiversity can be 'produced' in this way opens up vast new terrains for the expansion of capital into the natural world. For no industry has this proven more appealing than finance, which has seized upon the speculative prospects of this new frontier. Over recent years, financial firms and products have sprung up dedicated to new natural assets: EKO Asset Management Partners, for example, which was founded in 2008 before merging with another firm, described itself as 'a specialised investment firm focused on discovering and monetizing unrealized or unrecognized environmental assets.'[78] According to the firm's now defunct website, they sought investing opportunities in 'land with undeveloped or unrecognised environmental assets with a view to developing these assets and profiting from their sale in emerging environmental markets.'[79] In the summer of 2021, the fund management arm of French banking giant, BNP Paribas, launched its 'Ecosystem Restoration' fund, which offers investors 'exposure to companies engaged in the restoration and preservation of global ecosystems and natural capital',[80] while other firms have made a business of 'design[ing] solutions for public and private investors willing to invest in nature-based solutions.'[81] Real estate investors have also shown interest in the opportunities provided by environmental markets for 'developing' land in new ways, as well as the cash flows to be generated from creating or restoring (even if ineffectually) habitats and biodi-versity. The 'Real Wild Estates' initiative, for example, aims to bring together 'visionary investors and landholders' as well as high net worth individuals and private wealth management firms to 'bio-diversify and future-proof their investments.'[82]

Indeed, as soon as nature began to be parcelled into assets, finance found mechanisms for 'securitising' these, bundling their promises of future financial flows into new financial assets. For instance, in 2009, a team of researchers proposed that the occupants of service and natural capital-rich land in low-income countries could mortgage the value associated with this capital, using it as collateral for credit products from investors.[83] These proposals have since ventured a step further into the realm of financial derivatives. As outlined in Chapter 2, derivatives are meant to allow investors to 'hedge' against the risk of price movements: by owning both an asset, hoping its value appreci-ates, and a derivative, which promises a pay-out if the value declines, an investor can mitigate the risk of losses from price movements. In the case of derivatives like 'futures' contracts on oil, derivatives are meant to achieve a balance between sellers' hopes for rising prices and consumers' demand for them to fall. In practice, derivatives have also become a vehicle for specula-tion on those same movements in price, and their proliferation has often been accompanied by increasing volatility in prices.[84] The logic of their application to species and ecosystem conser-vation is thus highly suspect.

Advocates for creating 'biodiversity derivatives' argue that governments could offer 'modified derivatives contracts [that] sell species' extinction risk to market investors and stakehold-ers', and in doing so take 'advantage of the market to reduce costs in conservation.'[85] The contracts would be priced in part based on the likelihood of species decline, with the implication that species at greater risk of extinction would be considered more valuable. In theory, these contracts could 'create markets around biodiversity conservation, providing an insurance policy against species jeopardy while also providing incentives for environmental stewardship.'[86] In practice, we have to ask whether cost efficiency, in partnership with the risk of conservation funding tied to speculative price volatility, is at all a reasonable or effective approach to conservation – particularly when the mechanism could simply promote the protection of 'high value' species at risk of extinction in lieu of holistic biodiversity. The derivatives market for agricultural commodities offers sobering lessons in this respect, with high levels of speculative activity contributing to a food price crisis in 2007–8.[87] Beyond volatility, as Frédéric Hache of the Green Finance Observatory argues, the decision to single out only specific ecosystem services or species and ignore complex ecological interdependencies, 'greatly improves the cost-effectiveness of the market, but at the cost of environmental integrity and ... the creation of new externalities', alongside new financial risks.[88]

Unknowable nature

Ultimately, the case for market mechanisms in conservation, from quantifying ecosystem services to markets in biodiversity offsetting and derivatives, rests on the significant assumption that market incentives are either inherently superior to direct regulation of environmental challenges, or in the very least necessary because regulation has failed to emerge. In other words, let the perfect not be the enemy of the good – even a too low carbon price or a volatile species value is better than doing nothing. Are these assertions valid? For a market system to support ecologically effective rather than simply least-cost stewardship and restoration of ecosystems and biodiversity, in the very least the units being exchanged in the market should have some relationship to underlying ecological systems and needs. This implies that accounting frameworks for establishing the value of different 'ecosystem services' and natural capital 'stocks' can and must have a high degree of equivalence to their ecological importance. On their own, the non-substitutability of species and ecological phenomena alongside their abstraction from the complexity and interconnectedness of the systems in which they're situated make this a virtual impossibility. Despite this, methodologies have been developed that attempt to do so.

The prevailing techniques for establishing the value of ecological 'goods and services' rely on approaches related to consumer preferences and other proxy values. The former might include valuations based on, for instance, how much individuals would be willing to pay to travel to an ecologically rich area or how much more they would be willing to pay for a house in an area with clean air relative to – all other things being equal – polluted air, known as 'revealed preferences'. Stated preferences, meanwhile, involve simply asking individuals how much they would be willing to pay to preserve, say, an old growth forest. Otherwise, proxy values might be determined based on opportunity cost, according to which the value of preserving an area of land for forest instead of converting it to agricultural use implies the forest is at least equivalent to what the property would be worth if farmed. With respect to appraising the value (monetary or otherwise) of the environment, these might sound ludicrously simplistic. However, they are widely used: the stated preference method was, notoriously, a basis for determining the value of damages from the 1989 Exxon Valdez oil spill.[89] Similarly, the REMEDE toolkit, an early project in this area funded by the European Commission, provided guidance for determining the damages of a polluted river based on the lost revenue from fishing trips.[90] In effect, it's difficult to see how these methods, in combination with the problems inherent to separating ecological systems into apparently discrete units of value, could ever provide a representative figure of the value of the natural world even in purely economic terms – let alone their intrinsic worth.

Depoliticised nature

At the core of neoliberal thought is the argument that the global economy is so complex as to render any attempts to plan or even fully measure it futile, giving birth to the price system as the ideal arbiter of information. There is a certain irony to be found in the fact that the same humility about the inherent unknowability of the biosphere and the dazzling web of life-forms within it is distinctly absent. There is also irony in the fact that the enormous effort required to fully quantify natural capital and ecosystem services and agree unified methods for their trade in newly constructed markets is likely to be immeasurably more complex than the supposedly bulky direct regulatory approach it is meant to avoid.

The construction of novel markets for nature and biodiversity is an enormous project, from the development of agreed methodologies to the creation and monitoring of the architectures of exchange. Despite this, an implicit argument underlying the supposed pragmatism of market-based approaches is the idea that so-called 'command-and-control' regulation is politically and bureaucratically expensive, requiring a vast state apparatus for enforcement and maintenance that is prone to error – something markets help to avoid. However, these assertions of markets' simplicity and efficiency obscure the considerable workings of the state in both constructing and maintaining them. Nor are market-based approaches immune to becoming mired in the thorniness of political lobbying and obstruction.

The European Union's effort to establish a 'green taxonomy' for what is considered a sustainable investment asset has been a years-long and politically fraught process. Lobbying has watered down the framework so extensively as to make it an almost meaningless definition, with fossil gas power plants designated as 'green' despite contributing to fossil fuel infrastructure lock-in and an outsized contribution to highly potent methane emissions.[91] To argue for constructing markets to address ecological crisis, then, requires adherence to one of two positions. First is a genuine commitment to the belief, as articulated above, that despite all evidence to the contrary, constructing artificial markets for trade in artificial commodities like ecosystem services or carbon emissions is necessarily more bureaucratically and legislatively streamlined than traditional regulation. Alternatively, in line with the neoliberal view of government's purpose, legislative effort and bureaucratic complexity are worthwhile – welcome, even – so long as they are in service of new arenas for marketisation. Better still if doing so can shift the locus of decision-making power out of the political and democratically contestable domain and into the private authority of the market.

The idea that private control over and ownership of land and nature is the only way to protect it from over-exploitation has a long history. Indeed, the 'tragedy of the commons' is by now a cliché, with its implication widely internalised: commonly shared resources are doomed, by the self-interested nature of humankind, to be destroyed. The concept has its popular roots in a now seminal (if often misrepresented) 1968 paper by Garrett Hardin, exemplified through a thought experiment based on farmers' assumed tendency to overuse a shared pasture;[92] over time, the intuitive appeal of the idea has enabled it to permeate common sense. It has been evoked time and again as evidence of the need for private property rights over common resources and for pricing nature. The paper, however, relies on the premise that the only possibilities for governing commons are lawlessness – giving rise to inevitable tragedy and ruin – or substantial coercive control. For advocates of the market-based approach, this can be resolved by the power of the price signal.[93]

The idea that there are no alternative systems was later refuted in Elinor Ostrom's *Governing the Commons*, which empirically evaluated several cases of alternative commons governance structures, finding them overwhelmingly effective in stewarding shared resources. A more recent review of over 80,000 land acquisitions published in *Nature* similarly called the supposed ecological superiority of private control over natural resources into question, finding that in the vast majority of cases, exclusive purchases – whether made by private companies or foreign governments – resulted not in robust stewardship as a by-product of self-interest, but rather in accelerated deforestation, biodiversity loss and negative outcomes for local communities.[94] There is no silver-bullet method for collective stewardship of common resources; Ostrom herself advocated for a diversity of methods unique to local needs and conditions. What is clear is that market-based approaches for doing so are far from guaranteed to be effective in protecting or restoring thriving ecosystems, and even less likely to do in a way that is just.

The turn to market-based solutions for the most complex and urgent challenges of our time can thus be viewed as a metastatic advance of neoliberal instincts – an adherence to the idea that the state's role should be limited to facilitating functioning markets, rather than seeking (and, in the view of neoliberals, inevitably failing) to achieve specific goals. In the proliferation of carbon markets, a significant degree of public, democratic prerogative was handed to the private authority of firms. The diffusion of natural capital, 'ecosystem services', and the blur of financial products these frameworks support will only further this process. These approaches are in keeping with the onward march of the Wall Street Consensus explored in Chapter 4. Indeed, a recent influential report endorsed by the likes of Mark Carney, Michael Bloomberg and Kristalina Georgieva, the managing director of the IMF, lays the ground-work for markets in natural capital and ecosystem services to serve as the core tools for global conservation efforts, envision-ing 'de-risking' approaches and 'financial innovations' to shep-herd private capital into new nature-based asset classes.[95] Here again, the effect of the Wall Street Consensus will be to transfer the governance of a common and public good to private, profit-motivated authority, while using public investing capacity to guarantee investors' profits.

Neo-colonial nature

The extraction of resources like fossil fuels and lithium from the Global South has long been understood as a neo-colonial project, insofar as these processes of exchange enable wealthy and primarily Northern countries to exploit the resource wealth of the South for their desired purposes, enforced through the architectures of international trade and finance explored in Chapter 5. The creation of 'nature-based solutions', biodiversity offsets, and markets in ecological 'services' is a new frontier along which these processes can operate. At the same time, new financial products, such as the 'sovereign green bonds' with interest rates pegged to achieving climate and environmental outcomes recently proposed in Uruguay, open up the possibility for transferring sovereignty over the governance of nature to private investors. At a glance, this may sound like an appealing model, both in terms of obtaining financing for and enforcing governments' environmental targets.[96] In practice however, this mechanism risks creating new avenues through which private investors can discipline sovereign governments, particularly of low-income states, and in doing so 'entangle environmental management strategies with the unpredictable play of competing profitable domains of speculative investment and hedging activity.'[97] In the world of rising private investor ownership of poorer countries' sovereign debt, the financialisation of ecological conservation therefore represents a pathway toward further neo-colonial control. The world's dominant capitalist economies are haunted by climate and ecological crisis. They confront systemic financial risks, risks to profitability and aggregate growth, and ultimately to their reproduction. But they are also haunted by the recognition that addressing these risks is increasingly a balancing act between exploiting the land, labour and resources of 'elsewheres' for the conventionally profitable ventures of extraction and production, and their use as sinks to sustain the wastes and impacts of ever-greater demand and consumption, whether carbon emissions, biodiversity loss, or the disruption of ecological resilience, from crop failure to disease. Until recently, the latter has been outside the realm of the market.

Internalising ecological degradation to the market is, within the logics and economic principles of green capitalism, the necessary, if not inevitable, route to achieving this balance. In doing so, the logic goes, threats from a climate and biosphere on the brink can be mitigated, while profitability and expansion can, instead of being hindered by ecological limits, simply be transplanted to new domains. However, as with (and indeed frequently overlapping with) the carbon pricing and offsetting regimes that came before them, these efforts at internalisation create a devastating mix of new externalities for both ecosystems and people throughout the world.

In short, to maintain itself, green capitalism in globally affluent centres requires the appropriation of nature elsewhere. This condition is exemplified through, for example, the issuance of 'green' or 'climate bonds' – typically certified by finance industry-funded NGOs in the Global North – to finance ecologically destructive projects. For example, a bond issuance to support the Bolsonaro government's plan for building a grain transporting railway through the heart of the Amazon recently received a stamp of approval from the London-based civil society organisation Climate Bonds Initiative, despite staunch resistance from Indigenous communities in the area and clear destructive impacts on the Amazon rainforest's biodiversity.[98] The creation of biodiversity offsetting regimes and markets, meanwhile, is a pathway to cordoning off land and ecologies for conservation credits to service the consumption and wealth accumulation of the globally affluent. In many instances, these initiatives have driven land grabs and forced expulsion, or undermined the livelihoods of subsistence farmers. Among the Baiga people of central India, biodiversity offset programmes have conscripted local farmers into planting mono-species teak plantations, forcefully fencing off residents' access to the fields on which they had based their livelihoods.[99] In Madagascar, meanwhile, global mining giant Rio Tinto purchased a forest to offset the ecological damage of one of its mines, in the process excluding local people from accessing the previously common forest.[100]

This is neo-colonialism in its most distilled form: the forcible transfer of sovereignty from the people who occupy the land to those with sufficient monetary and coercive power to ensure it is used in their interest. In the process, the inhabitants of these natural capital-rich or service-producing areas – overwhelmingly Indigenous or subsistence farming communities in 'underdeveloped' regions of the Global South – are reduced to 'service providers' or custodians for the demands of the global economy.[101] Proposals like the 'Global Deal for Nature' – which advocates sequestering 30% of the Earth for nature by 2030 (with an additional 20% designated to 'climate stabilisation') and is backed by a coalition of 50 countries as well as countless conservation organisations – arrive cloaked in the amenable and necessary ambition of preserving and restoring the biosphere. In doing so, they evade the essential questions: which land? Where?

There is, unquestionably, an urgent need to halt the destruction of the ecosystems and lifeforms that remain, and the science underlying the Global Deal reflects the best understanding of how to relieve the immense pressures we have placed on the biosphere which ultimately sustains us. However, by advocating land simply be set aside for 'nature' rather than 'human activities', the Global Deal obscures, deliberately or otherwise, that this selective production of nature is in support of the continuation of particular types of human activities, for particular people.[102]

What's the value of a whale?

The ability for the commodification and financialisation of nature to creep, silently, across the agendas of the world's governing bodies and institutions is the legacy of a profound and deepening alienation from it. For generations of capitalist development, the embodied reality of the natural environment has been abstracted away, rendered to a spectral form which features only as a metabolic input. As a result of this enforced blindness, the environment in which we are so precariously situated has been pushed to such an extreme that the ghost has once again taken solid form, pushing against the exuberance of concentrated accumulation and unequal expansion. Ahead of us are two diverging roads. Along one, explored further in the conclusion, is a confrontation with the illusions, injustices and inherent instability of the economic systems that presently govern and mould life on Earth. Along the second is the entrenchment of those prevailing systems. It's a future in which sections of this planet and its inhabitants are claimed by, or sacrificed in service of maintaining, our unequal present. And it's a future in which those things we save from a rapidly disappearing world are solely those natural 'assets' and 'services' we deem billable. Perhaps, in this future calculus, $2 million for a whale will make their conservation a worthy investment – or at least those subspecies whose combined financial contributions to eco-tourism and carbon sequestration are the greatest. Or perhaps, situated within an ever-expanding ledger of abstracted values, $2 million each will simply be deemed too costly relative to other expenditures. Perhaps whales, too, are destined to become ghosts.

Between the devil and the deep blue sea: should we accept green capitalist solutions?

> The risk of Armageddon has risen dramatically. Stay bullish on stocks over the next twelve months. –BCA Global Investment Solutions[1]
>
> The child in each of us knows paradise. –Octavia Butler[2]

In February 2022, the Intergovernmental Panel on Climate Change published its latest summary of the impacts of our rapidly changing climate. It is a vast document, reaching nearly 3,700 pages compiling all available evidence on the myriad transformations, insecurities and catastrophes both looming on the horizon and already affecting many around the world. In thousands of pages of scientific findings, it might be easy for essential points to be lost. Fortunately, the report's final line offers no shortage of clarity: 'The cumulative scientific evidence is unequivocal … Any further delay in concerted anticipatory global action on adaptation and mitigation will miss a brief and rapidly closing window of opportunity to secure a liveable and sustainable future for all (*very high confidence*).'[3] This was not the only revelation buried in the report's pages. For the first time,

the IPCC acknowledged the role of the private sector in foment-
ing not only misinformation on the climate crisis, but another
phenomenon, which it termed 'maladaptation'. In the words
of the report's authors, maladaptation describes those actions
that may be designed to help mitigate or adapt to a changing climate, but in doing so 'lead to increased risk of adverse
climate-related outcomes, including via increased greenhouse
gas emissions, increased or shifted vulnerability to climate
change, more inequitable outcomes, or diminished welfare,
now or in the future.' Whether by compromising livelihoods or
accelerating biodiversity loss, maladaptive responses 'can create
lock-ins of vulnerability, exposure and risks that are difficult
and expensive to change and exacerbate existing inequalities'.
In most cases, the authors argue, maladaptation is likely to be
an 'unintended consequence'.[4] In a sense, the authors described
(unintentionally or otherwise) the trouble with green capitalism.

This book began with a question: how is it that we remain
so off course for meeting even the outer limits of safety when it
comes to the climate and nature crises? Throughout the chapters that followed, I have tried to sketch an answer, the details
of which fell broadly into one of two categories: the systems,
ideas and political-legal architectures that facilitate deepening
inequality and, as a consequence, ecological harm; and the
false or maladaptive solutions that stem from them. However,
in the effort to answer the original question, a second, persistent one has emerged: given the urgency of the context and the
weight of politics supporting the systems and ideas underlying
the green capitalist framework – should we accept green capitalist solutions? Is something – anything – better than nothing?
If, in curbing emissions or protecting biodiversity, some financiers and development firms make an exorbitant profit, is that

really so big a problem as to merit scrapping the whole project? We live in a society structured and defined by capitalist relations, and the idea that market-based solutions are the best and most pragmatic path to resolving most problems is powerfully ingrained common sense. Asset management firms and other large corporate interests have outsized power in shaping the perspectives of governments and international institutions. This makes any programme for confronting these interests an uphill battle, which must advance across incredibly unfavourable terrain. At the same time, ecological crisis – as I have repeated perhaps too often throughout these pages – is at every turn advancing along the fastest trajectories scientists have offered. Time is not a luxury we can afford. If the entirety of this book thus far has been devoted to answering the questions I first posed – namely, how did we get here? Why are we *still* here? – in what remains I'll do my best to answer the second: should we accept green capitalist solutions?

To answer this question, it first helps to establish criteria for what constitutes a 'solution' worth pursuing. Throughout this book I have evaluated green capitalist solutions against what I believe to be two essential criteria. The first, with which I'm confident anyone concerned with ecological crisis will agree, is that a solution must have a material impact: it must actually slow or reverse the industrial flow of emissions into the atmosphere or the collapse of biodiversity; failing this, it must reduce vulnerability to the impacts of these processes or contribute to adaptation. Crucially, it must accomplish one of these tasks on a timescale that reflects the urgency of accelerating ecological crisis. Second, and perhaps more divisively, it must contribute to necessarily radical shifts in the distributions of wealth, consumption and power in the global economy. As I have previously argued, this isn't a question of equality or justice in a moralising sense. Both of these are worth pursuing in their own right. To many (myself included), this makes meeting them a necessarily high bar for any approach to addressing these challenges. However, even for those interested solely in the question of effectiveness – that is, does a solution reduce emissions or ecological degradation – achieving these, as has been argued throughout this book, is also a practical necessity.

The evidence that affluent consumption is the primary driver of ecological crisis is expansive.[5] While technological progress has, to date, produced some reductions in material throughput and waste, these gains have been entirely negated by rising consumption.[6] However, while affluent consumption matters in absolute terms, inequalities in these patterns of consumption and waste are just as critical. In part, this reflects the 'zero-sum game' of rising consumption: relative income is one of the strongest determinants of happiness, with the result that the forms and rates of consumption that signal one's position are driven overwhelmingly by the super-affluent, and in turn drive consumption up across the board with diminishing returns to wellbeing.[7] The need to address these inequalities also reflects the deepening extent to which the nature and scale of consumption and waste among the affluent demands 'cheap' and invisible land, resources and labour – whether this is dumping industrial refuse near communities of colour or shipping hundreds of containers of plastic waste from Canadian consumers to be dealt with by Malaysian labourers.[8] In this sense, the 'freedom' implied by consumption and choice within markets ultimately rests on the profound unfreedom of countless others, kept just out of sight. This is a strategy that is reaching the end of its road. The supply of these invisible people, ecologies and dumping sites for waste is rapidly dwindling.[9] Indeed, as Jason Moore argues: 'The end of cheap garbage may loom larger than the end of cheap resources.'[10] These then, are my criteria for evaluating any approach to confronting ecological crisis. The first assures we secure a present and a future that are safe and habitable. The second does this as well, while also trying to make that future one worth living in.

Do green capitalist solutions work?

As this book has consistently argued, the primary argument invoked in favour of market-based solutions to climate and ecological crisis is cost efficiency. Considerably less attention tends to be devoted to the urgent question of whether, in practice, these solutions have delivered on their purported target outcomes, from swiftly cutting emissions to restoring a biodiverse ecosystem. Perhaps this is for good reason: the evidence reviewed throughout these chapters as to the material impact of existing green capitalist solutions offers little reason for optimism. Among the greatest triumphs of carbon pricing mechanisms, for instance, is the EU ETS which – while it reports emissions reductions of close to 40% within the sectors it covers – has, over 15 years, scarcely left a dent on the region's overall emissions. Nor has it delivered the 'innovations' in decarbonised energy and industry assumed by carbon pricing advocates; rather, most gains to date have been the result of temporary transitions from coal to gas. Sustainable finance is pitched as a perfect alignment between the profit motive and altruism – doing well by doing good – yet for the moment it seems to be, at best, an immaterial exercise in branding, and at worst, an excuse for inaction from policymakers. Furthermore, under the evolving conditions of asset manager capitalism, the role of the state has been firmly oriented toward de-risking and shepherding private sector profits, rather than using its capacities for direct investment and action. The evidence in favour of biodiversity offset programmes is perhaps the least compelling, thus far generating poor to catastrophic outcomes for biodiversity, while creating new opportunities to profit from new markets in conservation. But beyond the failure for these market mechanisms to drive substantial impacts to date, there are many reasons to believe they never will. In part, this reflects the pervasiveness of unsupported assumptions and biases, from neglecting the systemic embeddedness of fossil fuels in global systems of energy and production to prioritising cost efficiency over actual ecological outcomes. But it also reflects capitalism's drive to externalise costs, such that all these efforts to 'internalise' climate and ecological damage to the market have and will continue to generate new and painful 'externalities'. This is where the question of materiality begins to bleed into the question of justice.

Freedom, democracy, justice: the illusions of green capitalism

In ecological crisis, capitalism confronts both an unprecedented threat to its fundamental operating logics, and an opportunity to turn (for a finite period) the mitigation of that threat into a new terrain for profit. Green capitalism, as defined here, reflects this blend of threat and opportunity, and is centred around two broad strategies for minimising the former while maximising the latter. The first strategy is to commodify and

273

render market-compliant the governance of phenomena from carbon emissions to the 'services' provided to the economy by ecosystems and biodiversity. The second is to use the state as a facilitator of new market domains and as a 'de-risker' of private capital, in line with the Wall Street Consensus articulated by Daniela Gabor.[11] In lieu of public investment and capacity, green capitalist approaches thus advocate the use of state capacity – particularly for handling risk – to safeguard and shepherd private capital into previously undesirable areas through a heady blend of market making, incentive, and guarantee. In practice, these approaches operate in a somewhat blurred sequence, with the establishment of markets for trading emissions permits, for instance, immediately followed and supplanted by the market for derivatives and other financial products based on these new commodities, with financial risk often shifted, willingly, onto the state and public.

Within both of these strategies – and running through the numerous green capitalist policies and solutions explored in this book – is a central thread: the effort to privatise the response to ecological crisis. In other words, green capitalist solutions seek to transfer the complex, ethically and socially fraught, and inherently political questions presented by ecological crisis from democratically contestable terrain to the private authority of markets, with outcomes ultimately driven by the self-interest of rational actors motivated by profit. For disciples of 'free market' economic liberalism, the idea that green capitalism seeks to shift authority over the collective response to ecological crisis to the private sphere will appear as a grave misreading of the market and the price mechanism as the ultimate terrain of democracy. To quote Ludwig von Mises, among the most prominent free market thinkers: 'The capitalist system of production is an economic democracy in which every penny gives a right to vote.'[12] In this view, the market is an innately democratic system, in which actors arrive freely as equals and make their voices heard through spending or withholding their money. As a result, the market is also an arbiter of justice and good democratic governance, as it penalises those businesses or actors whose actions or offerings are deemed undesirable.[13]

Any casual observer of the political systems of the US or UK, among others, will understand immediately that this vision is a fantasy. The scale of economic power exercised by the vast corporate persons and financial firms that today dominate the global economy all but erases the power any individual has in making their voice heard. Indeed, corporations routinely have outsized sway in formal political democratic processes as well, with lobbying power and political donations often setting incredibly narrow terms within which politicians can operate. Distributions of wealth are radically unequal and their increasingly strict relationship to asset ownership makes the ever-elusive aspiration of 'social mobility' increasingly untenable.[14] We produce more than enough food every day to feed everyone on Earth, yet each year over 1 billion tonnes is left to waste, as an estimated 800 million live in hunger and 'chronic malnourishment'.[15] The freedom to consume affordable goods is increasingly predicated on the reciprocal unfreedom and exploitation of those within the supply chains of those goods, from garment workers to seasonal agricultural labourers. It is difficult, even in this vanishingly small survey of the ills currently supported by market outcomes, to maintain that this is a system defined by its promotion of democracy, genuine freedom, or justice.

In fairness, free market thinkers acknowledge that expansive inequalities exist and indeed that people may take issue with them; within the market-led value system, however, these are not problematic. To borrow again from Mises: 'It is true that the various individuals have not the same power to vote. The richer man casts more ballots than the poorer fellow. But to be rich and to earn a higher income is, in the market economy, already the outcome of the previous election.'[16] Thus, the issue of the enormously unjust 'pre-distribution' of wealth and, correspondingly, democratic power, is deemed entirely fair – the reflection of democratic will previously exercised.[17] Similarly, as the first chapter explored, substantive equality is not of concern, provided the conditions of formal equality are met, such that the prince and pauper are both equally free to sleep beneath the bridges of Paris.

This relative disinterest in substantive inequality is integral rather than incidental to market-led economics and systems of governance. As theorist Stuart Hall wrote, this 'liberal' approach to governance embodies an inescapable tension 'between its universalistic claims on behalf of all citizens and its alignment with the interests of particular sections of society; between its commitment to representative government and its doubts about universal democracy.'[18] It is a disinterest that also, ultimately, deals the strongest blow to the prospects of green capitalism as a viable or desirable programme for confronting ecological crisis. Vast tree planting projects in service of carbon offset demands are already driving major land grabs across many regions of the Global South, and their widespread uptake – in combination with other non-solutions such as massive scaling up of crops for bioenergy – is placing the stability of the global food supply at additional risk.[19] Resistance to the perception of anti-democratic 'elite' climate politics perceived to place unjust burdens on the working poor is widespread (if not always in good faith), from the *gilets jaunes* in France to the UK parliament's 'Net Zero Scrutiny Group'. At the same time, the foregrounding of profit-motivated solutions risks exacerbating the very inequalities driving ecological crisis in the first instance. It is for this reason that the solutions of green capitalism – whether carbon pricing, ESG or habitat banking – are self-defeating.

So: should we accept green capitalist solutions? The answer, to me, is clear. Market-based solutions do not offer a path to safety for the world's majority, let alone a future that is defined by collective abundance and wellbeing. At best, green capitalist solutions are a deadly distraction from the urgent task of actually slowing, reversing, and adapting to climate and ecological crisis; at worst, they are actively undermining our ability to do so.

Democracy, freedom, justice: demanding the Earth

As stated at the outset, the purpose of this book is not to provide a manifesto of solutions to ecological crisis. That could form the subject of many other books at least as long as this one. Nor is its purpose to convince people of the urgency of ecological crisis. Frankly, I take for granted that anyone reading this is convinced of this point. Rather, the purpose of this book has been to take stock of where we are, and to try to cohere under a single logic the many actors, ideas and systems keeping the world so off track. In doing so, I hope that someone might come away from it newly convinced that we are currently travelling fast in the wrong direction. For others already troubled by this feeling, I hope to have provided some clarity and actionable detail with respect to why that might be. For both these intended readers, I also hope to leave you convinced that something different is possible.

The elephant in the room in all mainstream proposals for governing and responding to ecological crisis is pious adherence to the tenets of market-led economics and statecraft. The inevitability of the price mechanism and market rationality are embedded throughout countless aspects of our lives. In this sense, green capitalism is not limited to a specific approach to policy design or type of solution; it also reflects an entrenched cultural sense of what is possible, reasonable and good. For instance, a study of media articles found that four in every five articles discussing the economy used positive language about economic growth, without the need (or perhaps the ability) to specify what the benefits of growth might be.[20] Received common sense is that growth is a rising tide that 'lifts all boats', even if the gains are distributed extremely unequally, and even when this tide is lifting us toward catastrophe. This perspective – adhering to the fairness and naturalness of markets, the goodness of aggregate growth, and the inevitability of capitalism as a perhaps flawed but ultimately insurmountable system for organising our lives – dominates the governance and functioning of the global economy, as well as the prevailing agenda for confronting ecological crisis. Market-led economics and governance also hold a monopoly over what is deemed 'utopian' – in other words, a fruitless, silly exercise that fails to engage with practical realities. In this way, green capitalism has been allowed to function as 'the adult in the room', to the detrimental exclusion of alternative perspectives on how best to confront ecological crisis.

As cited above, according to Dieter Helm, the trouble with utopian thinking is that it is 'at best a distraction, and at worst an excuse for not engaging with the world as it is'. The implication is that market-based solutions like natural capital accounting and carbon pricing *do* engage with the world as it is. This is a big claim. Certainly, market-based solutions accept and work within the terms of our existing economic model as they are. But they don't do so in a way that is useful, either with respect to ecological impact or justice. And crucially, though they accept the confines of capitalism, there is much about the world that they obscure or wilfully ignore – the accelerating and increasingly desperate pace of climate and ecological breakdown; the failure of capitalism to provide basic welfare and freedom for the world's majority; the boundless possibility for things to be different.

Given this entrenched perspective, it is unsurprising that resistance to the kinds of bold changes we need to secure a habitable planetary future for all and a safe present for many tends to focus on what we stand to lose. Undeniably, available evidence suggests that 'addressing environmental breakdown may require a direct downscaling of economic production and consumption in the wealthiest countries.'[21] This is an uncomfortable idea to grapple with, but as philosopher Kate Soper writes: 'If we have a cosmopolitan care for the well-being of the poor of the world, and a concern about the quality of life for future generations, then we have to campaign for a change of attitudes to work, consumption, pleasure, and self-realisation in affluent communities.'[22] There is the sense that this future is necessarily austerian, anti-progress and defined by lack. Indeed, the same media study cited above found discussion of economies defined by the absence of growth to focus on bleakness and stagnation.[23] Comparatively little attention is directed at what we stand to gain – but there is much to be gained. Understanding what requires us to ask what the existing system currently fails to provide, from universal access to health care and education, to basic material security, to free time. It certainly does not offer a secure planetary future, let alone one in which all life can thrive. And it does not offer genuine democracy, justice or freedom for most. Absent these, what purpose is 'the economy' meant to serve?

I can't offer a definitive answer to this question; indeed, it's an answer that should reflect collectively determined and freely given priorities, wishes and needs. At the moment, we live under a system that mechanically assures the opposite. It should come as no surprise that ideas for an alternative would likely spell the end of capitalism as we know it. Perhaps this is utopian thinking. But amidst an accelerating planetary crisis propelled with devastating force by cumulative and ongoing inequalities in consumption, wealth and power, it shouldn't be. In the words of the late David Graeber: 'We cling to what exists because we can no longer imagine an alternative that wouldn't be even worse.'[24] The time is long overdue for imagining, and fighting for, that alternative.

*****

Whales have not always lived in the sea: 50 million years ago, the fossil record suggests they were land-dwelling, and may have been hoofed. Eventually, responding to various threats – predation, competition for food sources, or some equivalent – whales made the transition over the span of some ten million years into the water. They've spent the 40 million-odd years since becoming perfectly adapted to the ocean's demands. Over the span of just a few human lifetimes, great whales were almost wiped from the planet's ledger, with their populations reduced almost to extinction. Today, the entire whale population is affected by our activities and our remaking of the planet and its systems. Six out of thirteen great whales are threatened or endangered; 300,000 whales, porpoises and dolphins die each year ensnared in the nets of commercial fishing operations. In their effort to escape the deafening pulses of naval sonar and shipping channels, many whales have beached themselves, some with bleeding ears.[25]

Whales are considered a 'sentinel species' for our own climatic and ecological fate. Their biology is a lesson in the finely calibrated balance achieved by this planet's systems. In an inconceivably brief window of time, we have sent these systems teetering toward a point of no return. Fossils set down over millions of years are, in the span of moments, combusted and converted to the energy that fuels our lives. Much of this has been instrumental to the survival and wellbeing of humankind. Much has not. We have reached the point at which expanding the former imperative, while discarding the latter, is both necessary and urgent. Deciding whether and how we do this is ultimately a question of what we value. What, then, is the value of a whale? Do we consider them worth saving? Or would we notice if, silently, the last whale slipped into the glossy black of the sea, and never resurfaced?

The bodies of whales are scored with the histories of capitalism's impact on the Earth and its inhabitants. To ask what a whale is worth is to ask whether we can resituate ourselves on this planet, re-embedding 'the economy' within the inescapable social and ecological systems that support its reproduction, and to ask whether its imperatives can be subjugated to the needs of life and collective thriving. To answer these questions, we'll have to stop searching in the wrong places.

Notes

Preface

1 'Intensive Search Underway for Survivors of Destructive Flooding in Western Europe', *CBS News*, 17 July 2021, www.cbsnews.com/news/flooding-western-europe-germany-intensive-search-survivors/ (accessed 1 March 2022).

2 Nicola Jones, 'How the World Passed a Carbon Threshold – and Why it Matters', *Yale School of the Environment*, 26 January 2017, https://e360.yale.edu/features/how-the-world-passed-a-carbon-threshold-400ppm-and-why-it-matters (accessed 1 March 2022).

3 For example, see Naomi Oreskes, *Merchants of Doubt* (London: Bloomsbury, 2011); Kate Aronoff, *Overheated: How Capitalism Broke The Planet – and How We Fight Back* (New York: Bold Type Books, 2021).

Introduction

1 Ralph Chami et al., 'Nature's Solution to Climate Change', *Finance and Development* 56, no. 4 (2019), www.imf.org/external/pubs/ft/fandd/2019/12/natures-solution-to-climate-change-chami.htm (accessed 1 March 2022).

2 Daniel Cressey, 'World's Whaling Slaughter Tallied at 3 Million', *Nature* 519, no. 752 (2015), doi: 10.1038/519140a.

3 R.C. Moore et al., 'Microplastics in Beluga Whales (Delphinapterus Leucas) From the Eastern Beaufort Sea', *Marine Pollution Bulletin* 150, no. 110723 (2020), doi: 10.1016/j.marpolbul.2019.110723.

4 Rebecca Giggs, *Fathoms: The World in the Whale* (London: Scribe, 2020).

5 Robert Costanza et al., 'The Value of the World's Ecosystem Services and Natural Capital', *Nature* 387 (1996): 253–260.

6 World Economic Forum, 'Nature Risk Rising: Why the Crisis Engulfing Nature Matters for Business and the Economy', *World Economic Forum*, 19 January 2020, www.weforum.org/reports/nature-risk-rising-why-the-crisis-engulfing-nature-matters-for-business-and-the-economy (accessed 1 March 2022).

7 Isak Stoddard et al., 'Three Decades of Climate Mitigation: Why Haven't We Bent the Global Emissions Curve?', *Annual Review of Environment and Resources* 46 (2021), doi: 10.1146/annurev-environ-012220-011104.

8 Ibid.

9 Joe Turner and Dan Bailey, 'Ecobordering: Casting Immigration Control as Environmental Protection', *Environmental Politics* 33, no. 1 (2021), doi: 10.1080/09644016.2021.1916197.

10 Erik M. Conway and Naomi Oreskes, *Merchants of Doubt* (London: Bloomsbury, 2010); Phoebe Keane, 'How the Oil Industry Made us Doubt Climate Change', *BBC News*, 20 September 2020, www.bbc.co.uk/news/stories-53640382 (accessed 1 March 2022).

11 William Booth and Karla Adam, 'Boris Johnson Used to Mock "Eco-Doomsters". Now he's a Climate Champion', *The Washington Post*, 3 November 2021, www.washingtonpost.com/world/europe/boris-johnson-climate-cop26/2021/11/02/ffbc2526-3b79-11ec-bd6f-da376f47304e_story.html (accessed 1 March 2022).

12 Conservative and Unionist Party, 'Get Brexit Done, Unleash Britain's Potential: The Conservative and Unionist Party Manifesto 2019', www.conservatives.com/our-plan/conservative-party-manifesto-2019 (accessed 1 March 2022).

13 Malte Meinshausen et al., '1.9°C: New COP26 Pledges Bring Projected Warming to Below 2°C for the First Time in History' (2021), *Climate Resource*, https://data.climateresource.com.au/ndc/20211103-ClimateResource-below2C.pdf (accessed 1 March 2022).

14 For detailed texts examining these histories, see: Erik M. Conway and Naomi Oreskes' seminal *Merchants of Doubt* (London: Bloomsbury, 2010); Naomi Klein, *This Changes Everything: Capitalism vs. the Climate*

(New York: Simon & Schuster, 2014); and Kate Aronoff, *Overheated: How Capitalism Broke the Planet – and How We Fight Back* (New York: Bold Type Books, 2021).

15 William Nordhaus, 'Can We Control Carbon Dioxide? [1975]', *The American Economic Review* 109, no. 6 (2019), www.jstor.org/stable/26737880 (accessed 10 September 2021).

16 Carbon Brief Staff, 'The History of Climate Change's Speed Limit', *Carbon Brief*, 8 December 2014, www.carbonbrief.org/two-degrees-the-history-of-climate-changes-speed-limit (accessed 1 March 2022).

17 The economics profession does not, technically, have a Nobel prize within the formal awards established by Alfred Nobel. Though often referred to in the shorthand as the 'Nobel Prize in Economics', the economics profession established its own separate prize – the rather less punchy 'Sveriges Riksbank Prize in Economic Sciences in Memory of Alfred Nobel' – several decades after the original Nobels were created.

18 When I saw 'we' here, I mean to imply the aggregate actions of global society. In other words, there is an incredible diversity of perspectives, plans and actions underway across the world striving to grapple with ecological crisis. Nonetheless, at the aggregate level, the world is pulled in the direction which I am describing here – and the collective 'we' along with it.

19 These data are explored in depth in Chapter 2. See also Kristoffer Tigue, 'Why Do Environmental Justice Advocates Oppose Carbon Markets? Look at California, They Say', *Inside Climate News*, 25 February 2022, https://insideclimatenews.org/news/25022022/why-do-environmental-justice-advocates-oppose-carbon-markets-look-at-california-they-say/ (accessed 1 March 2022).

20 This turn of phrase is borrowed from Servaas Storm, 'Capitalism and Climate Change: Can the Invisible Hand Adjust the Natural Thermostat?', *Development and Change* 40, no. 6 (2009), doi: 10.1111/j.1467-7660.2009.01610.x.

21 Jeremy B. Rudd, 'Why Do We Think Inflation Expectations Matter for Inflation? (And Should We?)', *Federal Reserve Board* (2021), doi: 10.17016/FEDS.2021.062.

22 Katharina Pistor, *The Code of Capital: How the Law Creates Wealth and Inequality* (Princeton, NJ: Princeton University Press, 2019).

23 See e.g. T. Weidmann et al., 'Scientists' Warning on Affluence', *Nature Communications* 11, no. 3107 (2020), www.nature.com/articles/

s41467-020-16941-y (accessed 1 March 2022); Joel Millward-Hopkins et al., 'Providing Decent Living with Minimum Energy: A Global Scenario', *Global Environmental Change* 65 (2020), doi: 10.1016/j.gloenv cha.2020.102168; Jun Lan et al., 'A Structural Decomposition Analysis of Global Energy Footprints', *Applied Energy* 163 (2016), doi: 10.1016/j. apenergy.2015.10.178; T. Parrique et al., 'Decoupling Debunked: Evidence and Arguments Against Green Growth as a Sole Strategy for Sustainability', *European Environmental Bureau* (2019), https://eeb. org/library/decoupling-debunked/ (accessed 1 March 2022).

24 Aaron Benanav, *Automation and the Future of Work* (London: Verso, 2020).

25 Damian Carrington, 'Orca "Apocalypse": Half of Killer Whales Doomed to Die from Pollution', *The Guardian*, 27 September 2018, www.theguardian.com/environment/2018/sep/27/orca-apocalyp se-half-of-killer-whales-doomed-to-die-from-pollution (accessed 1 March 2022).

Chapter 1: Gatekeepers

1 William Nordhaus, *The Climate Casino: Risk, Uncertainty and Economics* (New Haven and London: Yale University Press, 2013).

2 Niels Bohr, as quoted in Otto Robert Frisch, *What Little I Remember* (Cambridge: Cambridge University Press, 1979) p. 95.

3 James C. Scott, *Seeing Like a State* (New Haven, CT: Yale University Press, 1998).

4 Phil McManus, 'History of Forestry: Ideas, Networks and Silences', *Environment and History* 5, no. 2 (1999): 185–208, www.jstor.org/ stable/20723100 (accessed 25 March 2022).

5 This description of German forestry science draws on Scott, *Seeing Like a State*.

6 Ibid.

7 McManus, 'History of Forestry'.

8 Scott, *Seeing Like a State*.

9 Ibid.

10 Benjamin Franta, 'Weaponizing Economics: Big Oil, Economic Consultants, and Climate Policy Delay', *Environmental Politics* (2021), doi: 10.1080/09644016.2021.1947636.

11 Ibid.

12 Quinn Slobodian, *Globalists: The End of Empire and the Birth of Neoliberalism* (Cambridge, MA: Harvard University Press, 2018).

13 Ibid., p. 95.

14 Ibid.

15 David Harvey, *A Brief History of Neoliberalism* (Oxford: Oxford University Press, 2005).

16 It's for this reason that the work of James C. Scott with which this chapter began – though he describes himself as a 'crude Marxist' – is nonetheless popular among neoliberal and libertarian groups such as the Cato Institute. See, for example, The Cato Institute, 'A Conversation with James C. Scott', *Cato Unbound*, September 2010, www.cato-unbound.org/print-issue/487/ (accessed 11 January 2022).

17 Ibid.

18 Milton Friedman, *Capitalism and Freedom* (Chicago: University of Chicago Press, 1962), p. 200, as quoted in Werner Bonefeld, *The Strong State and the Free Economy* (Maryland: Rowman and Littlefield International, 2017), p. 62.

19 Rep. Alexandria Ocasio-Cortez, 'H.Res.109 – Recognizing the Duty of the Federal Government to Create a Green New Deal', *United States Congress*, 2 July 2019, www.congress.gov/bill/116th-congress/house-resolution/109/text (accessed 3 March 2022).

20 Servaas Storm, 'Capitalism and Climate Change: Can the Invisible Hand Adjust the Natural Thermostat?', *Development and Change* 40, no. 6 (2009), doi: 10.1111/j.1467-7660.2009.01610.x.

21 William Nordhaus, *The Spirit of Green: The Economics of Collisions and Contagions in a Crowded World* (Princeton, NJ: Princeton University Press, 2020).

22 Martin L. Weitzman, 'A Review of *The Stern Review on the Economics of Climate Change*', *Journal of Economic Literature* 45 (2007): 703–723.

23 UNDP, *Human Development Report 2007/8* (New York: Palgrave Macmillan, 2007).

24 Larry Lohmann, 'Financialisation, Commodification and Carbon: The Contradictions of Neoliberal Climate Policy', *The Stocialist Register* 48 (2012), https://socialistregister.com/index.php/srv/article/view/15647 (accessed 3 March 2022).

25 Christian Gollier and Mar Reguant, 'Climate Change', in Olivier Blanchard and Jean Tirole (eds), *Major Future Economic Challenges: International Commission* (Government of France, 2021).

26 Nordhaus, *The Spirit of Green*.

27 P.S. Dasgupta and G.M. Heal, *Economic Theory and Exhaustible Resources* (Cambridge: Cambridge University Press, 1979).

28 Storm, 'Capitalism and Climate Change'.

29 Cedric Durand, 'Energy Dilemma', *New Left Review: Sidecar*, 5 November 2021, https://newleftreview.org/sidecar/posts/energy-dilemma (accessed 10 January 2022).

30 For a detailed history of how 'efficiency' came to be the assumed goal of environmental policy as well as an assumed feature of emissions and pollution trading schemes, see Richard Lane, 'The Promiscuous History of Market Efficiency: The Development of Early Emissions Trading Systems', *Ecological Politics* 21, no. 4 (2012), doi: 10.1080/09644016.2012.688355.

31 The account that follows draws on Steve Keen, 'The Appallingly Bad Neoclassical Economics of Climate Change', *Globalizations* 18, no. 7 (2020), doi: 10.1080/14747731.2020.1807856.

32 William Nordhaus, 'World Dynamics: Measurement Without Data', *The Economic Journal* 83, no. 332 (1973): 1156–1183.

33 William Nordhaus, 'To Slow or Not to Slow: The Economics of the Greenhouse Effect', *The Economic Journal* 101, no. 407 (1991): 920–937.

34 Ibid.

35 Simon Dietz and Nicholas Stern, 'Endogenous Growth, Convexity of Damage and Climate Risk: How Nordhaus's Framework Supports Deep Cuts in Carbon Emissions', *The Economic Journal* 125, no. 583 (2015): 574–620, doi: 10.1111/ecoj.12188.

36 Arent et al., 'Key Economic Sectors and Services', in C.B. Field, V.R. Barros, D.J. Dokken et al. (eds), *Climate Change 2014: Impacts, Adaptation, and Vulnerability* (Cambridge: Cambridge University Press, 2014), p. 662.

37 For instance, the National Atmospheric and Oceanic Society in the United States estimated that in 2021, the costs of climate and weather-related disasters totalled near $150 billion, while insurance firm Munich Re estimated that in 2020, climate-related disasters cost the global economy $210 billion in damages, predicting the climate crisis would substantially exacerbate these losses. See 'Record Hurricane Season and Major Wildfires – The Natural Disaster Figures for 2020', *Munich Re*, 1 July 2021, www.munichre.com/en/company/media-relations/media-information-and-corporate-news/media-information/2021/2020-natural-disasters-balance.html (accessed 13 December 2021).

38 Arent et al., 'Key Economic Sectors', p. 668.

39　See e.g. William Nordhaus's influential book: *The Climate Casino: Risk, Uncertainty and Economics for a Warming World* (New Haven, CT: Yale University Press, 2014).

40　Kevin Anderson quoted in Kate Aronoff, *Overheated: How Capitalism Broke the Planet – and How We Fight Back* (New York: Bold Type Books, 2021).

41　Simon Dietz et al., 'Economic Impacts of Tipping Points in the Climate System', *Proceedings of the National Academy of Sciences* 118, no. 34 (2021), doi: 10.1073/pnas.2103081118.

42　Steve Keen et al., 'Economists' Erroneous Estimates of Damages from Climate Change' (2021), *The Royal Society Publishing*, https://arxiv.org/pdf/2108.07847.pdf (accessed 12 December 2021).

43　David Anthoff, Francisco Estrada, and Richard S.J. Tol, 'Shutting Down the Thermohaline Circulation'. *American Economic Review* 106, no. 5 (2016): 602–606, doi: 10.1257/aer.p20161102.

44　Damian Carrington, 'Climate Crisis: Scientists Spot Warning Signs of Gulf Stream Collapse', *The Guardian*, 5 August 2021, www.theguardian.com/environment/2021/aug/05/climate-crisis-scientists-spot-warning-signs-of-gulf-stream-collapse (accessed 13 November 2021).

45　For further evaluation see Delavane Diaz and Frances Moore, 'Quantifying the Economic Risks of Climate Change', *Nature Climate Change* 7 (2017): 774–782, www.nature.com/articles/nclimate3411 (accessed 3 March 2022).

46　Adair Turner, 'The Dangerous Delusion of Optimal Global Warming', *Project Syndicate*, 1 August 2019, www.project-syndicate.org/commentary/misguided-nordhaus-model-optimal-climate-change-by-adair-turner-2019-08 (accessed 3 March 2022).

47　William Nordhaus, 'Expert Opinion on Climatic Change', *American Scientist* 82 no. 1 (1994): 45–51, www.jstor.org/stable/29775100 (accessed 25 March 2022).

48　Ibid.

49　Ibid.

50　Though many governments do establish a standard rate for their own policy decisions, such as the rate fixed within the UK Treasury's 'Green Book'.

51　Nordhaus, for example, advocated a rate closer to 4% in his response to The Stern Review. See William Nordhaus, 'A Review of *The Stern Review on the Economics of Climate Change*', *Journal of Economic Literature* 45 (2007): 686–702.

52 Laurie T. Johnson and Chris Hope, 'The Social Cost of Carbon in U.S. Regulatory Analyses: An Introduction and Critique', *Journal of Environmental Studies and Sciences* 2 (2012), doi: 10.1007/s13412-012-00 87-7.

53 Frédéric Hache, '50 Shades of Green: The Rise of Natural Capital Markets and Sustainable Finance. Part I, Carbon' (2019), *Green Finance Observatory*.

54 Partha Dasgupta, 'Discounting Climate Change', *Journal of Risk and Uncertainty* 37, no. 2/3 (2008), www.jstor.org/stable/41761456 (accessed 25 March 2022).

55 John Whibey, 'Understanding the Social Cost of Carbon', *Yale Climate Connections*, 12 February 2015, https://yaleclimateconnections. org/2015/02/understanding-the-social-cost-of-carbon-and-connecting-it-to-our-lives/ (accessed 3 March 2022).

56 Isabella Backman, 'Stanford Explainer: Social Cost of Carbon', *Stanford News*, 7 June 2021, https://news.stanford.edu/2021/06/07/professors-explain-social-cost-carbon/#Definition (accessed 6 September 2021).

57 Ibid.

58 The account that follows in the next paragraphs draws on the exceptionally clear summary of damage function limitations outlined in Delavane Diaz and Frances Moore, 'Quantifying the Economic Risks of Climate Change', *Nature Climate Change* 7 (2017): 744–782, www.nature.com/articles/nclimate3411 (accessed 3 March 2022).

59 Frank Ackerman, Elizabeth A. Stanton and Ramon Bueno, 'Fat Tails, Exponents, Extreme Uncertainty: Simulating Catastrophe in DICE', *Ecological Economics* 69, no. 8 (2010): 1657–1665.

60 For a complete breakdown of common critiques of major IAMs, see Table 2 in Diaz and Moore, 'Quantifying the Economic Risks'.

61 Jonathan M. Harris, Brian Roach and Anne-Marie Codur, 'The Economics of Global Climate Change' (2017), *Global Development and Environment Institute at Tufts University*.

62 See e.g. W. Kip Viscusi and Clayton J. Masterman, 'Income Elasticities and Global Values of a Statistical Life', *Journal of Benefit-Cost Analysis* 8, no. 2 (2017): 226–250, doi: 10.1017/bca.2017.12; and Ted R. Miller, 'Variations Between Countries in Values of Statistical Life', *Journal of Transport Economics and Policy* 34, no. 2 (2000): 169–188.

63 Richard Richels et al., 'The Trump Administration Cooks the Climate Change Numbers Once Again', *The Hill*, 18 July 2020, https://thehill.

com/opinion/energy-environment/507929-the-trump-administration-cooks-the-climate-change-numbers-once (accessed 6 September 2021).

64 David Malakoff, Robert F. Service and Warren Cornwall, 'Trump Team Targets Changes to Key Metric that Calculates Social Cost of Carbon', *Science: Insider*, 16 December 2016, www.science.org/content/article/trump-team-targets-changes-key-metric-calculates-social-cost-carbon (accessed 6 September 2021).

65 H.W. Arndt, *The Rise and Fall of Economic Growth: A Study in Contemporary Thought* (Melbourne: Longman Cheshire, 1978).

66 Vacliv Smil, *Growth: From Microorganisms to Megacities* (Boston: MIT Press, 2019). As cited in Richard Seymour, 'Patterning Slowdown' (2021), *New Left Review*, https://newleftreview.org/issues/ii131/articles/richard-seymour-patterning-slowdown (accessed 3 March 2022).

67 This account draws on Richard Lane, 'The American Anthropocene: Economic Scarcity and Growth During the Great Acceleration', *Geoforum* 99 (2019): 11–21, doi: 10.1016/j.geoforum.2019.01.003.

68 Ibid., p. 13.

69 President's Materials Policy Commission, 'Resources for Freedom: Volume 1, Foundations for Growth and Security' (1952), *United States Government*. Via Lane, 'The American Anthropocene'.

70 Lane, 'The American Anthropocene'.

71 Ibid.

72 J.R. McNeill and P. Engelke, *The Great Acceleration: An Environmental History of the Anthropocene Since 1945* (Cambridge, MA: Belknap Press, 2014).

73 Seymour, 'Patterning Slowdown'.

74 Ibid.

75 J.R. McNeill, *Something New under the Sun: An Environmental History of the World in the 20th Century* (London: Penguin, 2001).

Chapter 2: Sirens

1 Karl Marx, *Capital: A Critique of Political Economy, Volume I* (New York: Vintage Books, 1977).

2 Frédéric Hache, '2021: A Carbon Markets Odyssey' (2022), *Green Finance Observatory*.

3 Kaisa Amaral, 'Europe's Industry Polluters Make €50 Billion in Carbon Market Windfall Profits', *Carbon Market Watch*, 7 June 2021,

https://carbonmarketwatch.org/2021/06/07/europes-industry-poll
uters-make-e50-billion-in-carbon-market-windfall-profits/ (accessed
1 March 2022).

4 With thanks to Frédéric Hache for this clarifying framing.
5 Jessica Green, 'Does Carbon Pricing Reduce Emissions? A Review of
   Ex-Post Analyses', *Environmental Research Letters* 16, no. 4 (2021), https://
   iopscience.iop.org/article/10.1088/1748-9326/abdae9 (accessed 1
   March 2022).
6 Ibid. See 'The EU Emissions Trading System in 2021: Trends and
   Projections', *The European Environment Agency*, 12 January 2022, www.
   eea.europa.eu/publications/the-eu-emissions-trading-system-2/the-eu-
   emissions-trading-system (accessed 1 March 2022).
7 Patrick Bayer and Michael Aklin, 'The European Union Emissions
   Trading System Reduced CO_2 Emissions Despite Low Prices',
   Proceedings of the National Academy of Sciences 117, no. 16 (2020), doi:
   10.1073/pnas.1918128117.
8 Examples of such praise abound, but for prominent mainstream
   examples see e.g.: William Nordhaus, *The Spirit of Green* (Princeton, NJ:
   Princeton University Press, 2021); Tim Harford, 'The Climate Won't
   Wait. We Need a Carbon Price Now', *The Financial Times*, 29 October
   2021, www.ft.com/content/d666b9a8-f2a9-4a51-9c85-fb4223c556b0
   (accessed 1 March 2022); 'The World Urgently Needs to Expand its
   Use of Carbon Prices', *The Economist*, 23 May 2020, www.economist.
   com/briefing/2020/05/23/the-world-urgently-needs-to-expand-its-
   use-of-carbon-prices (accessed 1 March 2022).
9 Kate Aronoff, *Overheated: How Capitalism Broke the Planet – and How We
   Fight Back* (New York: Bold Type Books, 2021).
10 Green, 'Does Carbon Pricing Reduce Emissions?' See also M.A.
   Mehling, G.E. Metcalf and R.N. Stavins, 'Linking Climate Policies to
   Advance Global Mitigation', *Science* 359 (2018): 997–998.
11 Ian Parry, 'Putting a Price on Pollution', *Finance and Development* 56
   no. 4 (2019), www.imf.org/external/pubs/ft/fandd/2019/12/the-
   case-for-carbon-taxation-and-putting-a-price-on-pollution-parry.htm
   (accessed 1 March 2022).
12 Worse still, evidence suggests that any reductions in CO_2 emissions
   to be gained in the switch to fossil gas may be wholly negated by
   increases in upstream methane leakage resulting from gas production
   processes. Via Gareth Bryant, *Carbon Markets in a Climate-Changing
   Capitalism* (Cambridge: Cambridge University Press, 2020).

13 See e.g. Pietro Quercia, 'Polluting for Profit: The Paradox of the EU's Emissions Trading System', *Instituto Affari Internationali*. 7 June 2019, www.iai.it/en/pubblicazioni/polluting-profit-paradox-eus-emissions-trading-system (accessed 1 March 2022); Sabine Frank, 'The EU Emission Trading System – Carbon Pricing as an Important Tool to Achieve the Objectives of the Green Deal', *Climate Change & Audit Journal*, 23 June 2020, https://carbonmarketwatch.org/2020/06/23/the-eu-emission-trading-system-carbon-pricing-as-an-important-tool-to-achieve-the-objectives-of-the-green-deal/ (accessed 1 March 2022).

14 Andreas Kluth, 'Here's How Good Climate Policy Could Go Bad', *Bloomberg*, 17 May 2021, www.bloomberg.com/opinion/articles/2021-05-12/europe-shows-how-good-climate-policy-goes-bad (accessed 1 March 2022).

15 Brian Walsh, 'Why the Climate Bill Died', *TIME*, 26 July 2010, https://science.time.com/2010/07/26/why-the-climate-bill-died/ (accessed 1 March 2022).

16 The scheme was replaced with the ineffectual 'Emissions Reduction Fund' by the Abbott government, which enables businesses to earn credits for storing or 'avoiding' emissions in their activities. Quotation sourced from Leah Stokes and Matto Mildenberger, 'The Trouble with Carbon Pricing', *Boston Review*, 24 September 2020, https://bostonreview.net/articles/leah-c-stokes-matto-mildenberger-tk/ (accessed 1 March 2022).

17 Walsh, 'Why the Climate Bill Died'.

18 Natalie Sauer, 'We Were Ecologists Before the Capitalists', *Climate Home News*, 20 March 2019, www.climatechangenews.com/2019/03/20/ecologists-capitalists-gilets-jaunes-climate-justice/ (accessed 1 March 2022).

19 Stokes and Mildenberger, 'The Trouble with Carbon Pricing'.

20 Gilbert E. Metcalf, 'How to Set a Price on Carbon Pollution', *Scientific American*, 1 June 2020, www.scientificamerican.com/article/how-to-set-a-price-on-carbon-pollution/ (accessed 1 March 2022).

21 'Three Degrees of Global Warming is Quite Plausible and Truly Disastrous', *The Economist*, 24 July 2021, www.economist.com/briefing/2021/07/24/three-degrees-of-global-warming-is-quite-plausible-and-truly-disastrous (accessed 1 March 2022).

22 Robert Pindyck, 'The Social Cost of Carbon Revisited', *Journal of Environmental Economics and Management* 94 (2019), doi: 10.1016/j.jeem.2019.02.003.

23 Gollier and Reguant, 'Climate Change'.

24 Parry, 'Putting a Price on Carbon'.

25 Anthony Patt and John Lilliestam, 'The Case Against Carbon Prices', *Joule*, 2 (2018): 2494–2498.

26 Eric Lonergan and Corinne Sawers, 'The Wrong Chapter of the Textbook', *Philosophy of Money*, 9 January 2022, www.philosophy ofmoney.net/the-wrong-chapter-of-the-textbook/ (accessed 12 February 2022).

27 For further elaboration see Patt and Lilliestam, 'The Case Against Carbon Prices'.

28 Ibid.

29 F. Geels, *Technological Transition and System Innovations: A Co-Evolutionary and Socio-Technical Analysis* (Cheltenham: Edward Elgar Press, 2005).

30 Lonergan and Sawers, 'The Wrong Chapter'.

31 For a necessarily incomplete sample from economists with varying per-spectives, see: Green, 'Does Carbon Pricing Reduce Emissions?'; Patt and Lilliestam, 'The Case Against Carbon Prices'; Nordhaus *The Spirit of Green*, p. 275, in which he writes that most experts agree on the prin-ciple that 'in a market context … the carbon price should be equal in every sector and every country'; the IMF's advocacy of a global carbon price 'floor', in Vitor Gaspar and Ian Parry, 'A Proposal to Scale up Global Carbon Pricing', *IMF Blog*, 28 June 2021, https://bl ogs.imf.org/2021/06/18/a-proposal-to-scale-up-global-carbon-pricing/ (accessed 1 March 2022); and a similar argument in Stefano Carattini, 'COP26: Set a Minimum Global Carbon Price for Emissions', *Nature*, 26 October 2021, www.nature.com/articles/d41586-021-02881-0 (accessed 1 March 2022); World Economic Forum and PwC, 'Increasing Climate Ambition: Analysis of an International Carbon Price Floor', *World Economic Forum*, 3 November 2021, www.weforum.org/reports/increa sing-climate-ambition-analysis-of-an-international-carbon-price-floor (accessed 1 March 2022); and Joseph Stiglitz, 'Keynote Speech: Sharing the Burden of Saving the Planet: Global Social Justice for Sustain-able Development' (2008), *International Economic Association*.

32 Though it's beyond the scope of this chapter, carbon border adjust-ments enacted by wealthy governments are also likely to create sig-nificantly unjust outcomes by economically penalising poorer nations who have contributed significantly less to the climate crisis than, for instance, the countries of the European Union. These issues will be explored in Chapter 5.

33 Storm, 'Capitalism and Climate Change'.

34 'Economists' statement on carbon dividends', *Climate Leadership Council*, 17 January 2019, https://clcouncil.org/economists-statement/ (accessed 1 March 2022).

35 Matto Mildenberger et al., 'Limited Impacts of Carbon Tax Rebate Programmes on Public Support for Carbon Pricing', *Nature Climate Change* 12 (2022): 141–147, www.nature.com/articles/s41558-021-01268-3 (accessed 1 March 2022).

36 Michael Aklin and Matto Mildenberger, 'Prisoners of the Wrong Dilemma: Why Distributive Conflict, Not Collective Action, Characterizes the Politics of Climate Change', *Global Environmental Politics* 20, no. 4 (2020): 4–27, doi: 10.1162/glep_a_00578.

37 Manuel Pastor, 'Up in the Air: Revisiting Equity Dimensions of California's Cap-and-Trade System', *University of Southern California Dornsife Equity Research Institute*, 1 February 2022, https://dornsife.usc.edu/eri/up-in-the-air/ (accessed 1 March 2022).

38 Larry Lohmann, 'The Endless Algebra of Carbon Markets', *Capitalism Nature Socialism* 22, no. 4 (2011), doi: 10.1080/10455752.2011.617507.

39 Worse still, evidence suggests that any reductions in CO_2 emissions to be gained in the switch to fossil gas may be wholly negated by increases in upstream methane leakage resulting from gas production processes. Via Gareth Bryant, *Carbon Markets in a Climate-Changing Capitalism* (Cambridge: Cambridge University Press, 2020).

40 For instance, see T. Weidmann et al. (2020) 'Scientists' Warning on Affluence', *Nature Communications* 11, no. 3107 (2020), 11, www.nature.com/articles/s41467-020-16941-y (accessed 1 March 2022). This question will be explored further in Chapter 6.

41 Physicians for Social Responsibility, 'Compendium of Scientific, Medical, and Media Findings Demonstrating Risks and Harms of Fracking (Unconventional Gas and Oil Extraction): Seventh Edition', *Physicians for Social Responsibility*, 14 December 2020, www.psr.org/blog/resource/fracking-compendium/ (accessed 1 March 2022); Nina Lakhani, 'Living Near Fracking Sites Raises Risk of Premature Death for Elderly, US study finds', *The Guardian*, 27 January 2022, www.theguardian.com/environment/2022/jan/27/people-living-closer-us-oil-and-gas-wells-higher-risk-dying-prematurely-study (accessed 1 March 2022).

42 For example, see ActionAid, 'Caught in the Net: How "Net-Zero Emissions" Will Delay Real Climate Action and Drive Land Grabs', *ActionAid*, 3 June 2015, https://actionaid.org/publications/2015/caught-net-how-net-zero-emissions-will-delay-real-climate-action-an

d-drive-land (accessed 1 March 2022); IATP and the National Farm Family Coalition, 'Why Carbon Markets Won't Work for Agriculture' (2020), *Institute for Agriculture and Trade Policy*, www.iatp.org/sites/default/files/2020-02/2020_01_CarbonMarketsAndAg_FINAL.pdf (accessed 1 March 2022).

43 The phrase 'externalising machine' is borrowed from Storm, 'Capitalism and Climate Change'.

44 'Press Release: COP26 Ends with a Strong Result on Carbon Markets and an International Call to Action for the Most Urgent Climate Priorities', *Environmental Defense Fund*, 13 November 2021, www.edf.org/media/cop26-ends-strong-result-carbon-markets-and-international-call-action-most-urgent-climate (accessed 1 March 2022).

45 'Business Roundtable', *InfluenceMap*, https://lobbymap.org/influencer/Business-Roundtable (accessed 13 February 2022).

46 InfluenceMap, 'American Petroleum Institute's "Carbon Price" Policy', *InfluenceMap*, https://influencemap.org/pressrelease/American-Petroleum-Institute-s-carbon-price-policy-2e62fb8756be1dc5c5e40f9aff65aebf (accessed 1 March 2022).

47 Nichola Groom, 'Big Oil Outspends Billionaires in Washington State Carbon Tax Fight', *Reuters*, 31 October 2018, www.reuters.com/article/us-usa-election-carbon-idUSKCN1N51H7 (accessed 1 March 2022).

48 Chris McGreal, 'ExxonMobil Lobbyists Filmed Saying Oil Giant's Support for Carbon Tax a PR Ploy', *The Guardian*, 30 June 2021, www.theguardian.com/us-news/2021/jun/30/exxonmobil-lobbyists-oil-giant-carbon-tax-pr-ploy (accessed 1 March 2022).

49 Gareth Bryant, *Carbon Markets in a Changing Climate* (Cambridge: Cambridge University Press, 2018). Bryant offers a brilliantly clear and fulsome explanation of the politics of carbon markets.

50 Ibid.

51 Quoted in Stuart Hall, 'Variants of Liberalism' (1986) in Stuart Hall and Gregor McLennan (edS), *Selected Writings on Marxism* (Durham, NC: Duke University Press, 2021).

52 Hall, 'Variants of Liberalism'.

53 Hache, '50 Shades of Green. Part I'.

54 Ben Elgin, 'These Trees Are Not What They Seem: How the Nature Conservancy, the World's Biggest Environmental Group, Became a Dealer of Meaningless Offsets', *Bloomberg Green*, 9 December 2020, www.bloomberg.com/features/2020-nature-conservancy-carbon-offsets-trees/ (accessed 1 March 2022).

Notes

55 'BP Sets Ambition for Net Zero by 2050, Fundamentally Changing Organisation to Deliver', *BP*, 12 February 2020, www.bp.com/en/global/corporate/news-and-insights/press-releases/bernard-looney-announces-new-ambition-for-bp.html (accessed 1 March 2022).

56 This account draws on reporting by Stephen Stapczynski, Akshat Rathi and Godfrey Marawanyika, 'How to Sell "Carbon Neutral" Fossil Fuel That Doesn't Exist', *Bloomberg*, 11 August 2021, www.bloomberg.com/news/features/2021-08-11/the-fictitious-world-of-carbon-neutral-fossil-fuel (accessed 1 March 2022).

57 Frank Watson, 'COP26: Voluntary Carbon Market Value Tops $1 Bill in 2021: Ecosystem Marketplace', *S&P Global*, 11 November 2021, www.spglobal.com/commodity-insights/en/market-insights/latest-news/energy-transition/111121-cop26-voluntary-carbon-market-value-tops-1-bil-in-2021-ecosystem-marketplace (accessed 1 March 2022).

58 Stapczynski, Rathi and Marawanyika, 'How to Sell "Carbon Neutral" Fossil Fuel That Doesn't Exist'.

59 Ibid.

60 The Conservancy has been criticised over its tenure, including close ties to ExxonMobil and other prominent forces of climate denial, and its highly corporate approach to conservation. For further detail, see Elgin, 'These Trees Are Not What They Seem'.

61 Camilla Hodgson, 'US Forest Fires Threaten Carbon Offsets as Company-Linked Trees Burn', *The Financial Times*, 3 August 2021, www.ft.com/content/3f89c759-eb9a-4dfb-b768-d4af1ec5aa23 (accessed 1 March 2022).

62 Justine Calma, 'If Forests Go Up in Smoke, so Can Carbon Offsets', *The Verge*, 13 September 2019, www.theverge.com/2019/9/13/20859156/forests-fires-carbon-offsets-amazon-california (accessed 1 March 2022).

63 Lisa Song, 'An Even More Inconvenient Truth: Why Carbon Credits for Forest Preservation May Be Worse Than Nothing', *Pro Publica*, 22 May 2019, https://features.propublica.org/brazil-carbon-offsets/inconvenient-truth-carbon-credits-dont-work-deforestation-redd-acre-cambodia/ (accessed 1 March 2022).

64 Ibid.

65 Adam Bumpus and D.M. Liverman, 'Carbon Colonialism? Offsets, Greenhouse Gas Reductions, and Sustainable Development', in Richard Peet et al. (eds), *Global Political Ecology* (Abingdon: Routledge, 2011).

66 Martin Kames et al., 'How Additional is the Clean Development Mechanism?' (2016), *Institute for Applied Ecology*, https://ec.europa.eu/clima/system/files/2017-04/clean_dev_mechanism_en.pdf (accessed 1 March 2022).

67 'Novartis Carbon-Sink Forestry Projects', *Novartis*, October 2017. www.novartis.com/sites/novartis_com/files/novartis-carbon-sink-forestry-projects.pdf (accessed 1 March 2022).

68 ActionAid International, 'Not-Their-Lands: The Land Impact of Royal Dutch Shell's Net Zero Climate Commitment', *ActionAid*, 17 May 2021, https://actionaid.org/publications/2021/not-their-lands-land-impact-royal-dutch-shells-net-zero-climate-target (accessed 1 March 2022).

69 Josh Gabbatiss, 'Analysis: Shell Says New "Brazil-Sized" Forest Would be Needed to Meet 1.5C Climate Goal', *CarbonBrief*, 12 February 2021, www.carbonbrief.org/analysis-shell-says-new-brazil-sized-forest-would-be-needed-to-meet-1-5c-climate-goal (accessed 1 March 2022); see also Shell, 'Sky: Meeting the Goals of the Paris Agreement' (2021).

70 Nafeez Ahmed, 'World Bank and UN Carbon Offset Scheme "Complicit" in Genocidal Land Grabs – NGOs', *The Guardian*, 3 July 2014, www.theguardian.com/environment/earth-insight/2014/jul/03/world-bank-un-redd-genocide-land-carbon-grab-sengwer-kenya (accessed 1 March 2022).

71 David Sheppard and Leslie Hook, 'Eni to Plant Vast Forest in Push to Cut Greenhouse Gas Emissions', *The Financial Times*, 15 March 2019, www.ft.com/content/7c4d944e-470d-11e9-b168-96a37d002cd3 (accessed 1 March 2022).

72 See e.g. Ahmed, 'World Bank and UN'; Connor Cavanagh and Tor A. Benjaminsen (2013) 'Virtual Nature, Violent Accumulation: The "Spectacular Failure" of Carbon Offsetting at a Ugandan National Park', *Geoforum* 56: 55–65, doi: 10.1016/j.geoforum.2014.06.013; C. Lang and T. Byakola, 'A Funny Place to Store Carbon: UWA-FACE Foundation's Tree Planting Project in Mount Elgon National Park, Uganda', *World Rainforest Movement* (2006), www.forestpeoples.org/sites/default/files/publication/2010/08/ugandacarbonprojwrmdeco6eng.pdf (accessed 1 March 2022).

73 'The Maipo Valley's Hydroelectric Nightmare: When "Clean" Development Harms People and their Environment', *Centre for International Environmental Law*, November 2019. www.ciel.org/

the-maipo-valleys-hydroelectric-nightmare/ (accessed 15 August 2021).

74 Broadly defined as a contemporary form of Marx's original 'primitive accumulation', 'accumulation by dispossession' entails the concentration of wealth through the conversion of collective or common property, such as land, to private ownership through contemporary tools including financialisation, privatisation of public assets like housing or utilities, and the state's management of crises in the interests of the private sector. For further elaboration see David Harvey, *A Brief History of Neoliberalism* (Oxford: Oxford University Press, 2005).

75 Kevin Anderson, 'The Inconvenient Truth of Carbon Offsets', *Nature* 484, no. 7 (2012), www.nature.com/articles/484007a (accessed 1 March 2022).

76 Bank of England, 'Climate Change: What are the Risks to Financial Stability?', *The Bank of England*, 10 January 2019, www.bankofengland. co.uk/knowledgebank/climate-change-what-are-the-risks-to-financi al-stability (accessed 1 March 2022).

77 Some prominent organisations in this area include: Carbon Disclosure Project, which provides a repository of voluntary corporate disclosures, and awards letter grades depending on disclosures' completeness (though not their contents); Carbon Tracker, which is at the forefront of analysing stranded asset risk; and 2 Degrees Investing Initiative, which analyses financial portfolios' exposure to risk based on various transition scenarios.

78 Julia Kollewe, 'BlackRock's Larry Fink: Climate Policies are About Profits, Not Being "Woke"', *The Guardian*, 18 January 2022, www. theguardian.com/environment/2022/jan/18/blackrock-larry-fink-cl imate-policies-profits-woke (accessed 1 March 2022).

79 Larry Fink, 'Larry Fink's 2020 Letter to CEOs: A Fundamental Reshaping of Finance', *BlackRock*, 2021, www.blackrock.com/cor porate/investor-relations/2020-larry-fink-ceo-letter (accessed 7 July 2021).

80 Ibid.

81 Knightian uncertainty is so named because of its original articulation by Frank Knight in 1921. For a detailed discussion of the concept's implications for climate-related financial policy upon which this section draws, see Hugues Chenet, Josh Ryan-Collins and Frank van Lerven, 'Climate-Related Financial Policy in a World of Radical Uncertainty: Towards a Precautionary Approach',

UCL Institute for Innovation and Public Purpose Working Paper Series, 23 December 2019, www.ucl.ac.uk/bartlett/public-purpose/publica tions/2019/dec/climate-related-financial-policy-world-radical-un certainty (accessed 1 March 2022).

82 Chenet, Ryan-Collins and van Lerven, 'Climate-Related Financial Policy'; Geoff Mann, 'Check Your Spillover', *London Review of Books* 10, no. 3 (2022), www.lrb.co.uk/the-paper/v44/n03/geoff-mann/ check-your-spillover (accessed 1 March 2022).

83 Andreas Kluth, 'A Liberal Manifesto in a Time of Inequality and Climate Change', *Bloomberg*, 18 January 2020, www.bloombergquint. com/business/how-liberalism-can-solve-inequality-and-climate-cha nge (accessed 1 March 2022).

84 Max Ajl, *A People's Green New Deal* (London: Pluto Press, 2021).

85 Importantly, in recognition of this, financial markets and regulators are increasingly seeking mechanisms to place a monetary value on ecosystems, species and beyond. The considerable problems with this approach are discussed in Chapter 6.

86 Adam Tooze 'Why Inflation and the Cost-Of-Living Crisis Won't Take us Back to the 1970s', *The New Statesman*, 4 February 2022, www. newstatesman.com/ideas/2022/02/why-inflation-and-the-cost-of-living-crisis-wont-take-us-back-to-the-1970s (accessed 1 March 2022).

87 Stokes and Mildenberger, 'The Trouble with Carbon Pricing'.

88 Cedric Durand, 'Energy Dilemma', *New Left Review: Sidecar*, 5 November 2021, https://newleftreview.org/sidecar/posts/energy-dilemma (accessed 1 March 2022).

89 Nathalie Berta, Emmanuelle Gautherat and Ozgur Gun, 'Transactions in the European Carbon Market: A Bubble of Compliance in a Whirlpool of Speculation', *Cambridge Journal of Economics* 41, no. 2 (2017): 575–593, doi: 10.1093/cje/bew041.

90 Claudia Kettner et al., 'Price Volatility in Carbon Markets: Why it Matters and How it Can be Managed', *Österreichisches Institut für Wirtschaftsforschung*, 2011; Frédéric Hache, '2021: A Carbon Markets Odyssey – Policy report on the EU ETS review', *Green Finance Observatory*, 2022.

91 Ewa Krukowska, 'EU Urged to Protect Carbon Market From Excessive Speculation', *Bloomberg*, 15 December 2021, www.bloomb erg.com/news/articles/2021-12-15/eu-urged-to-protect-carbon-mar ket-from-excessive-speculation (accessed 15 January 2022). Note that certain carbon markets such as China's comparatively nascent

emissions trading scheme have implemented some controls to limit speculative trading, but these examples are scarce and, critically, represent an additional source of complexity in constructing a market for which a primary justification is to mitigate the need for complex state regulation and enforcement in the first place.

92 Nicholas Bouleau, *Le Monsenge de Finance: Les Mathematiques, Le Signal-Prix, et La Planete* (Paris: Atelier, 2018). As quoted (and translated) in Hache, '50 Shades of Green. Part I'.

Chapter 3: Titans

1 Antonio Gramsci, translated from the original Italian in *La Citta Futura* (1917), as quoted in Giovanni Tiso, 'I Hate the Indifferent', *Overland Journal*, 18 March 2013, https://overland.org.au/2013/03/i-hate-the-indifferent/ (accessed 2 October 2021).

2 Jeff Goodell, "The Fuse Has Been Blown', and the Doomsday Glacier is Coming for Us All', *Rolling Stone*, 29 December 2021, www.rollingstone.com/politics/politics-features/doomsday-glacier-thwaites-antarctica-climate-crisis-1273841/ (accessed 1 March 2022).

3 IPCC, 'Global warming of 1.5°C' (2018), *Intergovernmental Panel on Climate Change*, www.ipcc.ch/sr15/ (accessed 1 March 2022).

4 Timothy Lenton et al., 'Climate Tipping Points: Too Risky to Bet Against', *Nature* 575 (2019): 592–596.

5 Ivan Ascher, *Portfolio Society: On the Capitalist Mode of prediction* (Princeton: Zero Books, 2017).

6 Ibid.

7 Wolfram Schlenker and Charles A. Taylor, 'Market Expectations about Climate Change' (2019), *National Bureau of Economic Research*, www.nber.org/papers/w25554 (accessed 1 March 2022).

8 This insight, drawing on the work of Katharina Pistor, is explored in further depth in Chapter 5. See Katharina Pistor, *The Code of Capital: How the Law Creates Wealth and Inequality* (Princeton, NJ: Princeton University Press, 2019).

9 Yun Li and Nate Rattner, 'S&P 500 Doubles from its Pandemic Bottom, Marking the Fastest Bull Market Rally since WWII', *CNBC*, 16 August 2021, www.cnbc.com/2021/08/16/sp-500-doubles-from-its-pandemic-bottom-marking-the-fastest-bull-market-rally-since-wwii.html (accessed 1 March 2022).

Notes

10 https://twitter.com/jbarro/status/1354464982981877762 (accessed 1 March 2022).

11 Doug Henwood, 'The GameStop Bubble is a Lesson in the Absurdity and Uselessness of the Stock Market', *Jacobin*, 27 January 2021, www.jacobinmag.com/2021/01/gamestop-stock-market-reddit (accessed 1 March 2022).

12 Lisa Adkins, Melinda Cooper and Martijn Konings, *The Asset Economy: Property Ownership and the New Logic of Inequality* (Bristol: Polity Press, 2020).

13 Doug Henwood, *Wall Street: How it Works and For Whom* (London: Verso, 1997).

14 Mathew Lawrence et al., 'Commoning the Company', *Common Wealth*, 17 April 2020, www.common-wealth.co.uk/reports/commoning-the-company (accessed 1 March 2022).

15 By real assets I mean, for instance, the housing market, which received substantial government assistance in the UK, for example, in the form of tax breaks and other incentives to keep house prices elevated.

16 Yakov Feygin, 'The Deflationary Bloc', *Phenomenal World*, 9 January 2021. www.phenomenalworld.org/analysis/deflation-inflation/ (accessed 10 September 2021).

17 Ibid.

18 Adkins, Cooper and Konings, *The Asset Economy*.

19 Andrew Haldane, 'Age of the Asset Manager?' (2014), speech given at the London Business School, www.bankofengland.co.uk/-/media/boe/files/speech/2014/the-age-of-asset-management.pdf (accessed 1 March 2022). See also Thomas Piketty, *Capital in the 21st Century* (Cambridge, MA: Harvard University Press, 2014).

20 Oddny Helgadottir, 'Banking Upside Down: The Implicit Politics of Shadow Banking Expertise', *Review of International Political Economy* 23, no. 6 (2016): 1–26, doi: 10.1080/09692290.2016.1224196.

21 Edward Stevenson, 'The Rise of Non-Bank Lenders', *IQEQ,* 8 December 2021, https://iqeq.com/insights/rise-non-bank-lenders (accessed 1 March 2022).

22 Isabel Schnabel, 'The Rise of Non-Bank Finance and its Implications for Monetary Policy Transmission: Speech by Isabel Schnabel', *European Central Bank*, 16 September 2021, www.bis.org/review/r210916f.htm (accessed 1 March 2022).

23 Gillian Tett, 'ETFs are the Canary in the Bond Coal Mine', *The Financial Times*, 29 July 2020, www.ft.com/

301

content/6bdc7747-3ab9-4410-a4b2-ba9acbe204e8 (accessed 1 March 2022).

24 Bank of England, 'Assessing the Resilience of Market-Based Finance', *Bank of England*, 13 July 2021, www.bankofengland.co.uk/report/ 2021/assessing-the-resilience-of-market-based-finance (accessed 1 March 2022).

25 Ibid.

26 Shares in ETFs are traded on exchanges like a stock throughout the day, rather than their purchase being restricted to end-of-day transactions via fund management companies, as is the case for a traditional mutual fund. Figures from Crystal Kim, 'The ETF Business is Dominated by the Big Three. The SEC is Suddenly Concerned', *Barrons*, 5 April 2019, www.barrons.com/articles/etfs-are-dominated-by-blackrock-vanguard-and-state-street-the-sec-is-con cerned-51554512133 (accessed 1 March 2022).

27 Lubasha Heredia et al., 'The $100 Trillion Machine: Global Asset Management 2021', *Boston Consulting Group*, 8 July 2021, www.bcg. com/publications/2021/global-asset-management-industry-report (accessed 1 March 2022).

28 This coordinating power was so profound as to prompt Marx, along-side various socialist thinkers, to view them as an embryonic model for a planned economy.

29 Stefan Avdjiev et al., 'Tracking the International Footprints of Global Firms', *Bank for International Settlements Quarterly Review*, 11 March 2018, www.bis.org/publ/qtrpdf/r_qt1803f.htm (accessed 1 March 2022).

30 For a survey of ecological and social harms enabled by the specific legal benefits of corporate personhood, see David Whyte, *Ecocide: Kill the Corporation Before it Kills Us* (Manchester: Manchester University Press, 2021).

31 In practice, many corporate managers are also shareholders, with their remuneration packages typically offering large numbers of shares vested over their tenure at the company. In the process, the interests of management have been formally aligned with those of the shareholder.

32 Paddy Ireland, 'Company Law and the Myth of Shareholder Ownership', *Modern Law Review* 62, no. 1 (1999), www.jstor.org/ stable/1097073 (accessed 25 March 2022).

33 Productive investment measured here as the ratio of CapEx to Depreciation and Amortization, sourced from Adrienne Buller and

Benjamin Braun, 'Under New Management: Share Ownership and the Rise of UK Asset Manager Capitalism', *Common Wealth*, 7 September 2021, www.common-wealth.co.uk/reports/under-new-management-share-ownership-and-the-growth-of-uk-asset-manager-capitalism (accessed 1 March 2022).

34 The fraction of this corporate debt considered 'junk' or 'non-investment grade' also rose markedly over the same period. Figures from S. Çelik, G. Demirtaş and M. Isaksson, 'Corporate Bond Market Trends, Emerging Risks and Monetary Policy', *OECD: Capital Market Series*, 2020, www.oecd.org/corporate/ca/Corporate-Bond-Market-Trends-Emerging-Risks-Monetary-Policy.pdf (accessed 1 March 2022).

35 'S&P 500 Buybacks Set A Record High', *S&P Dow Jones*, 21 December 2021. www.spglobal.com/spdji/en/corporate-news/article/sp-500-buybacks-set-a-record-high/ (accessed 4 March 2022).

36 Benjamin Braun, 'Asset Manager Capitalism as a Corporate Governance Regime', *SocArXiv* (2020, doi: 10.31235/osf.io/v6gue.

37 Ibid.

38 Ibid.

39 Ibid.

40 Though there are some disputes as to their exact definitions and equivalence, I use these terms interchangeably throughout this book to mean those financial products whose portfolios are allocated based on tracking an index. Similarly, I use 'active' to denote those funds with portfolios that are constructed based on manager discretion, while acknowledging that in practice some funds may use a blended approach.

41 For example, a poster published by the Leuthold Group of investors, shortly after the first index fund was launched, featured a very concerned Uncle Sam 'stamping out' index funds, emblazoned with the tagline 'Index Funds are UnAmerican!'

42 David McWilliams, 'Quantitative Easing was the Father of Millennial Socialism', *The Financial Times*, 1 March 2019, www.ft.com/content/cbed81fc-3b56-11e9-9988-28303f70fcff (accessed 1 March 2022).

43 See e.g. David Thorpe 'The Passive Perspective', *The Financial Times Adviser*, 18 March 2021, www.ftadviser.com/investments/2021/03/18/the-passive-perspective/ (accessed 1 March 2022). Additional links between QE and the success of passive investing is the propensity for QE to benefit heavily indebted companies, which, supposedly,

active managers might traditionally avoid, thereby 'turn[ing] active management on its head'. See Tom Landstreet, 'The Big Idea: End of QE Sets New Stage for Active v Passive Debate', *CityWire*, 25 October 2017, https://citywireamericas.com/news/the-big-idea-end-of-qe-se ts-new-stage-for-active-v-passive-debate/a1062816 (accessed 1 March 2022).

44 Even the largest pension funds have begun to allocate their assets via passive strategies, marking a significant shift for an industry once relatively confined to the stability of government bonds. Figures sourced from Robin Wigglesworth, 'Global Passive Assets hit $15 trillion as ETF Boom Heats Up', *The Financial Times*, 9 May 2021, www.ft.com/content/7d5c2468-619c-4c4b-b3e7-b0da015e939d (accessed 1 March 2022).

45 In the UK, for example, passive funds now represent nearly 40% of net fund assets, and even once-stalwart active investors such as Legal & General have reoriented toward index-tracking products. Via Chris Hayes, 'Passive Attack: Charting the Rise of Passive Index Trackers', *Common Wealth*, 17 December 2021, www.common-wealth.co.uk/reports/passive-attack (accessed 1 March 2022).

46 David McLaughlin and Annie Massa, 'The Hidden Dangers of the Great Index Fund Takeover', *Bloomberg*, 9 January 2020, www.bloomberg.com/news/features/2020-01-09/the-hidden-dangers-of-th e-great-index-fund-takeover (accessed 1 March 2022).

47 Lucian Bebchuk and Scott Hirst, 'Index Funds and the Future of Corporate Governance: Theory, Evidence, and Policy', *Columbia Law Review* 119, no. 8 (2019), https://columbialawreview.org/content/index-funds-and-the-future-of-corporate-governance-theory-evidence-and-policy/ (accessed 1 March 2022).

48 For example, Rio Tinto, a diversified mining company, divested its thermal coal mining assets and operations following shareholder pressure (among other factors, such as waning expectations of profitability).

49 Jon Hale, 'The ESG Advisor: Index Funds Pose Problems for Asset Manager Net-Zero Commitments', *MorningStar*, 12 November 2021, www.morningstar.com/articles/1067786/the-esg-advisor-index-funds-pose-problems-for-asset-manager-net-zero-commitments (accessed 1 March 2022).

50 Lucie Pinson, 'An Inconvenient truth: How Passive Investing is Blocking Climate Progress', *ESG Clarity*, 5 August 2021, https://

esgclarity.com/an-inconvenient-truth-how-passive-investing-is-block
ing-climate-progress/ (accessed 1 March 2022).

51 Reuters Staff, 'BlackRock Suspends Purchases of Russian Securities in
Active and Index-Linked Funds', *Reuters*, 3 March 2022, www.reuters.
com/article/ukraine-crisis-blackrock-idCAKCN2L024H (accessed 4
March 2022).

52 Robin Wigglesworth, *Trillions: How a Band of Wall Street Renegades
Invented the Index Fund and Changed Finance Forever* (London: Penguin
Random House, 2021).

53 Ibid.

54 Ibid.

55 Ibid.

56 John Authers, 'Indices Don't Just Measure Markets – They Drive
Performance', *The Financial Times*, 23 June 2018, www.ft.com/con
tent/ebcb8e88-7572-11e8-aa31-31da4279a601 (accessed 1 March
2022).

57 Ibid.

58 Michael Dathan and Sergei Davydenko, 'Debt Issuance in the Era
of Passive Investment' (2020), https://papers.ssrn.com/sol3/papers.
cfm?abstract_id=3152612 (accessed 21 October 2021).

59 Christopher K. Merker, 'How Passive Investment Dulls the Green
Wave', *Financial Times*, 13 February 2020, http://sustainablefinance
blog.com/2020/02/13/how-passive-investment-dulls-the-green-wave-
ft/ (accessed 1 March 2022).

60 Anusha Chari, 'Seminar: Are Index Funds Harmful for Global
Financial Stability?' (2022), *Peterson Institute for International Economics*,
www.youtube.com/watch?v=C5lbPnF-2hs&ab_channel=PetersonIn
stituteforInternationalEconomics (accessed 1 March 2022).

61 Hugues Chenet, Josh Ryan-Collins and Frank van Lerven, 'Climate-
Related Financial Policy in a World of Radical Uncertainty:
Towards a Precautionary Approach', *UCL Institute for Innovation and
Public Purpose Working Paper Series*, 23 December 2019, www.ucl.ac.uk/
bartlett/public-purpose/publications/2019/dec/climate-related-fin
ancial-policy-world-radical-uncertainty (accessed 1 March 2022).

62 The Sunrise Project, 'The Passives Problem and the Paris Goals: How
Index Investing Trends Threaten Climate Action' (2019), *The Sunrise
Project*, https://sunriseproject.org/wp-content/uploads/2020/01/
Sunrise-Project-Report-The-Passives-Problem-and-Paris-Goals.pdf
(accessed 1 March 2022). See also Adrienne Buller and Chris Hayes,

'Passive Revolution', *Common Wealth*, 2022, www.common-wealth. co.uk/reports/the-passive-revolution.

63 Johannes Petry, Jan Fichtner and Eelke Heemskerk, 'The New Gatekeepers of Financial Claims: States, Passive Markets, and the Growing Power of Index Providers', in Kai Koddenbrock and Benjamin Braun (eds), *Capital Claims: Following Finance Across Borders* (London: Routledge, 2022).

64 Ibid.

65 Wigglesworth, *Trillions*.

66 Richard Henderson and Own Walker, 'BlackRock's Black Box: The Technology Hub of Modern Finance', *The Financial Times*, 24 February 2020, www.ft.com/content/5ba6f40e-4e4d-11ea-95a0-43d1 8ec715f5 (accessed 1 March 2022).

67 Ibid.

68 Ibid. Impressively, with over $250 billion in assets, if it were an independent firm, Apple's investment subsidiary, Braeburn Capital, would be among the world's largest asset managers.

69 'Press Release: BlackRock Unveils New Offering to Power Investors' Transition to Net Zero Emissions', *BlackRock*, 1 December 2020, www.blackrock.com/corporate/newsroom/press-releases/article/cor porate-one/press-releases/blackrock-unveils-new-offering (accessed 25 October 2021).

70 Chenet, Ryan-Collins and Van Lerven, 'Climate-Related Financial Risk'.

71 Servaas Storm, 'Capitalism and Climate Change: Can the Invisible Hand Adjust the Natural Thermostat?', *Development and Change* 40, no. 6 (2019): 1011–1038, doi: 10.1111/j.1467-7660.2009.01610.x.

72 ETFs and index-tracking funds are often conflated. In reality, while many index-tracking funds are also ETFs, they need not be, and there is a significant market in index-tracking traditional mutual funds. Likewise, ETFs can be actively managed. Put plainly, while passive vs. active (or 'index tracking') describes a fund's *strategy*, the distinction between ETF and mutual (or other type of fund) describes the mechanics of the fund.

73 Wigglesworth, *Trillions*.

74 Ibid.

75 This literature is discussed at length in, e.g., Mariana Mazzucato, *The Value of Everything: Making and Taking in the Global Economy* (London: Allen Lane, 2018).

Notes

Notes

76 Bebchuk and Hirst, 'Index Funds and the Future of Corporate Governance'.

77 For an exceptional distillation of the logic of 'universal' or 'common ownership', see Madison Condon, 'Externalities and the Common Owner', *Washington Law Review* 95, no. 1 (2020), https://digitalcom mons.law.uw.edu/wlr/vol95/iss1/4 (accessed 2 March 2022).

78 'Shell Announces Comprehensive Carbon Emissions Reductions Commitment with Climate Action 100+ Investors', *Climate Action 100+*, 3 December 2018, www.climateaction100.org/news/shell-announces-comprehensive-carbon-emissions-reductions-commitment-with-climate-action-100-investors/ (accessed 2 March 2022).

79 These voting patterns are discussed in depth in the next chapter.

80 Robert G. Monks and Nell Minow, *Corporate Governance: Fifth Edition* (Chichester: John Wiley & Sons, 2011).

81 Common Wealth and the High Pay Centre, 'Do Dividends Pay Our Pensions?' *The Trades Union Congress*, 10 January 2022, www.tuc.org.uk/research-analysis/reports/do-dividends-pay-our-pensions (accessed 2 March 2022).

82 John Sabelhaus and Alice Henriques Volz, 'FEDS Notes: Are Disappearing Employer Pensions Contributing to Rising Wealth Inequality?', *The United States Federal Reserve*, 1 February 2019, www.fed eralreserve.gov/econres/notes/feds-notes/are-disappearing-employer-pensions-contributing-to-rising-wealth-inequality-20190201.htm (accessed 11 January 2022).

83 Robert Gebeloff, 'Who Owns Stocks? Explaining the Rise in Inequality During the Pandemic', *The New York Times*, 26 January 2021, www.nytimes.com/2021/01/26/upshot/stocks-pandemic-ine quality.html (accessed 2 March 2022).

84 See, for example, David Dayen, 'Larry Fink and his BlackRock Team Poised to Take Over Hillary Clinton's Treasury Department', *The Intercept*, 2 March 2016, https://theintercept.com/2016/03/02/larry-fink-and-his-blackrock-team-poised-to-take-over-hillary-clintons-trea sury-department/ (accessed 2 March 2022).

85 Benjamin Braun and Adrienne Buller, 'Titans', *Phenomenal World*, 6 November 2021, www.phenomenalworld.org/analysis/blackrock-asset-manager-capitalism/ (accessed 2 March 2022); BlackRock Investment Institute, 'Dealing with the Next Downturn: From Unconventional Monetary Policy to Unprecedented Policy Coordination', *BlackRock*, 15 August 2019, www.blackrock.com/cor

porate/insights/blackrock-investment-institute/publications/global-macro-outlook/august-2019 (accessed 2 March 2022).

86 Leslie P. Norton, 'BlackRock is Biggest Beneficiary of Fed Purchases of Corporate Bond ETFs', *Barrons*, 1 June 2020, www.barrons.com/articles/blackrock-is-biggest-beneficiary-of-fed-purchases-of-corporate-bond-etfs-51591034726 (accessed 2 March 2022).

87 Annie Massa and Caleb Melby, 'In Fink We Trust: BlackRock is Now the Fourth Branch of Government', *Bloomberg*, 21 May 2020, www.bloomberg.com/news/articles/2020-05-21/how-larry-fink-s-blackrock-is-helping-the-fed-with-bond-buying (accessed 27 August 2021).

88 Jeanna Smialek, 'Top U.S. Officials Consulted with BlackRock as Markets Melted Down', *The New York Times*, 24 June 2021, www.nytimes.com/2021/06/24/business/economy/fed-blackrock-pandemic-crisis.html (accessed 27 August 2021).

Chapter 4: Alchemists

1 Robert Frost, 'Nothing Gold Can Stay', *The Yale Review* (1923).

2 Jonathan Watts, '"Airpocalypse" Hits Siberian City as Heatwave Sparks Forest Fires', *The Guardian*, 20 July 2021, www.theguardian.com/environment/2021/jul/20/airpocalypse-hits-siberian-city-as-heatwave-sparks-forest-fires (accessed 2 March 2022).

3 Newsround, 'What are Zombie Fires and Why is the Arctic on Fire?', *BBC News*, 20 May 2021, www.bbc.co.uk/newsround/57173570 (accessed 22 July 2021).

4 Robert MacFarlane, *Underland: A Deep Time Journey* (London: W.W. Norton & Company, 2020), p. 284.

5 'Secret Cold War Base Shifts Through Greenland Ice', *BBC News*, 2 August 2019, www.bbc.co.uk/news/blogs-news-from-elsewhere-49209510 (accessed 2 March 2022).

6 'Oil Auction in Arctic Wildlife Refuge Draws Scant Interest', *The Financial Times*, 6 January 2021, www.ft.com/content/bf1c671e-a032-43a0-8471-5cfc133c8fee (accessed 2 March 2022).

7 Total, 'Russia: Total Signs Definitive Agreements for Entry into Arctic LNG 2', 3 May 2019, https://totalenergies.com/media/news/press-releases/russia-total-signs-definitive-agreements-entry-arctic-lng-2 (accessed 5 July 2021).

8 Sanne Wass, 'Sustainability-Linked Bonds in "Rapid Growth" as More Firms Tap ESG Debt Market', *S&P Global*, 23 June 2021, www.spglobal.com/marketintelligence/en/news-insights/latest-news-head lines/sustainability-linked-bonds-in-rapid-growth-as-more-firms-tap-esg-debt-market-65049789 (accessed 2 March 2022).

9 Amanda Luhavalja, 'Equinor's Move to Halve Carbon Intensity, Scope 3 Emissions Both Praised, Panned', *S&P Global Market Intelligence*, 7 February 2020, www.spglobal.com/marketintelligence/en/news-insights/latest-news-headlines/equinor-s-move-to-halve-car bon-intensity-scope-3-emissions-both-praised-panned-56984504 (acc essed 2 March 2022).

10 Katherine Dunn, 'ESG Investing is Bigger Than Ever. Here's How You Can Save the World, and Your Portfolio', *Fortune*, 11 October 2020, https://fortune.com/2020/10/11/esg-investing-climate-social-impact-tips-advice-economic-social-governance-stocks/ (accessed 2 March 2022).

11 Bloomberg Intelligence, 'ESG Assets May Hit $53 Trillion by 2025, a Third of global AUM', *Bloomberg Professional Services*, 23 February 2021, www.bloomberg.com/professional/blog/esg-assets-may-hit-53-trillion-by-2025-a-third-of-global-aum/ (accessed 2 March 2022).

12 Ibid.

13 'Sustainable Bond Issuance Crossed the $1 Trillion Milestone in 2021', *Linklaters: Sustainable Futures*, 31 January 2022, https://sus tainablefutures.linklaters.com/post/102hhj6/sustainable-bond-iss uance-crossed-the-1-trillion-milestone-in-2021 (accessed 4 March 2022).

14 HM Treasury, Department for Work & Pensions, and Department for Business, Energy and Industrial Strategy, 'Greening Finance: A Roadmap to Sustainable Investing', *HM Treasury*, 18 October 2021, www.gov.uk/government/publications/greening-finance-a-roadmap-to-sustainable-investing (accessed 2 March 2022).

15 'Overview', *Task Force on Climate-Related Financial Disclosures*, March 2021, www.fsb-tcfd.org/publications/ (accessed 2 March 2022).

16 'Net Zero Asset Managers Fall Short of Targets Set by Scientists', *Bloomberg*, 10 November 2021, www.bloomberg.com/news/arti cles/2021-11-10/net-zero-asset-managers-fall-short-of-targets-set-by-sc ientists (accessed 2 March 2022).

17 Mark Carney, 'Building a Private Finance System for Net Zero' (2020), *COP26 Private Finance Hub*, https://ukcop26.org/wp-content/

uploads/2020/11/COP26-Private-Finance-Hub-Strategy_Nov-2020v4.
1.pdf (accessed 2 March 2022).

18 Daniela Gabor, 'The Wall Street Consensus', *Development and Change*
52, no. 3 (2021), doi: 10.1111/dech.12645.

19 'BlackRock Makes Energy Acquisition as U.S. Infrastructure Policy
Looms', *Reuters*, 1 February 2017, www.reuters.com/article/us-
blackrock-m-a-infrastructure-idUSKBN15G53D (accessed 2 March
2022).

20 Kate Bayliss and Elisa Van Waeyenberge, 'Unpacking the Public
Private Partnership Revival', *The Journal of Development Studies* 54, no. 4
(2018): 577–593.

21 Yannis Dafermos, Daniela Gabor and Jo Michell, 'The Wall Street
Consensus in Pandemic Times: What Does it Mean for Climate-
Aligned Development?', *Canadian Journal of Development Studies* 42,
no. 1–2 (2021): 238–251, doi: 10.1080/02255189.2020.1865137.

22 Ibid.

23 It should be noted that, in practice, certain funds or investors might
blend both the portfolio and stewardship approaches, though
this is less common, as the two can be, to an extent, mutually
exclusive.

24 To borrow a turn of phrase from an industry friend who will remain
anonymous.

25 MSCI ESG Research, 'Swipe to Invest: The Story Behind
Millennials and ESG Investing' (2020), *MSCI*, www.msci.com/
documents/10199/07e7a7d3-59c3-4d0b-b0b5-029e8fd3974b (accessed 2 March 2022).

26 Witold Henisz, Tim Koller and Robin Nuttall, 'Five ways that ESG
creates value', *McKinsey Quarterly*, November 2019, www.mckinsey.
com/business-functions/strategy-and-corporate-finance/our-insigh
ts/five-ways-that-esg-creates-value (accessed 2 March 2022).

27 Siobhan Riding, 'ESG Funds Attract Record Inflows During Crisis',
The Financial Times, 10 August 2020, www.ft.com/content/27025f35-
283f-4956-b6a0-0adbfd4c7a0e (accessed 2 March 2022).

28 Esther Whieldon and Robert Clark, 'ESG Funds Beat Out S&P 500
in 1st year of COVID-19; How 1 Fund Shot to the Top', *S&P Global
Market Intelligence*, 6 April 2021, www.spglobal.com/marketintelligen
ce/en/news-insights/latest-news-headlines/esg-funds-beat-out-s-p-500-
in-1st-year-of-covid-19-how-1-fund-shot-to-the-top-63224550 (accessed 2 March 2022).

29 Robert Armstrong, 'The Fallacy of ESG Investing', *The Financial Times*, 23 October 2020, www.ft.com/content/9e3e1d8b-bf9f-4d8c-baee-0b25c3113319 (accessed 2 March 2022).

30 Reed Albergotti, 'Apple's Longtime Supplier Accused of Using Forced Labor in China', *The Washington Post*, 29 December 2020, www.washingtonpost.com/technology/2020/12/29/lens-technology-apple-uighur/ (accessed 2 March 2022).

31 Richard Phillips, Jenaline Pyle and Ronen Palan, 'The Amazon Method: How to Take Advantage of the International Tax System to Avoid Paying Tax' (2020), *Die Linke IM Europarlamant*, https://left.eu/content/uploads/2021/05/THEamazonMETHOD-1.pdf (accessed 2 March 2022).

32 Aneesh Raghunandan and Shiva Rajgopal, 'Do ESG Funds Make Stakeholder-Friendly Investments?' (2021), *Columbia Business School*, https://ssrn.com/abstract=3826357 (accessed 2 March 2022).

33 Jeanne Martin et al., 'Voting Matters 2020', *ShareAction*, December 2020, https://api.shareaction.org/resources/reports/Voting-Matters-2020.pdf (accessed 2 March 2022).

34 Ibid.

35 BlackRock, 'Pursuing Long-Term Value for Our Clients: BlackRock Investment Stewardship' (2021), *BlackRock*, p. 41, www.blackrock.com/corporate/literature/publication/2021-voting-spotlight-full-report.pdf (accessed 2 March 2022).

36 Ibid.

37 Friends of the Earth, 'Doubling Down on Deforestation: How the Big Three Asset Managers Enable Consumer Goods Companies to Destroy the World's Forests' (2020), *Friends of the Earth*, https://foe.org/resources/doubling-down-on-deforestation/ (accessed 2 March 2022).

38 Siobhan Riding and Attracta Mooney, 'Investors blast EU's omissions of oil from ESG disclosures', *The Financial Times*, 3 May 2020, www.ft.com/content/07083de6-c4d4-4f1b-8dc4-c4490e670216 (accessed 2 March 2022).

39 Attracta Mooney and Patricia Nilsson, 'Why Did So Many ESG Funds Back Boohoo?', *The Financial Times*, 27 July 2020, www.ft.com/content/ead7daea-0457-4a0d-9175-93452f0878ec (accessed 2 March 2022).

40 For instance, in 2019 I examined the holdings of a series of funds marketed explicitly with the phrase 'fossil fuel reserves free' in their names, only to find a number had shares in major thermal coal producers

such as Germany's RWE and Brazil's Vale. See: InfluenceMap, 'Climate Funds and Fossil Fuels' (2019), *InfluenceMap*, https://influencemap.org/report/Climate-Funds-and-Fossil-Fuels-8f2c813ed814f e5b1eef61b48497b592 (accessed 2 March 2022).

41 Jamie Powell, 'ESG without the S', *The Financial Times*, 22 May 2020, www.ft.com/content/d8a77b40-990e-4329-8629-a18ddbb39f0c (accessed 2 March 2022).

42 Adrienne Buller, 'Doing Well By Doing Good? Examining the rise of Environmental, Social, Governance Investing', *Common Wealth*, 20 December 2020, www.common-wealth.co.uk/reports/doing-well-by-doing-good-examining-the-rise-of-environmental-social-governan ce-esg-investing (accessed 2 March 2022).

43 Nadia Ameli, Sumit Kothari and Michael Grubb (2021) 'Misplaced Expectations from Climate Disclosure Initiatives', *Nature Climate Change* 11 (2021): 917–924, www.nature.com/articles/s41558-021-01174-8 (accessed 2 March 2022).

44 Ibid.

45 Raghunandan and Rajgopal, 'Do ESG Funds Make Stakeholder-Friendly Investments?'

46 Ameli, Kothari and Grubb, 'Misplaced Expectations'.

47 Tariq Fancy, 'The Secret Diary of a "Sustainable Investor" – Part 1', *Medium*, 20 August 2021, https://medium.com/@sosofancy/the-secret-diary-of-a-sustainable-investor-part-1-70b6987fa139 (accessed 2 March 2022).

48 Hugues Chenet, Josh Ryan-Collins and Frank van Lerven, 'Climate-Related Financial Risk in a World of Radical Uncertainty: Towards a Precautionary Approach', *UCL Institute for Innovation and Public Purpose*, 23 December 2019, www.ucl.ac.uk/bartlett/public-purpose/pub lications/2019/dec/climate-related-financial-policy-world-radical-un certainty (accessed 2 March 2022).

49 Christian Wilson and Ben Caldecott, 'Breaking the Bond: Primary Markets and Carbon-Intensive Financing', Oxford Sustainable Finance Programme, The Smith School of Enterprise and the Environment, Oxford University. 2021.

50 Robert Armstrong 'The ESG Investing Industry is Dangerous', *The Financial Times*, 24 August 2021. www.ft.com/content/eco 2fd5d-e8bd-45bd-b015-a5799ae820cf.

51 Andrew Ross Sorkin, 'BlackRock CEO Larry Fink: Climate Crisis Will Reshape Finance', *The New York Times*, 24 February 2020, www.

nytimes.com/2020/01/14/business/dealbook/larry-fink-blackrock-cli
mate-change.html (accessed 2 March 2022).

52 Benjamin Braun, 'Asset Manager Capitalism as a Corporate
Governance Regime', *SocArXiv* (2020, doi:10.31235/osf.io/v6gue.

53 Anusar Farooqui, 'Seeing like BlackRock', *Policy Tensor*, 9 July 2021,
https://policytensor.substack.com/p/seeing-like-blackrock (accessed
2 March 2022).

54 Michael Mankins, Karen Harris and David Harding, 'Strategy in the
Age of Superabundant Capital', *Harvard Business Review*, March–April
2017, https://hbr.org/2017/03/strategy-in-the-age-of-superabunda
nt-capital (accessed 2 March 2022).

55 David Dayen, 'Bipartisan Senate Infrastructure Plan is a Stalking
Horse for Privatization', *The American Prospect*, 21 June 2021, https://
prospect.org/politics/bipartisan-senate-infrastructure-plan-privatizat
ion-asset-recycling/ (accessed 2 March 2022).

56 'Financing the Green Transition: The European Green Deal
Investment Plan and Just Transition Mechanism', *The European
Commission*, 14 January 2020, https://ec.europa.eu/commission/
presscorner/detail/en/qanda_20_24 (accessed 5 July 2021).

57 Cedric Durand, 'Energy Dilemma', *New Left Review: Sidecar*, 5
November 2021, https://newleftreview.org/sidecar/posts/energy-
dilemma (accessed 2 March 2022).

58 Ibid.

59 Joseph Stiglitz, *Freefall: America, Free Markets and the Sinking of the World
Economy* (New York: W.W. Norton & Company, 2010).

60 Chris Flood, 'ETF Inflows Shoot Past 2020's Full-Year Record Total',
The Financial Times, 10 September 2021, www.ft.com/content/7148206f-
dcec-4dd7-b940-f81ddc77a5bf (accessed 2 March 2022).

61 Jason W. Moore and Raj Patel, *A History of the World in Seven Cheap
Things* (London: Verso, 2017).

Chapter 5: Time travellers

1 Sign at a demonstration at Plaza de Mayo, Buenos Aires, Argentina,
August 2019. As cited in Natalie Alcoba, 'Headed for Disaster':
Argentinians Protest Against IMF debt deal', *Al Jazeera*, 12 December
2021. www.aljazeera.com/news/2021/12/12/headed-for-disaster-argen
tinians-protest-against-imf-debt-deal (accessed 18 December 2021).

Notes

2 William Shakespeare, *Hamlet* (London: Wordsworth Editions, 1992).

3 Alexander Koch et al., 'Earth System Impacts of the European Arrival and Great Dying in the Americas after 1492', *Quaternary Science Reviews* 207, no. 1 (2019): 13–36, doi: 10.1016/j.quascirev.2018.12.004.

4 'Humanity's Immense Impact on Earth's Climate and Carbon Cycle', *The Economist*, 9 May 2020, www.economist.com/schools-brief/2020/05/09/humanitys-immense-impact-on-earths-climate-and-carbon-cycle (accessed 2 March 2022).

5 United Nations Framework Convention on Climate Change, 'Adoption of the Paris Agreement, 21st Conference of the Parties', *United Nations*, 12 December 2015, https://unfccc.int/resource/docs/2015/cop21/eng/l09r01.pdf (accessed 2 March 2022).

6 Jocelyn Timperley, 'The Broken $100-Billion Promise of Climate Finance – And How to Fix It', *Nature*, 20 October 2021, www.nature.com/articles/d41586-021-02846-3 (accessed 2 March 2022).

7 Elena Ares and Philip Loft, 'COP26: Delivering on $100 Billion Climate Finance', *UK Parliament: House of Commons Library*, 3 November 2021, https://commonslibrary.parliament.uk/cop26-delivering-on-100-billion-climate-finance/ (accessed 2 March 2022).

8 'Press release: PM Calls on Richest Countries to Meet $100 Billion Climate Pledge', *Prime Minister's Office, 10 Downing Street*, 20 September 2021, www.gov.uk/government/news/pm-calls-on-richest-countries-to-meet-100-billion-climate-pledge (accessed 5 November 2021).

9 'Prime Minister Announces Investment in Global Climate Change Action', *Prime Minister of Canada Justin Trudeau*, 27 November 2015, https://pm.gc.ca/en/news/news-releases/2015/11/27/prime-minister-announces-investment-global-climate-change-action (accessed 12 November 2021).

10 Valerie Volcovici, 'Biden Pledges to Double U.S. Climate Change Aid; Some Activists Unimpressed', *Reuters*, 21 September 2021, www.reuters.com/business/environment/us-seeks-double-climate-change-aid-developing-nations-biden-202-09-21/ (accessed 2 March 2022).

11 All figures in this paragraph are sourced from: Simon Evans, 'Analysis: Which Countries are Historically Responsible for Climate Change?', *Carbon Brief*, 5 October 2021, www.carbonbrief.org/analysis-which-countries-are-historically-responsible-for-climate-change (accessed 2 March 2022).

12 Jason W. Moore, 'The Capitalocene, Part I: On the Nature and Origins of our Ecological Crisis', *The Journal of Peasant Studies* 44, no. 3 (2017): 594–630, doi: 10.1080/03066150.2016.1235036.

13 Ibid. See also Simon Lewis and Mark Maslin, 'Defining the Anthropocene', *Nature* 519 (2015), www.nature.com/articles/nature14258 (accessed 2 March 2022).

14 Hannah Ritchie and Max Roser, 'CO2 and Greenhouse Gas Emissions', May 2017, https://ourworldindata.org/co2-and-other-greenhouse-gas-emissions (accessed 2 March 2022).

15 Quoted in Stephen M. Gardiner, *A Perfect Moral Storm: The Ethical Tragedy of Climate Change* (Oxford: Oxford University Press, 2013).

16 Zia Weise and Karl Mathiesen, 'EU, US block effort for climate disaster funding at COP26, *Politico*, 13 November 2021, www.politico.eu/article/eu-us-block-financial-support-climate-change-cop26/ (accessed 2 March 2022).

17 Fiona Harvey and Rowena Mason, 'Alok Sharma "Deeply Frustrated" by India and China Over Coal', *The Guardian*, 14 November 2021, www.theguardian.com/environment/2021/nov/14/alok-sharma-deeply-frustrated-by-india-and-china-over-coal (accessed 2 March 2022).

18 'Confronting Carbon Inequality', *Oxfam*, 21 September 2020, https://oxfamilibrary.openrepository.com/bitstream/handle/10546/621052/mb-confronting-carbon-inequality-210920-en.pdf (accessed 4 March 2022).

19 T. Weidmann et al., 'Scientists' Warning on Affluence', *Nature Communications* 11, no. 3107 (2020): 11, www.nature.com/articles/s41467-020-16941-y (accessed 2 March 2022).

20 Bill Gates, *How to Avoid a Climate Disaster. The Solutions We Have and the Breakthroughs We Need* (London: Allen Lane, 2021).

21 Evidence of this effect is reviewed in Weidmann et al., 'Scientists' Warning on Affluence'; see also J. Lan et al., 'A Structural Decomposition Analysis of Global Energy Footprints'. *Applied Energy* 163 (2016): 436–451, doi: 10.1016/j.apenergy.2015.10.178.

22 'Humanity's Immense Impact on Earth's Climate and Carbon Cycle', *The Economist*, 9 May 2020, www.economist.com/schools-brief/2020/05/09/humanitys-immense-impact-on-earths-climate-and-carbon-cycle (accessed 2 March 2022).

23 Saikat Chatterjee and Thyagaraju Adinarayan, 'Buy, Sell, Repeat! No Room for "Hold" in Whipsawing Markets', *Reuters*, 3 August

2020, www.reuters.com/article/us-health-coronavirus-short-termis m-anal-idUSKBN24Z0XZ (accessed 2 March 2022).

24 The scholarship on this relationship is both expansive and vital reading. For a necessarily brief list of recent perspectives: Broulaye Bagayoko, 'Colonial Debt and Reparations', in Harpreet Kaur Paul and Dalia Gebrial (eds), *Perspectives on a Global Green New Deal* (Berlin: Rosa Luxemburg-Stiftung, 2021); Olúfẹ́mi O. Táíwò, *Reconsidering Reparations* (Oxford: Oxford University Press, 2022); Leon Sealey-Huggins (2018) 'The Climate Crisis is a Racist Crisis: Structural Racism, Inequality and Climate Change', in Azeezat Johnson, Remi Joseph-Salisbury, and Beth Kamunge (eds), *The Fire Now: Anti-Racist Scholarship in Times of Explicit Racial Violence* (London: Zed Books, 2018), pp. 99–113; Francoise Verges, 'Racial Capitalocene', in Gay Theresa Johnson and Alex Lubin (eds), *Futures of Black Radicalism* (London: Verso, 2017).

25 Walter Rodney, *How Europe Underdeveloped Africa* (London: Verso, 2018). Originally published 1972 by Bogle-L'Ouverture Publications.

26 Ibid.

27 Léonce Ndikumana, 'Capital flight from Africa: Resource Plunder and the Poisoned Paradises in Tax Havens', *Tax Justice Network*, 24 March 2021, https://taxjustice.net/2021/03/24/capital-flight-from-africa-resource-plunder-and-the-poisoned-paradises-in-tax-havens/ (accessed 4 March 2022).

28 See for example 'Managing Capital Inflows to Reduce Resource Transfer from Developing to Developed Countries', *United Nations Conference on Trade and Development*, 9 December 2019.

29 2019 was selected as a reference point as the pandemic induced unrepresentative patterns of aid spending. OECD, 'Aid by DAC Members Increases in 2019 With More Aid to the Poorest Countries' (2022) www.oecd.org/dac/financing-sustainable-development/dev elopment-finance-data/ODA-2019-detailed-summary.pdf (accessed 28 February 2022).

30 Curt Tarnoff, 'U.S. Agency for International Development (USAID): Background, Operations, and Issues', *Congressional Research Service* 7–5700, 21 July 2015, https://sgp.fas.org/crs/row/R44117. pdf (accessed 2 March 2022).

31 Raphael S. Cohen, 'Why We "Send Them Money"', *The Hill*, 30 December 2020, https://thehill.com/opinion/international/532044-why-we-send-them-money (accessed 12 August 2021).

32 Peter Beaumont, 'DfID Scheme Accused of "Putting UK Aid in Pockets of Wealthy Companies"', *The Guardian*, 14 August 2020, www.theguardian.com/global-development/2020/aug/14/dfid-sch eme-accused-of-putting-uk-aid-in-pockets-of-wealthy-companies (accessed 2 March 2022).

33 Ann Pettifor, *The Production of Money: How to Break the Power of Bankers* (London: Verso, 2018).

34 David Graeber, *Debt: The First 5000 Years* (New York: Melville House Publishing, 2011).

35 Notably, after the Wall Street crash of 1929, an array of regulatory efforts, both domestic and international, helped bring about a period of relative financial stability through to the 1970s. See, for example, Mariana Mazzucato, *The Value of Everything: Making and Taking in the Global Economy* (London: Allen Lane, 2018).

36 Ibid.

37 For an insightful discussion of the racially and geopolitically exclusionary construction of the Bretton Woods system, I recommend listening to 'Financial Empire with Daniela Gabor and Ndongo Samba Sylla', *The Dig*, 4 February 2022, www.thedigradio.com/podcast/financial-empire-w-daniela-gabor-ndongo-samba-sylla/ (accessed 2 March 2022).

38 Quinn Slobodian, *Globalists: The End of Empire and the Birth of Neoliberalism* (Cambridge, MA: Harvard University Press, 2018).

39 Michel J. Crozier, Samuel P. Huntington and Joji Watanuki (1975) 'The Crisis of Democracy: Report on the Governability of Democracies to the Trilateral Commission', *The Trilateral Commission* (1975), https://ia800305.us.archive.org/29/items/TheCrisisOfDemocracy-TrilateralCommission-1975/crisis_of_democracy_text.pdf (accessed 25 February 2022).

40 Martin Joseph, 'Henry Paulson: Save Globalisation to Secure the Future', *The Financial Times*, 17 April 2020, https://thakoni.com/henry-paulson-save-globalisation-to-secure-the-future/ (accessed 2 March 2022).

41 Kristin J. Forbes, 'The Microeconomic Evidence on Capital Controls: No Free Lunch' (2005), NBER Working Papers 11372, *National Bureau of Economic Research*, https://ideas.repec.org/p/nbr/nberwo/11372.html (accessed 2 March 2022).

42 Helene Ray, 'Dilemma Not Trilemma: The Global Financial Cycle and Monetary Independence' (2015), NBER Working Papers 21162,

National Bureau of Economic Research, www.nber.org/papers/w21162 (accessed 2 March 2022).

43 'Managing Capital Inflows to Reduce Resource Transfer from Developing to Developed Countries', *United Nations Conference on Trade and Development*, 9 December 2019, https://unctad.org/webflyer/ managing-capital-inflows-reduce-resource-transfer-developing-devel oped-countries (accessed 2 March 2022).

44 Ibid.

45 M. Ahyan Kose and Eswar Prasad, 'Capital Account: To Liberalise or Not?', *International Monetary Fund Finance and Development Magazine*, 24 February 2020, www.imf.org/external/pubs/ft/fandd/basics/ capital.htm (accessed 2 March 2022).

46 Importantly, the sources of foreign lending have, particularly since the 2008 Financial Crisis, begun to shift decisively away from Northern economies and the World Bank and toward China. China is now the world's largest bilateral creditor, particularly for low- and middle-income economies. By some estimates, their total lending is now greater than the World Bank, IMF and OECD governments combined. See Sebastian Horn et al., 'How Much Money Does the World Owe China?', *Harvard Business Review*, 26 February 2020, https://hbr.org/2020/02/how-much-money-does-the-world-owe-ch ina (accessed 2 March 2022).

47 Michael Thomson, Alexander Kentikelenis and Thomas Stubbs, 'Structural Adjustment Programmes Adversely Affect Vulnerable Populations: A Systematic-Narrative Review of Their Effect on Child and Maternal Health', *Public Health Reviews* 38, no. 13 (2017), doi: 10.1186/s40985-017-0059-2.

48 David Kaimowitz, Graham Theele and Pablo Pacheco, 'The Effects of Structural Adjustment on Deforestation and Forest Degradation in Lowland Bolivia', *World Development* 27, no. 3 (1999): 505–520.

49 Timon Forster et al., 'How Structural Adjustment Programs Affect Inequality: A Disaggregated Analysis of IMF Conditionality, 1980–2014', *Social Science Research* 80 (2019): 83–113, doi: 10.1016/j. ssresearch.2019.01.001.

50 Doris A. Oberdabernig, 'The Effects of Structural Adjustment Programs on Poverty and Income Distribution', *The Vienna Institute for International Economic Studies* (2010), https://wiiw.ac.at/the-effects- of-structural-adjustment-programs-on-poverty-and-income-distribu tion-p-2016.html (accessed 2 March 2022).

51 Thomson, Kentikelenis and Stubbs, 'Structural Adjustment'.

52 Jubilee Debt Campaign and Islamic Relief, 'Unlocking the Chains of Debt: A Call for Debt Relief for Pakistan' (2013), *Jubilee Debt Campaign*, https://jubileedebt.org.uk/wp-content/uploads/2013/10/Unlockin g-the-chains-of-debt_Final-Version_05.13.pdf (accessed 6 September 2021).

53 York Bradshaw and Jie Huang, 'Intensifying Global Dependency: Foreign Debt, Structural Adjustment, and Third World Underdevelopment', *The Sociological Quarterly* 32, no. 3 (1991): 321–342, doi: 10.1111/j.1533-8525.1991.tb00162.x.

54 George Caffentzis and Silvia Federici, 'A Brief History of Resistance to Structural Adjustment', in Kevin Danaher (ed.), *Democratizing the Global Economy* (Monroe, ME: Common Courage Press, 2001).

55 Stephanie Kelton, *The Deficit Myth* (London: John Murray Publishers, 2020).

56 Scott Ferguson, Maximilian Seijo and William Saas, 'The New Post-Colonial Economics with Fadhel Kaboub, *MR Online*, 7 July 2018, https://mronline.org/2018/07/07/the-new-postcolonial-economics-with-fadhel-kaboub/ (accessed 2 March 2022), cited in Stephanie Kelton, *The Deficit Myth* (London: John Murray Publishers, 2020).

57 Kelton, *The Deficit Myth*.

58 Samba Sylla, 'How Foreign Debt Undermines Sovereignty'.

59 John T. Harvey, *Currencies, Capital Flows and Crises: A Post Keynesian Analysis of Exchange Rate Determination* (London: Routledge, 2009).

60 Kimberley Amadeo, 'The Dollar is the World's Currency', *The Balance*, 18 July 2019, www.thebalance.com/world-currency-3305931 (accessed 2 March 2022).

61 Serkan Arslanalp and Chima Simpson-Bell, 'US Dollar Share of Global Foreign Exchange Reserves Drops to 25-Year Low', *International Monetary Fund Blog*, 5 May 2021, https://blogs.imf.org/2021/05/05/us-dollar-share-of-global-foreign-exchange-reserves-drops-to-25-year-low/ (accessed 2 March 2022).

62 Georgios Georgadis et al., 'Fundamentals vs. Policies: Can the US Dollar's Dominance in Global Trade be Dented?' (2021), Working Paper Series 2574, *European Central Bank*, www.ecb.europa.eu/pub/pdf/scpwps/ecb.wp2574~664b8e9249.en.pdf (accessed 2 March 2022).

63 David Adler and Andres Arauz, 'It's Time to End the Fed's "Monetary Triage"', *The Nation*, 23 March 2020, www.thenation.com/article/economy/economy-fed-imf/ (accessed 2 March 2022).

Notes

64 Mona Ali, 'Acute Dollar Dominance', *Phenomenal World*, 3 February 2022, www.phenomenalworld.org/analysis/acute-dollar-dominance/ (accessed 2 March 2022).

65 Adler and Arauz, 'It's Time to End the Fed's "Monetary Triage"'.

66 Gerardo García López and Livio Stracca, 'CGFS Papers No. 66: Changing Patterns of Capital Flows', *Bank for International Settlements*, 13 May 2021, www.bis.org/publ/cgfs66.htm (accessed 2 March 2022), as cited in Mona Ali, 'Acute Dollar Dominance'.

67 Ali, 'Acute Dollar Dominance'.

68 Ibid.

69 International Monetary Fund, 'Global Financial Stability Report: Markets in the Time of COVID-19', April 2020, www.imf.org/en/Publications/GFSR/Issues/2020/04/14/global-financial-stability-report-april-2020 (accessed 23 January 2022).

70 Ann Pettifor, 'Greenbank Greenback Dollar Bill', *Progressive International: Blueprint*, 1 May 2015, https://progressive.international/blueprint/6ab6a268-b1fd-43fc-8822-625a49d03b05-ann-pettifor-greenback-greenback-dollar-bill/en (accessed 2 March 2022).

71 Sebnem Kalemli-Ozcan, 'Emerging Market Capital Flows under COVID: What to Expect Given What We Know', *International Monetary Fund Special Series on Covid-19*, 16 September 2020, www.imf.org/en/Publications/SPROLLs/covid19-special-notes (accessed 2 March 2022).

72 Tim Jones, 'The G20's Debt Deal: Letting Private Lenders Off the Hook Again', *Jubilee Debt Campaign*, 17 November 2020, https://jubileedebt.org.uk/blog/the-g20s-debt-deal-letting-private-lenders-off-the-hook-again (accessed 2 March 2022).

73 Jubilee Debt Campaign, 'How the G20 Debt Suspension Initiative Benefits Private Lenders', October 2021, https://jubileedebt.org.uk/wp-content/uploads/2021/10/How-the-G20-debt-suspension-initiative-benefits-private-lenders_10.21.pdf (accessed 12 December 2021).

74 Ibid.

75 Ibid.

76 Ulrich Volz et al., 'Climate Change and Sovereign Risk 2020', *SOAS University of London, Asian Development Bank Institute, World Wide Fund for Nature Singapore, and Four Twenty Seven* (2020), https://doi.org/10.25501/SOAS.00033524.

77 Jerome E. Roos, *Why Not Default? The Political Economy of Sovereign Debt* (Princeton, NJ: Princeton University Press, 2019).

78 Jorgensen, Erika and Jeffrey D. Sachs, 'Default and Renegotiation of Latin American Foreign Bonds in the Interwar Period', in Barry Eichengreen and Peter H. Lindert (eds), *The International Debt Crisis in Historical Perspective* (Cambridge, MA: MIT Press, 1989).

79 Roos, *Why Not Default?*

80 Ibid.

81 Specifically, 63 of the lowest-income countries have seen their public debt repayments double as a fraction of government spending from 5.5% in 2011 to nearly 12.5% in 2019. Via Sara Murawski, 'Time to Resolve Debt Issues in the Global South', *Transnational Institute*, 17 April 2020, www.tni.org/en/article/time-to-resolve-debt-issues-in-the-global-south (accessed 2 March 2022).

82 Andrew Ross, 'Climate Debt Denial', *Dissent Magazine*, Summer 2013, www.dissentmagazine.org/article/climate-debt-denial (accessed 2 March 2022).

83 For instance, some scholarship has found domestic conflict over the costs of default is a major consideration. See Ugo Panizza, Federico Sturzenegger and Jeromin Zettelmeyer, 'The Economics and Law of Sovereign Debt and Default', *Journal of Economic Literature* 47, no. 3 (2009): 651–698, doi: 10.1257/jel.47.3.651. For a comprehensive analysis of economic dynamics relating to sovereign default from a more orthodox economic perspective, see Mark Aguiar and Manuel Amador, *The Economics of Sovereign Debt and Default* (Princeton, NJ: Princeton University Press, 2021).

84 Analysis of World Bank International Debt Statistics Database via 'Under the Radar: Private Sector Debt and Coronavirus in Developing Countries', *Jubilee Debt Campaign*, October 2020, https://jubileedebt.org.uk/wp-content/uploads/2020/10/Under-the-Radar-081020-1851.pdf (accessed 2 March 2022).

85 Roos, *Why Not Default?*

86 With thanks to Ann Pettifor for this useful framing.

87 Johannes Petry, Jan Fichtner and Eelke Heemskerk, 'The New Gatekeepers of Financial Claims: States, Passive Markets, and the Growing Power of Index Providers', in Kai Koddenbrock and Benjamin Braun (eds), *Capital Claims: Following Finance Across Borders* (London: Routledge, 2022).

88 Benjamin Robertson and Eric Lam, 'UBS Sees $121 Billion of EM Flows Amid "Seismic" Index Shifts', *Bloomberg*, 11 February 2019,

www.bloomberg.com/news/articles/2019-02-11/ubs-sees-121-billi
on-of-em-flows-amid-seismic-index-shifts (accessed 4 March 2022).

89 'Resources: Rating Agency' (2019), *Corporate Finance Institute*, https://
corporatefinanceinstitute.com/resources/knowledge/finance/rating-
agency/ (accessed 15 December 2021).

90 Note that Fitch is dually headquartered in New York and London.

91 'Credit-Rating Agencies are Back Under the Spotlight', *The
Economist*, 7 May 2020, www.economist.com/finance-and-econom
ics/2020/05/07/credit-rating-agencies-are-back-under-the-spotlight
(accessed 2 March 2022).

92 Mark Carl Rom, 'The Credit Rating Agencies and the Subprime
Mess: Greedy, Ignorant, and Stressed?', *Public Administration Review*
69, no. 4 (2019): 640–650, www.jstor.org/stable/27697910 (accessed
25 March 2022).

93 Rodrigo Olivares-Caminal, 'Moratorium on Debt for Africa? Be
Careful of Unintended Consequences', *The Conversation*, 10 May
2020, https://theconversation.com/moratorium-on-debt-for-africa-
be-careful-of-unintended-consequences-137406 (accessed 2 March
2022).

94 Andrew Harding, 'Madagascar on the Brink of Climate Change-
Induced Famine', *BBC News*, 25 August 2021, www.bbc.co.uk/
news/world-africa-58303792 (accessed 2 March 2022).

95 S&P, 'Climate Change is a Global Mega-Trend for Sovereign
Risk', *RatingsDirect*, 15 May 2014, New York, NY: Standard & Poor's
Ratings Services.

96 Robin Wigglesworth, *Trillions: How a Band of Wall Street Renegades
Invented the Index Fund and Changed Finance Forever* (London: Penguin
Random House, 2021).

97 Katharina Pistor, *The Code of Capital: How the Law Creates Wealth and
Inequality* (Princeton, NJ: Princeton University Press, 2019).

98 Ibid.

99 'The Energy Charter Treaty', *International Institute for Sustainable
Development*, June 2017, www.iisd.org/projects/energy-charter-treaty
(accessed 15 October 2021).

100 Sofia Balino, 'ECT Watch: New Dispute Reignites Debate Over
Treaty Protection for Fossil Fuel Investments', *International Institute
for Sustainable Development*, 19 February 2021, www.iisd.org/articles/
energy-charter-treaty-new-dispute-fossil-fuel-investments (accessed
2 March 2022).

101 Laura Basu, 'What's Wrong with Trade and Investment Agreements?', in Harpreet Kaur Paul and Dalia Gebrial (eds), *Perspectives on a Global Green New Deal* (Berlin: Rosa Luxemburg-Stiftung, 2021).

102 Kate Aronoff, 'The Obscure Treaty That Could Kill a Global Green Recovery', *The New Republic*, 8 July 2020, https://newrepublic.com/article/158397/obscure-treaty-kill-global-green-recovery (accessed 2 March 2022).

103 Mavluda Sattorova, 'Do Developing Countries Really Benefit from Investment Treaties? The Impact of International Investment Law on National Governance', *International Institute for Sustainable Development*, 21 December 2018, www.iisd.org/itn/en/2018/12/21/do-developing-countries-really-benefit-from-investment-treaties-the-impact-of-international-investment-law-on-national-governance-mavluda-sattorova/ (accessed 2 March 2020.

104 Ibid.

105 Dominic Npoanlari Dagbanja, 'The Environment, Human Rights, and Investment Treaties in Africa: A Constitutional Perspective', in J. Chaisse, L. Choukroune and S. Jusoh (eds), *Handbook of International Investment Law and Policy* (New York: Springer, 2020), pp. 1–30.

106 Pistor, *The Code of Capital*.

107 J. Timmons Roberts and Bradley C. Parks, 'Ecologically Unequal Exchange, Ecological Debt, and Climate Justice: The History and Implications of Three Related Ideas for a New Social Movement', *International Journal of Comparative Sociology* 50, no. 385 (2009), doi: 10.1177/0020715209105147.

108 R. Muradian and J. Martinez-Alier, 'Trade and the Environment: From a "Southern" Perspective', *Ecological Economics* 36 (2001): 281–297.

109 Ulrich Brand and Markus Wissen, *The Imperial Mode of Living* (London: Verso, 2016).

110 The Climate Finance Leadership Initiative is one among many examples of financial 'alliances' ostensibly aimed at tackling the climate crisis.

111 Keston K. Perry, 'Realising Climate Reparations: Towards a Global Climate Stabilization Fund and Resilience Fund Programme for Loss and Damage in Marginalized and Former Colonized Societies' (2020), https://ssrn.com/abstract=3561121.

112 Leon Sealey-Huggins, '"1.50C to stay alive": Climate Change, Imperialism and Justice for the Caribbean', *Third World Quarterly* 38, no. 11 (2017).

113 Ibid.

114 Kate Aronoff, 'The U.S. is Still Blocking Climate Progress', *The New Republic* 16 November 2021, https://newrepublic.com/article/164436/us-still-blocking-climate-progress-cop26.

115 Andreas Malm, *The Progress of This Storm* (London: Verso, 2018).

116 Naomi Oreskes, Michael Oppenheimer and Dale Jamieson, 'Scientists Have Been Underestimating the Pace of Climate Change', *Scientific American* 19 August 2019, https://blogs.scientificamerican.com/observations/scientists-have-been-underestimating-the-pace-of-climate-change/ (accessed 2 March 2022).

117 S.C. Sherwood et al., 'An Assessment of Earth's Climate Sensitivity Using Multiple Lines of Evidence', *Reviews of Geophysics* 58, no. 4 (2020), doi: 10.1029/2019RG000678.

118 Tim Palmer, 'Short-Term Tests Validate Long-Term Estimates of Climate Change', *Nature*, 26 May 2020, www.nature.com/articles/d41586-020-01484-5 (accessed 2 March 2022).

Chapter 6: Ghosts

1 Jacques Derrida, *Specters of Marx* (London: Routledge, 1993).

2 Elon Musk, discussing access to Bolivian lithium, https://twitter.com/panoparker/status/1318157559266762752?lang=en-GB (accessed 2 March 2022).

3 Emily A. Ury et al., 'Rapid Deforestation of a Coastal Landscape Driven by Sea-Level Rise and Extreme Events', *Ecological Applications* 31, no. 5 (2021), doi: 10.1002/eap. 2339.

4 Mikaela Weisse and Elizabeth Dow Goldman, 'We Lost a Football Pitch of Primary Rainforest Every 6 Seconds in 2019', *World Resources Institute*, 2 June 2020, www.wri.org/insights/we-lost-football-pitch-primary-rainforest-every-6-seconds-2019 (accessed 2 March 2022).

5 https://imazon.org.br/imprensa/desmatamento-na-amazonia-cresceu-33-de-janeiro-a-outubro-em-relacao-ao-ano-passado/ (accessed 2 March 2022).

6 J. Stropp et al., 'The Ghosts of Forests Past and Future: Deforestation and Botanical Sampling in the Brazilian Amazon', *Ecography* 43, no. 7 (2020), doi: 10.1111/ecog.05026.

7 Laura Parker, 'Plastic Trash Flowing into the Seas Will Nearly Triple by 2040 without drastic action', *National Geographic*, 23 June 2020,

www.nationalgeographic.com/science/article/plastic-trash-in-seas-will-nearly-triple-by-2040-if-nothing-done (accessed 2 March 2022).

8   Martin Arboleda, *Planetary Mine: Territories of Extraction Under Late Capitalism* (London: Verso, 2020).

9   Of course, the contributions both intra- and internationally to this transformation have been enormously unequal based on rates of growth and consumption, but such breakdowns are not, to my knowledge, available in this data. Yinon M. Bar-On, Rob Phillips and Ron Milo, 'The Biomass Distribution on Earth', *Proceedings of the National Academy of Sciences* 115, no. 25 (2018), doi: 10.1073/pnas.1711842115.

10 Pierre Legagneux et al., 'Our House is Burning: Discrepancy in Climate Change vs. Biodiversity Coverage in the Media as Compared to Scientific Literature', *Frontiers in Ecology and Evolution* (2018), doi: 10.3389/fevo.2017.00175.

11 'Global EV Outlook 2021', *International Energy Agency*, April 2021, www.iea.org/reports/global-ev-outlook-2021 (accessed 16 January 2022).

12 Vera Heck et al., 'Biomass-Based Negative Emissions Difficult to Reconcile with Planetary Boundaries', *Nature Climate Change* 8, no. 2 (2018): 151–155; Alister Doyle, 'Extracting Carbon from Nature Can Aid Climate but Will Be Costly: U.N'., *Reuters*, 26 March 2014, www.reuters.com/article/us-climatechange-ccs-idUSBREA2P1LK20140326 (accessed 2 March 2022).

13 There is extensive debate within those who theorise on the topic about where the boundaries of 'nature' should be drawn in relation to society, if it all, and indeed its utility as a term. Engaging properly with these debates is beyond the scope of this chapter, nor is being located firmly on one side of it necessary, in my opinion, for the arguments it sets out. In the interest of clarity and simplicity I therefore use nature to denote what others might term 'non-human natures' – both non-human species and entities such as 'natural resources', as well as those areas not occupied by or dedicated to human developments.

14 See, e.g. Joel Millward-Hopkins et al., 'Providing Decent Living with Minimum Energy: A Global Scenario', *Global Environmental Change* 65 (2020), doi: 10.1016/j.gloenvcha.2020.102168; T. Weidmann et al. (2020) 'Scientists' Warning on Affluence', *Nature Communications* 11, no. 3107 (2020), www.nature.com/articles/s41467-020-16941-y (accessed

1 March 2022); H. Haberl et al., 'A Systematic Review of the Evidence on Decoupling of GDP, Resource Use and GHG Emissions, Part II: Synthesizing the Insights', *Environmental Research Letters* 15 (2020), https://iopscience.iop.org/article/10.1088/1748-9326/ab842a (accessed 2 March 2022); T. Parrique, 'Decoupling Debunked: Evidence and Arguments Against Green Growth as a Sole Strategy for Sustainability', *European Environmental Bureau*, 8 July 2019, https://eeb.org/library/decoupling-debunked/ (accessed 2 March 2022).

15 Ibid.

16 See e.g. Financial Stability Board, 'The Implications of Climate Change for Financial Stability', *Financial Stability Board*, 23 November 2020, www.fsb.org/2020/11/the-implications-of-climate-change-for-financial-stability/ (accessed 2 March 2022); Simon Dietz et al., '"Climate Value at Risk" of Global Financial Assets', *Nature Climate Change* (2016), doi: 10.1038/nclimate2972; Brad Plumer, 'Companies See Climate Change Hitting Their Bottom Lines in the Next 5 Years', *The New York Times*, 4 June 2019, www.nytimes.com/2019/06/04/climate/companies-climate-change-financial-impact.html (accessed 2 March 2022).

17 Center for Biological Diversity, 'Tiehm's Buckwheat Proposed for Endangered Species Act Protection', 3 June 2021, https://biologicaldiversity.org/w/news/press-releases/tiehms-buckwheat-proposed-for-endangered-species-act-protection-2021-06-03/ (accessed 2 March 2022).

18 International Energy Agency, 'The Role of Critical Minerals in the Energy Transition', *International Energy Agency*, May 2021, www.iea.org/reports/the-role-of-critical-minerals-in-clean-energy-transitions (accessed 2 March 2022).

19 Jeffrey Kluger, 'A New Study Reveals How Humans Could Accidentally Murder Life on Mars', *TIME*, 15 November 2018, https://time.com/5455909/atacama-desert-mars-rain/ (accessed 20 November 2021).

20 Thea Riofrancos, 'The Rush to "Go Electric" Comes with a Hidden Cost: Destructive Lithium Mining', *The Guardian*, 14 June 2021, www.theguardian.com/commentisfree/2021/jun/14/electric-cost-lithium-mining-decarbonasation-salt-flats-chile (accessed 2 March 2022).

21 Robert Rapier, 'The World's Top Lithium Producers', *Forbes*, 13 December 2020, www.forbes.com/sites/rrapier/2020/12/13/the-worlds-top-lithium-producers/ (accessed 2 March 2022).

22 Riofrancos, 'The Rush to Go Electric'.

23 Dave Sherwood, 'In Chilean Desert, Global Thirst for Lithium is Fuelling a "Water War"', *Reuters*, 29 August 2018, www.reuters.com/article/us-chile-lithium-water-idUSKCN1LE16T (accessed 2 March 2022).

24 Benjamin Hitchcock Auciello et al., 'Recharge Responsibly: The Environmental and Social Footprint of Mining Cobalt, Lithium, and Nickel for Electric Vehicle Batteries' (2021), *Earthworks*, https://scalar.usc.edu/works/mere-hub/informes (accessed 2 March 2022).

25 Global Campus of Human Rights, 'Lithium: Mining Key Fossil Fuel Alternative Threatens Indigenous Rights in Latin America', https://gchumanrights.org/preparedness/article-on/lithium-mining-key-fossil-fuel-alternative-threatens-indigenous-rights-in-latin-ameri ca.html (accessed 2 March 2022).

26 Todd C. Frankel and Peter Whoriskey, 'Tossed Aside in the 'White Gold' Rush', *The Washington Post*, 19 December 2016, www.washingtonpost.com/graphics/business/batteries/tossed-aside-in-the-lithium-rush/ (accessed 2 March 2022).

27 Ibid.

28 Ibid.

29 Ulrich Brand and Markus Wissen, *The Imperial Mode of Living* (London: Verso, 2016).

30 Hallie Golden, 'Indigenous Tribes Tried to Block a Car Battery mine. But the Courts Stood in the Way', *The Guardian*, 15 October 2021, www.theguardian.com/environment/2021/oct/15/indigenous-tribes-block-car-battery-mine-courts (accessed 2 March 2022).

31 Michael Ash and James K. Boyce, 'Racial Disparities in Pollution Exposure and Employment at US Industrial Facilities', *Proceedings of the National Academy of Sciences* 115, no. 42 (2018), doi: 10.1073/pnas.1721640115.

32 'What We Are Monitoring and Why', *Tower Hamlets Council*, www.towerhamlets.gov.uk/lgnl/environment_and_waste/environmental_health/pollution/air_quality/Advanced_information_on_air_quality/What_we_are_monitoring_and_why.aspx (accessed 3 February 2022).

33 Thea Riofrancos, 'Shifting Mining From the Global South Misses the Point of Climate Justice', *Foreign Policy*, 7 February 2022, https://foreignpolicy.com/2022/02/07/renewable-energy-transition-critical-minerals-mining-onshoring-lithium-evs-climate-justice/ (accessed 9 February 2022).

34 Ibid.

35 Ibid.

36 Brand and Wissen, *The Imperial Mode of Living*.

37 OECD, 'Towards Green Growth: A Summary for Policy Makers', *Organisation for Economic Co-Operation and Development*, May 2011, www.oecd.org/greengrowth/48012345.pdf (accessed 2 March 2022).

38 Unless otherwise indicated, facts within this paragraph are drawn from Helmut Haberl et al., 'A Systematic Review of the Evidence on Decoupling of GDP, Resource Use and GHG Emissions, Part II: Synthesizing the Insights', *Environmental Research Letters* 15 (2020), doi: 10.1088/1748-9326/ab842a.

39 Ibid.

40 Jason Hickel and Giorgos Kallis, 'Is Green Growth Possible?', *New Political Economy* 25, no. 4 (2019), doi: 10.1080/13563467.2019.1598964.

41 Ibid. See also: Z. Wu et al., 'Does Economic Recession Reduce Material Use? Empirical Evidence Based on 157 Economies Worldwide', *Journal of Cleaner Production* 214 (2019), doi: 10.1016/j.jclepro.2019.01.015; Fridolin Krausmann et al., 'From Resource Extraction to Outflows of Wastes and Emissions: The Socioeconomic Metabolism of the Global Economy, 1900–2015', *Global Environmental Change* 52 (2018): 131–140, doi: 10.1016/j.gloenvcha.2018.07.003.

42 Krausmann et al. 'From Resource Extraction to Outflows of Wastes and Emissions.

43 Timothee Parrique et al., 'Decoupling Debunked: Evidence and Arguments Against Green Growth as a Sole Strategy for Sustainability', *European Environmental Bureau*, 8 July 2019, https://eeb.org/library/decoupling-debunked/ (accessed 2 March 2022).

44 Keston K. Perry, 'The "Green" New Deal Should Not be a New Imperial Masterplan', *Al Jazeera*, 4 June 2020, www.aljazeera.com/opinions/2020/6/4/the-green-new-deal-should-not-be-a-new-imperial-masterplan (accessed 2 March 2022); Leon Sealey-Huggins, '"Deal or no Deal?" Exploring the Potential, Limits and Potential Limits of Green New Deals', *Common Wealth*, 6 May 2021, www.common-wealth.co.uk/reports/deal-or-no-deal-exploring-the-potential-limits-and-potential-limits-of-green-new-deals (accessed 2 March 2022).

45 Robert Fletcher and Crelis Rammelt, 'Decoupling: A Key Fantasy of the Post-2015 Sustainable Development Agenda', *Globalizations* 14, no. 3 (2016): 450–467, doi: 10.1080/14747731.2016.1263077.

46 James Salzman et al., 'The Global Status and Trends of Payments for Ecosystem Services', *Nature Sustainability* 1 (2018): 136–144, www.nature.com/articles/s41893-018-0033-0 (accessed 2 March 2022).

47 'Press Release: UN adopts landmark framework to integrate natural capital in economic reporting', *United Nations*, 10 March 2021, www.un.org/sustainabledevelopment/blog/2021/03/un-adopts-landmark-framework-to-integrate-natural-capital-in-economic-reporting/ (accessed 2 March 2022); 'Natural Capital Accounting', *The European Commission*, https://ec.europa.eu/environment/nature/capital_accounting/index_en.htm (accessed 25 January 2022).

48 Dieter Helm, *Natural Capital: Valuing Our Planet* (New Haven, CT: Yale University Press, 2015), p. 87.

49 Ibid.

50 Rahul Basu and Scott Pegg, 'Minerals are a Shared Inheritance: Accounting for the Resource Curse', *The Extractive Industries and Society* 7, no. 4 (2020): 1369–1376, doi: 10.1016/j.exis.2020.08.001.

51 Patrick Bond and Rahul Basu, 'Intergenerational Equity and the Geographical Ebb and Flow of Resources: The Time and Space of Natural Capital Accounting', in Matthew Himley, Elizabeth Havice and Gabriela Valdivia (eds), *The Routledge Handbook of Radical Geography* (London: Routledge, 2021).

52 Herman Daly's farewell speech at the World Bank, as quoted in Bond and Basu, 'Intergenerational Equity'.

53 For an explanation of de-growth, see e.g. Hickel and Kallis, 'Is Green Growth Possible?'

54 Ibid., p. 37.

55 Hannah Ritchie, 'How Much of the World's Land Would we Need in Order to Feed the Global Population with the Average Diet of a Given Country?', *Our World in Data*, 3 October 2017, https://ourworldindata.org/agricultural-land-by-global-diets (accessed 2 March 2022).

56 Helen Briggs, 'Biodiversity Loss Risks "Ecological Meltdown" – Scientists', *BBC News*, 10 October 2021, www.bbc.co.uk/news/science-environment-58859105 (accessed 2 March 2022).

57 Shinichiro Fujimori, 'Land-Based Climate Change Mitigation Measures can Affect Agricultural Markets and Food Security', *Nature Food* 3 (2022): 110–121, www.nature.com/articles/s43016-022-00464-4 (accessed 2 March 2022).

58 www.swissre.com/media/news-releases/nr-20200923-biodiversity-and-ecosystems-services.html (accessed 2 March 2022).

59 Ibid.

60 This process is not new. Capitalism is predicated on creating methods for enclosing and extracting value from domains traditionally outside the formal reach of the market. Like the value-creating 'services' provided by nature for 'free', so too is value extracted from the unpaid labour of the foundational economy, such as care and domestic work.

61 David Hayes and Nicole Gentile, 'No Net Loss: How Mitigation Policy Can Spur Private Investment in Land and Wildlife Conservation', *Center for American Progress*, 1 November 2016, www.americanprogress.org/article/no-net-loss/ (accessed 2 March 2022).

62 Robert Costanza et al., 'The Value of the World's Ecosystem Services and Natural Capital', *Nature* 387 (1997): 253–260.

63 See, for example, Helm, *Natural Capital*; Partha Dasgupta, 'The Economics of Biodiversity: The Dasgupta Review', *HM Treasury*, 2 February 2021, www.gov.uk/government/publications/final-report-the-economics-of-biodiversity-the-dasgupta-review (accessed 2 March 2022).

64 Ibid.

65 Neil Smith, 'Nature as Accumulation Strategy', *Socialist Register*, 19 March 2009, https://socialistregister.com/index.php/srv/article/view/5856 (accessed 2 March 2022).

66 Smith, 'Nature as Accumulation Strategy'.

67 Tanya Latty and Timothy Lee, 'How Many Species on Earth? Why That's a Simple Question but Hard to Answer', *The Conversation*, 28 April 2019, https://theconversation.com/how-many-species-on-earth-why-thats-a-simple-question-but-hard-to-answer-114909 (accessed 2 March 2022).

68 Luis Villazon, 'How Many Species Have Yet to be Discovered?', *Science Focus*, www.sciencefocus.com/nature/how-many-species-have-yet-to-be-discovered/ (accessed 2 March 2022).

69 Eric Neumayer, 'Preserving Natural Capital in a World of Uncertainty and Scarce Financial Resources', *International Journal of Sustainable Development and World Ecology* 5, no. 1 (1998), doi: 10.1080/13504509809469967.

70 Holly P. Jones et al., 'Restoration and Repair of Earth's Damaged Ecosystems', *Proceedings of the Royal Society B* 285, no. 1873 (2018), doi: 10.1098/rspb.2017.2577.

71 This set of assumptions and their definition draws on Frédéric Hache, '50 Shades of Green: Part II, The Fallacy of Environmental

Markets', *Green Finance Observatory* (May 2019), doi: 10.2139/ssrn.3 547414.

72 Ibid.

73 James C. Scott, *Seeing Like a State: How Certain Schemes to Improve the Human Condition Have Failed* (New Haven, CT: Yale University Press, 1998).

74 Sian Sullivan, 'Banking Nature? The Spectacular Financialisation of Environmental Conservation', *Antipode* 45, no. 1 (2013): 198–217, doi: 10.1111/j.1467-8330.2012.00989.x.

75 Nature Conservation Council, 'Paradise Lost: The Weakening and Widening of NSW Biodiversity Offsetting Schemes, 2005–2016' (2016), *Nature Conservation Council*, https://assets.nationbuilder.com/nature org/legacy_url/2417/bio-offsetting-report_v14.pdf?1630462684 (accessed 2 March 2022).

76 Atte Moilanen and Janne S. Kotiaho, 'Planning Biodiversity Offsets: Twelve Operationally Important Decisions', *Nordic Council of Ministers* (2018), doi: 10.6027/TN2018-513.

77 'Habitat Banking Investment Scheme Wins Government Funding', *Berkshire, Buckinghamshire & Oxfordshire Wildlife Trust*, www.bbowt.org. uk/news/habitat-banking-investment-scheme-wins-government-fund ing (accessed 2 March 2022).

78 As cited in Sullivan, 'Banking Nature?'

79 Ibid.

80 'BNP Paribas Asset Management Launches Ecosystem Restoration Fund', 7 June 2021, https://mediaroom-en.bnpparibas-am.com/ news/bnp-paribas-asset-management-launches-ecosystem-restoration-fund-edaf-ofb7a.html (accessed 2 March 2022).

81 'Natural Capital', *Mirova*, www.mirova.com/en/invest/natural-cap ital (accessed 2 March 2022).

82 The Real Wild Estates Company, *The Real Wild Estates Company* (2021), www.realwildestates.com/wp-content/uploads/2021/12/rw ec-brochure.pdf (accessed 2 March 2022).

83 James T. Mandel et al., 'Debt Investment as a Tool for Value Transfer in Biodiversity Conservation. *Conservation Letters* 2, no. 5 (2009): 233–239, doi: 10.1111/J.1755-263X.2009.00070.x.

84 Hache, '50 Shades of Green. Part II'.

85 James T. Mandel, Josh Donlan and Jonathan Armstrong, 'A Derivative Approach to Endangered Species Conservation', *Frontiers in Ecology and the Environment* 8, no. 1 (2010): 44–49, doi: 10.1890/070170.

86 Ibid.

87 'Testimony of Michael W. Masters: Managing Member/Portfolio Manager Masters Capital Management LLC before the Committee on Homeland Security and Governmental Affairs United States Senate', www.hsgac.senate.gov/imo/media/doc/052008Masters. pdf (accessed 2 March 2022).

88 The argument against this is clear from an ecological perspective but is likely also important from a financial perspective. As a detailed analysis from the Green Finance Observatory articulates: "The decision to only consider and value certain ecosystem services while ignoring others, to artificially unbundle services and not fully account for inter-dependencies means that internalising environmental externalities via habitat banking is likely to create new externalities and the potential build-up of unmonitored risks. In finance, this is called a basis risk: you purchase an insurance against adverse price fluctuations and the insurance price is supposed to move in an opposite and equal direction to that of the asset being insured. If, however, the insurance does not perfectly cover your risk, you are exposed to a residual risk called basis risk: the risk that the insurance price might not move in normal, steady correlation with the price of the underlying asset, and that this fluctuation in the basis may negate the effectiveness of the hedging strategy'. See Hache, '50 Shades of Green. Part II'.

89 Richard T. Carson et al., 'Contingent Valuation and Lost Passive Use: Damages from the Exxon Valdez Oil Spill', *Environmental and Resource Economics* 25 (2003): 257–286, https://link.springer.com/arti cle/10.1023/A:1024486702104 (accessed 2 March 2022).

90 Hache, '50 Shades of Green. Part II'.

91 Kate Abnett, 'EU Proposes Rules to Label Some Gas and Nuclear Investments as Green', *Reuters*, 2 February 2022, www.reuters.com/ business/sustainable-business/eu-proposes-rules-label-some-gas-and-nuclear-investments-green-2022-02-02/ (accessed 2 March 2022).

92 Garrett Hardin, 'The Tragedy of the Commons', *Science* 162, no. 3859 (1968): 1243–1248, www.jstor.org/stable/1724745 (accessed 25 March 2022).

93 Helm, *Natural Capital*.

94 Kyle Frankel Davis et al., 'Tropical Forest Loss Enhanced by Large-Scale Land Acquisitions', *Nature Geoscience* 13 (2020): 482–488, www. nature.com/articles/s41561-020-0592-3?proof=tNature (accessed 2 March 2022).

95 The Paulson Institute, 'Financing Nature: Closing the Global Biodiversity Financing Gap' (2020), *The Paulson Institute*, www.paulsoninstitute.org/conservation/financing-nature-report/ (accessed 2 March 2022).

96 Fermin Koop, 'Uruguay Launches Sovereign Bond Linked to Climate Targets', *The Brazilian Report*, 31 December 2021, https://brazilian.report/latin-america/2021/12/31/uruguay-sovereign-bond-climate-targets/ (accessed 2 March 2022).

97 Sullivan, 'Banking Nature?'

98 Andrew Fishman, 'How Your 401(K) is Helping Destroy the Amazon Rainforest', *The Intercept*, 23 November 2021, https://theintercept.com/2021/11/23/brazil-amazon-deforestation-greenwashing-bonds-investment/ (accessed 2 March 2022).

99 'Why Nature-Based Solutions Won't Solve the Climate Crisis – They'll Just Make Rich People Even Richer', *Survival International*, October 2021, www.survivalinternational.org/articles/nature-based-solutions-wont-solve-climate-crisis (accessed 15 January 2022).

100 World Rainforest Movement and Re:Common (2016) 'Rio Tinto's Biodiversity Offset in Madagascar – Double Landgrab in the Name of Biodiversity?', *World Rainforest Movement*, 13 April 2016, www.wrm.org.uy/publications/rio-tintos-biodiversity-offset-in-madagascar-double-landgrab-in-the-name-of-biodiversity (accessed 2 March 2022).

101 Sullivan, 'Banking Nature?'

102 Gert van Hecken and Vijay Kolinjivadi, 'The "White Saviour" Deal for Nature', *Green European Journal*, 30 December 2021, www.greeneuropeanjournal.eu/the-white-saviour-deal-for-nature/ (accessed 2 March 2022).

Between the devil and the deep blue sea

1 BCA Global Investment Solutions, 'Rising Risk of a Nuclear Apocalypse', *BCA Global Investment Solutions*, 4 March 2022. Via Billy Bambrough, 'Vladimir Putin and Russia Could Trigger "Nuclear Apocalypse" And "Armageddon" – But Investors Told To "Stay Bullish"', *Forbes*, 6 March 2022.

2 Octavia Butler, *Parable of the Talents* (New York: Seven Stories Press, 1998).

3 Hans-O. Pörtner et al., 'Climate Change 2022: Impacts, Adaptation and Vulnerability – Summary for Policymakers' (2022), *Intergovernmental Panel on Climate Change*, www.ipcc.ch/report/sixth-assessment-report-working-group-ii/ (accessed 14 March 2022).

4 Ibid.

5 H. Haberl, 'A Systematic Review of the Evidence on Decoupling of GDP, Resource Use and GHG Emissions, Part II: Synthesizing the Insights', *Environmental Research Letters* 15 (2020), doi: 10.1088/1748-9326/ab842a.

6 Thomas Wiedmann et al., 'Scientists' Warning on Affluence', *Nature Communications* 11, no. 3107 (2020), cwww.nature.com/articles/s41467-020-16941-y (accessed 14 March 2022).

7 Ibid.

8 David Common, "We Are Going to Send This Back': Malaysia Returning Unwanted Canadian Plastic', *CBC News*, 28 May 2019, www.cbc.ca/news/world/we-are-going-to-send-this-back-malaysia-returning-unwanted-canadian-plastic-1.5152274 (accessed 14 March 2022).

9 Ulrich Brand and Markus Wissen, *The Imperial Mode of Living: Everyday Life and the Ecological Crisis of Capitalism* (London: Verso, 2021).

10 Jason W. Moore, *Capitalism in the Web of Life: Ecology and the Accumulation of Capital* (London: Verso, 2015), p. 305.

11 Daniela Gabor, 'The Wall Street Consensus', *Development and Change* 52, no. 3 (2021), doi: 10.1111/dech.12645.

12 Ludwig von Mises, *Planned Chaos* (Auburn, AL: Ludwig von Mises Institute, 2014).

13 William H. Peterson, 'The Meaning of Market Democracy', *The Free Market* 23, no. 12 (2003), https://mises.org/library/meaning-market-democracy (accessed 14 March 2022).

14 Hanna Szymborska and Jan Toporowski, 'Industrial Feudalism and Wealth Inequalities – Working Paper No. 174', *Institute for New Economic Thinking: Working Papers*, 18 January 2022, https://papers.ssrn.com/sol3/papers.cfm?abstract_id=4023748 (accessed 14 March 2022).

15 'Can we Feed the World and Ensure No One Goes Hungry?', *United Nations: UN News*, 3 October 2019, https://news.un.org/en/story/2019/10/1048452 (accessed 20 February 2022).

16 Mises, *Planned Chaos*.

17 Margaret Somers, 'The Moral Economy of the Capitalist Crowd: Utopianism, the Reality of Society, and the Market as a Morally

Notes

Instituted Process in Karl Polanyi's The Great Transformation', *Humanity* 11, no. 2 (2020).

18 Stuart Hall, 'Variants of Liberalism', in Stuart Hall and Gregor McLennan (ed.), *Selected Writings on Marxism* (Durham, NC: Duke University Press, [1986] 2021).

19 Shinichiro Fujimori et al., 'Land-Based Climate Change Mitigation Measures Can Affect Agricultural Markets and Food Security', *Nature Food*, 3 (2022): 110–121, www.nature.com/articles/s43016-022-00464-4 (accessed 14 March 2022).

20 J. Lewis, *Beyond Consumer Capitalism: Media and the Limits to Imagination* (Cambridge: Polity Press, 2013), pp. 124–178, as cited in Kate Soper, *Post-Growth Living: For an Alternative Hedonism* (London: Verso, 2020), p. 7.

21 T. Parrique et al., 'Decoupling Debunked: Evidence and Arguments Against Green Growth as a Sole Strategy for Sustainability' (2019), *European Environmental Bureau*, https://eeb.org/library/decoupling-debunked/ (accessed 14 March 2022).

22 Kate Soper, *Post-Growth Living: For an Alternative Hedonism* (London: Verso, 2020).

23 Lewis, *Beyond Consumer Capitalism*.

24 David Graeber, *Det: The First 5000 Years* (New York: Melville House, 2011).

25 'Does Military Sonar Kill Marine Wildlife?', *Scientific American*, 10 June 2009, www.scientificamerican.com/article/does-military-sonar-kill/#:~:text=Dear%20EarthTalk%3A%20Is%20it%20true,exercises%20actually%20kill%20marine%20wildlife%3F&text=Unfortunately%20for%20many%20whales%2C%20dolphins,to%20injury%20and%20even%20death (accessed 10 February 2022). See also Amia Srinivasan, 'What Have We Done to the Whale?', *The New Yorker*, 24 August 2020, www.newyorker.com/magazine/2020/08/24/what-have-we-done-to-the-whale (accessed 14 March 2022).

Index

Note: 'n' after a page number indicates the number of a note on that page

Index